Fairness, Inc.

Fairness, Inc.

*The Origins (and Billion-Dollar Bonuses) of
Rule 10b-5 as America's Insider
Trading Prohibition*

J. Scott Colesanti

PROFESSOR OF LEGAL WRITING
MAURICE A. DEANE SCHOOL OF LAW
HOFSTRA UNIVERSITY

CAROLINA ACADEMIC PRESS
Durham, North Carolina

Library of Congress Cataloging-in-Publication Data

Names: Colesanti, J. Scott, author.
Title: Fairness, inc. : the origins (and billion-dollar bonuses) of Rule
   10b-5 as America's insider trading prohibition / J. Scott Colesanti.
Description: Durham, North Carolina : Carolina Academic Press, LLC, 2018. |
   Includes bibliographical references and index.
Identifiers: LCCN 2017052810 | ISBN 9781531003746 (alk. paper)
Subjects: LCSH: Insider trading in securities--Law and legislation--United
   States. | Insider trading in securities--Law and legislation--United
   States--History. | United States. Securities and Exchange Commission. Rule
   10b-5.
Classification: LCC KF1073.I5 C59 2018 | DDC 345.73/0268--dc23
LC record available at https://lccn.loc.gov/2017052810

eISBN 978-1-53100-375-3

CAROLINA ACADEMIC PRESS, LLC
700 Kent Street
Durham, North Carolina 27701
Telephone (919) 489-7486
Fax (919) 493-5668
www.cap-press.com

Printed in the United States of America

For James and Giovanni, the fairest souls I've ever known …

Contents

Preface

Boundless Equity

Traditionally, the capitalist world accorded insiders the advantage of using their unique position for personal gain. The story tells of the European deputy commander of the national army being allowed to deposit the entirety of the nation's defense budget into his personal account (to live off the daily accumulating interest). When it came to the personal stock trades of corporate managers, the "majority rule" stated that such insiders owed no duty to shareholders to reveal confidential news. Between 1909 and 1933, distinct courts in the American system began acknowledging rare exceptions between buyers and sellers of corporate stock under the "special circumstances" rule.

The Great Depression (b. 1929) tested this nation's economic system and way of life like no challenge before. Wall Street was blamed for the majority of attendant ills. When Franklin Roosevelt took office, a New Deal was ushered in, with an accompanying but unspecific promise of restrictions on access and privilege. The resulting securities laws, in part, presumed certain stock transactions by company insiders to be illegal—under very detailed conditions.

As has been noted countless times, Congress did not then or at any point thereafter define the violation coined "insider trading." Nonetheless, the American insider trading prohibition ("Prohibition")—largely encapsulated within Securities and Exchange Commission[1] Rule 10b-5—has admirably trudged forward and grown to be the unquestioned worldwide standard. It now covers all parties and all trades. It is readily employed by the SEC, the Department of Justice, state regulators, stock exchanges, and private counsel. It is utilized to garner unfathomable monetary awards as decided by judges and juries; in turn, it cowers defendants to settle accusations, culminating in 2014 with an

---

1. Hereinafter "SEC" or "Commission."

epic $1.8 billion fine against a mammoth hedge fund firm. Such cartoonish recovery raises the question, how did the Rule meant to cabin excesses itself become such a tool for extravagant returns?

———————

I commenced work on my first insider trading investigation in 1989, within 6 months of graduating law school. I was shocked by the lack of statutory guidance. Further, the legal principles emanated solely from the SEC's stockpile of cases from various decades. Within our own regulator, we tried to follow local precedent and remain true to a list of aggravating factors rumored to exist solely within the market surveillance division (the exact list was never shown to me). "Do what you think is fair, and we can prove," I recall being told by superiors.

Years later, as an adjunct law professor, I focused on the sole hint at a statutory standard appearing in a federal securities law: "For the purpose of preventing the unfair use of information ..."[2] With those ten words, the 1934 Congress loosed generations of varied weapons against what has become a notorious economic crime.

Decades later, after serving as a securities arbitrator, full-time academic, compliance counsel, public speaker, and author, I can say that my nascent fears of ill-definition were amply justified. As a cause of action, the whole of Rule 10b-5 contains ever-changing parts. When broken into elements, some of them disappear. In sum, the Prohibition proves most ready to be a hodgepodge response to any perceived inequity—even when the ad hoc response runs counter to the intentions of its creators. To say that this standard is tied more to each generation's notion of fairness than to a persisting rule of law is a tragic understatement; the standard wholly varies with the perceived gravity of the financial privilege in each and every case.

To be sure, the free-form nature of the amorphous regulation has not escaped attention. A highly regarded legal treatise commenced with the sardonic dedication, "For all of those investors who have been protected from a crime that Congress has been unwilling or unable to define."[3] A Circuit Court said the theory supporting cases against those outside the subject corporation made us all "pawns in an overall litigation strategy known only to the SEC."[4] The Supreme

———————

2. Section 16(b) of the Securities Exchange Act, 15 U.S.C. §78p (2012).

3. Ralph C. Ferrara, Donna M. Nagy & Herbert Thomas, Ferrara On Insider Trading and The Wall iii (Law Journal Press 1995).

4. *United States v. Bryan*, 58 F.3d 933, 952–955 (4th Cir. 1995).

Court, which had twice struck down the government's attempt to render inside information contraband, similarly refused the first two attempts to expand the prohibition to non-insiders. Even when ultimately approving the theory by which the government charges "outsiders," the high Court acknowledged that informational disparities among investors are inevitable. Still, between 1961 and the present, the Prohibition has steadfastly traveled upwards to become the pinnacle business regulation in the history of commerce.

———————

The current Book is the story of a single word, a vague Rule, a few dozen people, and a cause memorized by rote. Perhaps the tale is a testament to the persistence of an agency that itself must sing for its supper from Congress on an annual basis. Indeed, the Commission has steadfastly expanded its insider trading arsenal, and the worldwide fear of the unique Prohibition arguably speaks foremost to the ambitious foresight of a bureaucratic goal.

Or maybe the story hinges on the action of Congress, which, when randomly drawn into the scuffle, has consistently empowered an agency and investors to seek higher fines through increased litigation.

But more likely, the Prohibition's raucous journey is a credit to the American judiciary, which, ably availing itself of our common law system, has proven uncannily flexible in bending the equities behind our unique disdain of insider privilege. Boundless Rule 10b-5, the proscription alternatively branded by the Congress that inspired it "a catchall" and later by the highest Court "not a catchall," has more often than not been warmly embraced in the widest of terms by jurists captivated by an undying quest for market equality.

And the enforcement of the Prohibition has most often equated wrong with dollars. Indeed, like the Cold War and the Crusades, efforts at combating insider trading have quite spectacularly launched careers and generated nearly incalculable bounties. When it comes to prosecuting insider trading, it appears that justice is sometimes blind, but it is always richly rewarded.

While many critiques parse the scant 81 words comprising Rule 10b-5, the more challenging analysis of the humble anti-fraud measure expediently drafted nearly 75 years ago may lie in its sole restriction: The claimant party's ability to justifiably invoke *fairness*. From the creation of the modern insider trading prohibition in 1961 through the present time, the *fairness* standard remains the sole discernible predictor in a body of law perennially racing to keep pace with the stock market, thus scattering SEC precedent into that infamous rabbit hole known as "case-by-case basis."

Fairness as contemplated by Congress, the Commission, the experts, or the courts.

Fairness as a lure to attract foreign investors to the highly regulated American markets.

Fairness as measuring rod to compensate the victims of greedy villains.

Fairness as a shibboleth, the recitation of which all but ensures a payday for its pronouncer.

Fairness as a Rorschach test with only one interpretation, should we wish the markets to appear equitable.

Fairness as its own means and end, interpreted on any given day by courts, administrative regulations, private sector guides, government press releases— even in televised docudramas pitting good vs. evil.[5] Ultimately, as this just cause grew, *fairness* towards the insider trader himself has been examined (when he appears to have acted more on serendipity than out of malicious intent). Indeed, like second and third generation photocopies of a favored picture, the fairness standard is now almost unrecognizable in case results.

Accordingly, this Book traces both the unfathomable growth and the consequential earning potential of a rule that transcends its own purpose and language. Indeed, SEC Rule 10b-5 has become the primary calibrant by which the efficacy of regulation is measured, creating estimable careers and fortunes for its best practitioners. The anti-fraud measure historically whipped up by a coterie of practical regulators in 1942 has swelled to premise fines and disgorgements now numbered in the billions. And those billions are shared by government attorneys, prosecutors, the SEC, class action lawyers, nominal plaintiffs, actual victims, educational charities, the Federal budget, and sometimes even whistleblowers (both foreign and domestic).

Ideally, the reader will learn both how the Prohibition developed and how it collaterally grew to become a profit center. Regrettably, as the precedents continue to multiply, the battle against insider trading has been institutionalized to such a degree that significant reform may not be possible.

---

5. In early 2016, a television program titled "Billions" routinely attracted over a million viewers per episode (and grew to have an open following among lawyers and law students). The fictitious show continues to pit a billionaire hedge fund owner of nefarious means against an overly aggressive federal prosecutor with equally questionable tactics. In one episode, a representative of the prosecutor's office pleaded in vain at a federal court hearing for the survival of an insider trading Complaint, arguing repeatedly for "fairness to the marketplace." *Billions* (Episode 10, "Quality of Life," original air date of March 27, 2016).

Nevertheless, it is ultimately for the fresh eyes of law students to decide if the far reach of this storied measure has been judiciously exercised to the benefit of investors, or if it has simply been opportunistically employed in the name of justice.

The Chinese proverb says, "The best way to predict the future is to invent it." No one could have predicted the various means by which regulatory and private fortunes have been generated by a weapon called *fairness*, but Rule 10b-5 most certainly invented them. The *fairness* standard is either a healthy subordination of law to a worthy Congressional goal or the ledger by which an unnamed but juggernaut corporation generates bonuses for all of its managers. Concomitantly, Rule 10b-5's exponential growth is alternatively a triumph of reason over formality or a cautionary tale of scapegoat profiteering. Either way, when it comes to insider trading, the Rule has essentially functioned as a corporation, garnering billions from (and for) those in its path.

J. Scott Colesanti, LL.M.
February 2018

Using This Book

This Book has a two-fold purpose: 1) Describing in detail the origins of American insider trading law, primarily effectuated through application of Securities and Exchange Commission Rule 10b-5, and 2) Detailing the reasons for the revenue streams therefrom. The Book's three parts deal with, in turn, the history of the Prohibition, its period of greatest challenge, and its current (and cowering) embodiment. In turn, each Chapter strives to meets its goal through 3–5 sections progressing from the people to the law to the result. After every three Chapters, a "Checkpoint" Chapter revisits the lessons of the preceding part while gauging the Prohibition's growth.

Footnotes in each Chapter provide direction to the source of a quote or new assertion. For broader reference, a selected bibliography concludes each Chapter; this listing attempts to both further corroborate the statements in each Chapter and to present a variety of views on the key cases and events discussed therein.

It is impossible to research this field without being struck by the sheer repetition of the term "fairness" by attorneys, policy makers, victims, legislators, and jurists. Accordingly, throughout the Book, the term is highlighted in bold.

Because the role of the lawyer is to offer solutions, the Book concludes with over a dozen short and long-term suggestions for a variation on the status quo.

The accompanying Teacher's Manual offers some additional timely questions and cases, as well as more food for thought.

About the Author

J. Scott Colesanti, LL.M., was the first law clerk to a Chief Hearing Officer of the New York Stock Exchange. He investigated his initial insider trading cases within a year of his law school graduation and subsequently served as the youngest Trial Counsel for the New York Stock Exchange Division of Enforcement during his 10-year tenure.

Professor Colesanti has taught at the law school level for over 17 years. In 2006, while serving as an adjunct, he was selected "Professor of the Year" by the Hofstra Law Review. He has developed and taught 10 courses and has had over 20 articles published by legal journals. His writings are included in treatises on securities law and as expert commentaries to seminal cases.

He has also served within the NYSE Office of the General Counsel, and as a securities industry arbitrator for over a decade. Professor Colesanti has handled appeals before the Securities and Exchange Commission, the Social Security Administration, the EEOC, and the New York State Division of Human Rights.

Professor Colesanti regularly lectures on the Financial Crisis and has lectured/taught abroad on securities fraud and insider trading. He served on the editorial board of the *Journal of Securities Law, Regulation and Compliance,* and is a former contributing co-editor of the *Business Law Professor Blog.* As of August 2017, Professor Colesanti was rated among the top 10% of authors ranked by downloads on the Social Science Research Network. "Fairness, Inc." is his third released book.

———————

Part One
Victory without Theory

Chapter I

Fairness over Madness: The Congressional Response to the Great Depression

A decade of false prosperity ended with the arrival of unprecedented stock market losses in the last ten days of October 1929. The early results left people holding empty accounts, their institutions bankrupted by inscrutable lending practices. The ensuing fallout lead to unfathomable facts: Unemployment at 25%, half of all New York Stock Exchange securities proven worthless, a ruined farming system, half of all residential homes in foreclosure, and over 3,000 banks shuttered.

The economic collapse devastated rich and poor alike. In 1932, Herbert Hoover was replaced, and the Republicans lost 101 seats in the House of Representatives. A new type of thinking and a meaningful change on a national scale was demanded. First, it would take political skills to communicate what had gone wrong, and who was to blame.

A. The People Behind Fairness

Franklin Delano Roosevelt, the country's 32nd President, is remembered by many as a beacon of hope. His first inaugural address (March 1933) is widely known for the persisting exhortation that Americans had "nothing to fear but fear itself." That impassioned introduction of the nation's new steward also proclaimed the "falsity of material wealth as the standard of success," while boasting that "The money changers have fled from their high seats in the temple of our civilization." Less recalled from that address was the progressive leader's promise of "strict supervision of all banking and credits and investments, so that there [would] be an end to speculation with other people's money."

The morose state of American life in the 1930s has been aptly chronicled. The prior decade's reckless speculation had been comically showcased: New York banks borrowed money from the federal government at 5% and then lent it at 12%. An Assistant U.S. Attorney was said to have called upon a brokerage and learned that its offices "were equipped with a peephole like a speakeasy." Concomitantly, "brokers loans" enabling mass speculation (i.e., buying stock on "margin") reached a total of six billion dollars by the end of 1928. Subsequently, the Depression's most obvious victims were pictured queuing up on soup kitchen lines or wandering aimlessly in search of jobs that had been eliminated. Account holders stormed banks that had run out of assets. Men bought crates of apples to sell their contents on street corners. Farms dried up into "dust bowls," and people slept in their cars, a safe haven because automobiles (unlike homes) had been purchased with cash. Rumors told of busted stockbrokers leaping to their deaths.

Faced with unprecedented domestic malaise and an unchartable foreign agenda, FDR (months before repealing the nationwide alcohol ban) prioritized vast legislative changes to banking and securities law. The remedial Bills focused on the securities market both federalized state common law principles and invented some new ones.

Despite the dire state of the economy and the nation, opposition by vested interest was still strong—a bold stance given that the average brokerage house had pledged 1 dollar of assets up to 10 times during the unregulated halcyon days of the '20s. But FDR the politician would not abandon his pledge to reform Wall Street, enlisting allies from varied walks of life to effectuate the New Deal. What the new President (a former State Senator and Governor of New York) lacked in experience with financial regulation he more than made up for with savvy use of villainous symbols. One notable ally in the campaign to publicize the cause of so much despair came not from Washington but a region much closer to Wall Street itself.

Ferdinand Pecora was first known as a stellar prosecutor in New York. An immigrant who arrived from Sicily as a boy in 1892, he rose to serve as acting District Attorney of Brooklyn County in the 1920s. Overall, he prosecuted in excess of 1,000 cases, some of which involved unlawful "bucket shops" (i.e., fraudulent purveyors of cheap stocks). At least one of his verdicts he himself upset upon learning of his witness' fraud. Ultimately, his doggedness and/or alienation of political forces stalled his career, relegating him to what he considered unfulfilling private practice.

But Pecora's career flaw of scrupulous ethics and resultant political stagnation ultimately benefited the country. A Senate subcommittee authorized during the Hoover administration to investigate short sale[1] abuse had lapsed into disuse. After the Democratic victory in both houses and the White House in 1932, Pecora was personally invited to reinvigorate the subcommittee as its new Counsel. Bored with his career, he accepted a pay cut to move to Washington, D.C. to fill a likely short-term position.

As 12,000 pages of testimony prove, the resulting Pecora Hearings were anything but short. It is now axiomatic that the former prosecutor's exemplary cross-examination of Wall Street titans on the Senate Floor exposed many of the business' corrupt practices of the 1920s to the public. Pecora revealed a world of interlocking corporate directorships, discriminatory pricing, "preferred lists," and other secret stock dealings. He had uncovered chieftains who did not pay taxes and companies that had packaged near worthless stocks. His determined attacks compelled legendary J.P. Morgan to confess that the mammoth concern made costly loans to other banks because, "They are friends of ours and we know that they are good, sound straight fellows."[2] The financial titan was deliberately humbled by photographers who sat a little person on his lap to snap a shot of the circus that American finance had become. So effective were these and Pecora's tactics that they caused the resignation of the CEO of the entity that was to become Citibank, and a utility magnate to flee the country (only to return upon Washington's pressure on Greece for extradition).

However, the greater contribution by Pecora may have been his ambitious interpretation of his subcommittee's scope. As originally charged, the Senate grouping was to investigate wrongful "bear raids," whereby company officials sold company stock short (an evil that Herbert Hoover had even disliked). Indeed, the misuse of corporate "inside" information had not been taken up on the Floor of Congress since 1913. A skilled strategist, Pecora impressed upon key Senators the freedom of the subcommittee under its original charge to investigate inadequate disclosure and many other ills of the pre-Crash market. The politicians liked the approach, and the expansion was memorialized in the Committee's Report of June 6, 1934. The Committee's new powers included:

---

1. "Selling short" involves the sale of a security borrowed or otherwise not yet owned. The practice, by itself, is not illegal.

2. CHARLES R. GEISST, WALL STREET, A HISTORY 224 (1997).

(1) To make a thorough and complete investigation of the operation by any person, firm, copartnership, company, association, corporation, or other entity, of the business of banking, financing, and extending credit; and of the business of issuing, offering, or selling of securities;

(2) To make a thorough and complete investigation of the business conduct and practices of security exchanges and of the members thereof;

(3) To make a thorough and complete investigation of the practices with respect to the buying and selling and the borrowing and lending of securities which are traded in upon the various security exchanges, or on the over-the-counter market, or on any other market; and of the values of such securities ...[3]

That tactical expansion of authority proved pivotal, as an "us versus them" mentality characterized the period of legislative reform. John Kenneth Galbraith, the chief chronicler of the Depression, concluded that "only one and a half million people out of a population of approximately 120 million" were associated with stock purchases. Accordingly, changes to that market avoided investor accountability and remained centered on the titans, whom Pecora through his hearings successfully branded as both predatory and dangerously situated. To be sure, a gospel-like call for modifications to duties was largely inevitable, thanks to a full half of the nation's $100 billion in securities proving to be worthless, and the related failure of 40% of all of the nation's banks. Concurrently, Pecora placed witnesses in the stand and forced them to speak their folly, thereby identifying the culprits behind dustbowl despair.

In sum, Pecora did not disappoint FDR. The Senate hearings bearing his name succeeded in salvaging the progressive President's push for the federalization of the securities laws.[4]

Indeed, when it came time to adopt the first of these measures, Congress was whipped into a veritable frenzy:

> *Mr. Sabath.* I cannot yield. We have today millions upon millions of shares of stock outstanding that were at the time of listing of ques-

---

3. Senate Committee on Banking and Currency, *Stock Exchange Practices*, Report No. 1455, 73rd Cong., 2d Sess. (June 6, 1934).

4. Namely, the Securities Act of 1933, otherwise known as the "Truth in Securities Act" ("the '33 Act"). The following year, the Securities Exchange Act ("the '34 Act") was adopted (collectively hereinafter "the Acts").

tionable value and now are of no value at all, but are still being manipulated in. The gentlemen who control and manipulate the stock exchanges, hungry as they are for profit and more profit, have listed stocks that should never have been listed, and they will continue for many years to unload worthless stocks upon the American people until we pass a law that will prevent them from perpetrating the frauds that have been practiced upon the people of this Nation for many years. [*Applause.*][5]

Armed with market suspicion that predated FDR and fervent populist support attending his inauguration, Congress acted broadly in adopting, in turn, the '33 Act and the '34 Act. New and unprecedented details were required to be shared by issuers. These details were ensured publicity through required filings and related private causes of action; those causes of action eradicated traditional pleading requirements of reliance and knowledge, and were even guided by roadmaps within the statutes. Additionally, states, stock exchanges, and investors were enlisted in the fight to encourage diligent disclosure through civil litigation, creating a veritable mosaic of securities regulation showcasing government, industry, and investors as tiles.

As for informational advantages among management, that particularized ill was but one of many Depression-era foils to be addressed.[6] A spokesman for courts' "minority approach" (i.e., the view that disclosure should attend all securities purchases) was needed in 1934. And here FDR turned to one of his political advisers and most celebrated young minds.

———————

Thomas Corcoran, a lawyer with a much higher pedigree than Pecora, is credited with helping Franklin Roosevelt obtain a variety of New Deal victories. Corcoran's fame as a bare-knuckle lobbyist is belied by his aristocratic background. He was valedictorian of his 1922 graduating class at Brown University. He subsequently graduated from Harvard Law School and served as a secretary for Oliver Wendell Holmes at the Supreme Court. He then worked in stock issuance on Wall Street and briefly for the Federal Reserve Board. Dubbed Felix Frankfurter's

———————

5. Congressional Record—House (May 1933), at 2915.

6. The Supreme Court later acknowledged that insider trading was but a minor concern of Congress in 1934, stating that "most of the proposed legislation was directed at regulation of the stock exchanges themselves and certain trading practices that were considered undesirable regardless of who performed them ... Most of the hearings, therefore, dealt with other problems." *Foremost-McKesson, Inc. v. Provident Securities Co.*, 423 U.S. 232, n. 22 (1976).

"favorite pupil," he was both confidant of and servant to FDR, who retained Corcoran—an appointee of outgoing Herbert Hoover—after the 1932 election.

The political tasks with which he assisted ranged from the laudatory (e.g., the successful passage of the '33 Act) to the questionable (e.g., the unsuccessful Court-packing plan of 1938). In between, he led the charge to adopt Section 16(b) of the Securities Exchange Act, the one and only Congressional measure ever to expressly define the improper use of "inside information."

Specifically, Corcoran told Congress in the spring of 1934 of the dire need for Section 16(b)'s admittedly "crude rule of thumb,"[7] a strict liability provision characteristic of what lawyers today call "prophylactic measures." Without examining intent, the cause of action would unsettle all of an insider's paired purchases and sales within a strict 6-month period in order to dissuade such short term trading. Outsiders of consequence were lumped together with insiders under the statute; for reasons explained only in the briefest of terms, ten percent shareholders were deemed equally suspicious with corporate insiders.

With such a full plate, Congress cast the regulation of insider trading as solely the duty of the private litigant—not an irrational choice given that the same '34 Act was creating anew the agency to enforce the Acts (i.e., the SEC). The singular attempt by the 1934 Congress (or any successor Congress) to define insider trading, that measure was stated in relevant part as follows:

> For the purpose of preventing the **unfair** use of information which may have been obtained by such beneficial owner, director, or officer by reason of his relationship to the issuer, any profit realized by him from any purchase and sale ... of any equity security of such issuer ... within any period of less than six months ... shall inure to and be recoverable by the issuer, irrespective of any intention on the part of such beneficial owner, director, or officer in entering into such transaction ...

Section 16(b) thus recouped from the "insider" (real or presumptive) any and all profits resulting from purchases and sales of company stock within a demi-year. As a net, it ensnared all subject traders, regardless of intent, prompting subsequent commenters to term the measure "a spring gun that can hit the innocent as easily as the guilty."[8] The balance to this overreach was a finite time

---

7. *See* THOMAS LEE HAZEN, SECURITIES REGULATION/CASES AND MATERIALS 603 (7th ed. 2006) (describing the 1934 Floor testimony of Mr. Corcoran).

8. LARRY D. SODERQUIST & THERESA A. GABALDON, SECURITIES REGULATION 524 (7th ed. 2010).

period (6 months) and a modest 2-year statute of limitations, as well as a plain remedy sounding in disgorgement of the entire profit in favor of the issuer. Likewise, the newly formed SEC was expressly granted the authority to exempt transactions "not comprehended within the purpose of this subsection."

The three men—FDR, Pecora, and Corcoran—together had succeeded in demonizing Wall Street, federalizing the securities laws, and outlawing profiteering by company officials/its largest shareholders. FDR's "three R's" (relief, recovery, reform) had been reordered, with reform to financial regulation quickly accomplished within 18 months of the progressive leader's taking office. The private citizenry would be deputized to assist the cause of corporate disclosure. Wrong would be measured in dollars, and judges would have a statute to interpret. While debating Section 16(b), Congress considered and rejected a provision that extended to all persons; critics thus routinely fault Section 16(b) for not going further. However, the measure's lasting contributions are still impressive.

B. The Law of Section 16(b)

Section 16(b) contributed a new vocabulary in the uniquely American title of "unfair use of information" (later branded, in turn, "inside information" and "material, nonpublic information"). No prior federal law had outlawed management's personal use of corporate advantages, and even state common law had branded the condemnation of such as "the minority approach."[9] No legislator, agency, official or scholar had yet publicly named "insider trading," and the foul was but one of many uncovered by the lingering autopsy of the 1920s market. Once codified, the fair notion that insiders should pay back the profits linked to their insider status needed help from both the SEC and federal courts tasked with enforcing the novel measure.

1. Early Interpretations

The strict liability provision was enabled by its preceding subsection (16(a)), which required subject individuals to file records of personal transactions in

---

9. The Supreme Court, almost 3 decades before the Acts, had identified a departure from common law in recognizing "special circumstances" which could trigger a corporate duty to disclose confidential facts before a securities transaction. *Strong v. Repide*, 213 U.S. 419 (1909). However, at the time of the adoption the Acts, the common law's "majority rule" still maintained that no such duty generally existed.

their company stock with the government. The operative language of 16(b) itself contains four determinations:

1) whether the subject party was a 10% beneficial shareowner, a director, or an officer;

2) whether there was a purchase and a paired sale (*i.e.*, a "swing trade" emerged);

3) whether such paired transactions resulted in a "profit realized"; and

4) whether the paired transactions occurred within six months.[10]

The first two of these goals have proven the most in need of Commission/judicial interpretation. An encapsulation of the first pair of these focal points appears below:

- Concerning subject companies and employees, Section 16(b), by its own terms, does not apply to all corporations. As initially drafted, the subject entity must have its stock listed on a national securities exchange; Commission rule amendments in 1954 extended coverage to OTC (i.e., unlisted) companies. Today, SEC Rule 12g ensnares all companies with assets exceeding $10 million and at least 500 shareholders. Notably, once a stock triggers 16(b)'s coverage, even private transactions thereof (i.e., away from a stock exchange) are fair game.

- Concerning the transactions to be paired, the subject purchase/sale must involve common stock or convertible debt, but different classes of securities (e.g., common stock and unsecured bonds) may be matched in the process.[11]

Debates over Section 16(b)'s proper scope have abounded since its adoption, as have seeming transgressions caused by vagaries. Interpretations can, at times, appear capricious. For example, for officers and directors, the reporting obligation commences upon assuming the title and ends upon forgoing the title. However, for beneficial owners, the reporting duty starts with the trade after accumulating 10% (and similarly ends with the trade after falling below the threshold).

Smolowe v. Delendo

The third and fourth focal points of 16(b) (i.e., the "profit realized," and the six-month period) were largely presumed self-explanatory until clarified by the federal bench in 1943. As the home of Wall Street, the Second Circuit was turned to — as it would be time and time again — to set the contours of the

---

10. A full version of Section 16(b) appears in the Appendices to this Book.
11. *Gund v. First Florida Banks*, 726 F.2d 682 (11th Cir. 1984).

new Prohibition. Specifically, in *Smolowe v. Delendo Corporation*,[12] two share-holders sued two Directors for purchases and sales during a six-month time frame in which insiders knew that a favorable tax settlement of the government would speed a profitable sale of the company. The District Court read Section 16(b) to maximize recovery and thus ordered "rescission" of approximately $19,000 from the Directors.

On appeal, the Second Circuit was asked to consider both the role of the Director's lack of bad faith and the calculation of the award. On the former point, the opinion readily concluded that Congress had not intended that plaintiffs prove misuse of inside information. Such an interpretation, felt the court, would "render senseless" both the six-month capture period and the two-year statute of limitation. On the latter point (the calculation), the ma-jority opinion disregarded the inability of the plaintiff to match share cer-tificates or purchases with sales. The rough analogy to IRS "first in, first out" accounting dictates attempted to be offered by Corcoran during Congressional debate was dignified; although a cruder "high-low" approach was ultimately favored, courts similarly to this day strain to match any pur-chase with any sale during the relevant time frame to maximize the recoverable gain.

In sum, *Smolowe* gave Section 16(b) teeth, claws, and fangs. As Judge Charles Edward Clark (an FDR appointee) neatly summarized, "The primary purpose of the Securities Exchange Act—as [its] declaration of policy in sec-tion 2 makes plain—was to insure a **fair** and honest market, that is, one which would reflect an evaluation of securities in the light of all available and pertinent data."[13] In penalty, the Section 16(b) assault—one which the Commission itself confesses was an "indirect attack" on insider trading—fo-cused solely on money, a dangerously uncontrollable remedy in years to come. But such a focus on recovery (not yet labeled "disgorgement") was ex-pedient, given that criminal referral and reports of trades by other private investors were both beyond the reach of private plaintiffs in 1943.

In addition to upholding the most unforgiving of protocols, *Smolowe* also set the precedent for a number of insider trading case staples. First, the lack of any criminal penalty (or civil penalty for information dissemination) within

---

12. *Smolowe v. Delendo Corp.*, 136 F.2d 231 (2d Cir. 1943). Interestingly, Milton V. Free-man, who later helped to draft Rule 10b-5, was among the attorneys representing the gov-ernment as "intervenor-appellee."

13. *Smolowe*, 136 F.2d at 235.

Section 16(b) were cited for the premise that Congress had eschewed these stances in general. Second, supporting authority spanned the spectrum, ranging from the Congressional record to Internal Revenue Code cases, to private litigation, and, of course, to SEC disciplinary decisions. Third, as an example of a case upholding a prophylactic measure, *Smolowe* can be cited as evidence that strict liability approaches seem to largely invite flouting and prolonged litigation. Trials over the scope of 16(b)'s purchase/sale requirement have risen to the Supreme Court level more often than any other form of insider trading dispute.[14] And, on a daily basis, intricacies such as the rules governing joint and custodial accounts continue to spur 16(b) claims.[15]

Separately, *Smolowe* may have repaired a flaw of the '34 Act by providing for attorney fees, which the court dramatically confirmed in the opinion's concluding sentence: "Since in many cases such as this the possibility of recovering attorney's fees will provide the sole stimulus for the enforcement of §16(b), the allowance of which must not be too niggardly." To be sure, there was little incentive in the Acts in general for the private Bar to wage such battles until payday for the plaintiff's lawyer was assured.

2. Other Generous Interpretations

Subsequent Second Circuit courts added to the largesse by clarifying that an attorney commencing a 16(b) action could be entitled to reimbursement for work done on the suit even where the company (as statutory party in interest) commences the litigation.[16] Further, recovery could be possible even where the attorney did nothing more than identify a successful claim for the shareholder.[17] Such measures, deemed necessary to effectuate the statutory

---

14. Namely, Section 16(b) has been ruled on by the Supreme Court in at least 5 cases: *Blau v. Lehman*, 368 U.S. 403 (1962) (refusing to find a partner's employer subject to the swing trading rule); *Reliance Elec. Co. v. Emerson Elec. Co.*, 404 U.S. 418 (1972) (allowing a 13% shareholder to break up sales to minimize reporting obligations); *Kern County Land Co. v. Occidental Petroleum Co.*, 411 U.S. 582 (1973) (finding that an option to sell securities attending an involuntary merger was an "unorthodox transaction" and not a covered "sale"); *Foremost-McKesson, Inc. v. Provident Securities Co.*, 423 U.S. 232 (excepting the initial purchase placing the tender offeror over the 10% threshold); and *Credit Suisse v. Simmonds*, 132 S. Ct. 1414 (2012) (refusing to extend 16(b)'s two-year statute of limitations).

15. *See, e.g.*, SEC Rule 16a-1(a)(2)(ii) (explaining when spouses will be deemed the beneficial owner of each other's account).

16. *Gilson v. Chock Full O' Nuts Corp.*, 331 F.2d 107, '61–'64 CCH Dec ¶91, 362 (2d Cir. 1964) (en banc).

17. *Blau v. Rayette-Faberge, Inc.*, 389 F.2d 469, '67–'69 CCH Dec. ¶92,150 (2d Cir. 1968).

plan, helped snowball the provision into a glaring tool of recovery. In one 2008 case alone, a settlement of $11 million was obtained by the plaintiffs.[18]

In terms of exclusivity, Section 16(b) was expressly found by the *Texas Gulf Sulphur* court (discussed in Chapter III) to not preclude additional insider trading remedies. Further, although rare, there does exist case law applying both Section 16(b) and Rule 10b-5 to the same conduct.[19] Thus, the seminal insider trading provision, although later weakened by application of Rule 10b-5, is still cumulative in nature. This is a truism that characterizes various Prohibition remedies to this day.

C. Observations

Indeed, the early cases interpreting Section 16(b) set the letter and tone for the Prohibition in many further, unexpected ways. These cases foretold of Prohibition battles to come; five lasting and varied observations are addressed below.

• SEC role as cop has grown

Section 16(a)'s reporting requirements have become a source of notable fines. Impressively, Section 16(a) of the '34 Act, by granting the Commission the authority to enforce the filing of beneficial ownership reports necessary to effectuate 16(b), has itself proven to be a money-earner. As late as 1966, the Commission sought injunctions to prevent violations of Section 16(a) via failure to report personal trades.[20] Since then, while not frequent, SEC enforcement actions imposing monetary fines have been spectacular.[21] In 2014, a number of companies were disciplined to the tune of $2.6 million, and, in 2017, one company alone paid $15 million (for section 16(a) and section 14(a) violations). Unlike disgorgement under Section 16(b), fines under Section 16(a) bear no relation to any profit.

---

18. *See* Willkie Farr & Gallagher, Client Memorandum, *Settlement of Section 16(b) Action Based Upon Equity Swap Positions* (December 19, 2008) (describing the settlement by a British concern titled Children's Investment Management Fund).

19. *See, e.g., Pappas v. Moss*, 257 F. Supp. 345 (D.N.J. 1966).

20. *See, e.g., SEC v. Great American Industries, Inc.*, 259 F. Supp. 99 (S.D.N.Y. 1966).

21. *See, e.g., In re. Infospace* (Dec. 2004) ($83 million in fines; Rule 13d reporting violations also present); *Childrens Investment Fund Management* (Dec. 2008) ($11 million in fines); various individuals disciplined in September 2014 ($2.6 million in fines; Section 16(a) and Rule 13d violations).

• Any company on a stock exchange can be a defendant

What has been consistently clear is that bad faith is irrelevant, and that the defendant company need not be tied to financial services in any fashion. Any year's list of Section 16(b) defendants runs the range of Fortune 500 enterprises. Simply put, with the listing of a class of securities on a stock exchange comes the augur of private suit under Section 16(b).

• Repeat lawsuits by the same plaintiffs are not uncommon

Even a cursory review of Rule 16(b) case law reveals repeat lawsuits brought by the same parties against different companies. Decades later, debates over private litigation would question the role of "professional plaintiffs" within the Prohibition.

• Vagaries persist despite regulatory attention

SEC rulemaking on Section 16(b) is perennial. For example, Rule 16a-1(f) defines "officer," and Rule 16b-3 defines the requirements of exempted employee benefit plan transactions. Such regulations are updated — for inflation, trends, and in response to industry assertions — more than those in many topical areas. Yet, the Section 16(b) suits continue, aided by the shortening of the required time frame for submission of trading reports in 2002, as well as the requirement that all companies file the same electronically in 2003.

• Malleable "theory" is born

Section 16(b) was without precedent — it aimed to punish a fraud but did not examine intent, while unsettling profits without imposing penalty. It thus stands alone within the Prohibition as a strict liability measure. Nonetheless, it indirectly spawned a host of measures subjugating mental states and other requirements to the goal of attaining fairness. The contribution by the 134th Congress of the language "For the purpose of preventing the unfair use of information" had both direct impact on corporate responsibilities and resurgent effect on discussions of compliance tactics. This dual consequence translated into daily practicalities for corporate counsel and their clients.

1. Daily Practicalities of 16(b)

By requiring subject individuals to report their trades in company stock, Section 16(a) of the '34 Act enabled the private cause of action created by Section 16(b). Per subsequent SEC rules, Section 16(b) took on life as a routine and formal reporting requirement for corporate management. The three categories of relevant filings are detailed below:

- "Form 3" serves as the initial filing, providing notice that an individual has become an officer or director, or, if an outsider, a 10% shareholder.
- "Form 4" serves as notice of the covered transaction (i.e., a purchase or sale of company stock or convertible debt).[22]
- "Form 5" serves as a deferred notice or summary of annual reporting.

Form 4 is thus the operative disclosure, as it notifies the public of insider transactions. While not illegal, these transactions—if matched within 6 months, for a profit, per the statute—create a right of recovery for the corporation. The modest Section 16(b) weapon against insider trading adopted by Congress in 1934 itself grew to be a profitable enterprise for a boutique industry of market watchers. Because all of the required documents for review existed in paper form at SEC headquarters in Washington, these law firms blossomed along the middle east coast. Law firms specializing in such matching thus sprung up, normally in the Chesapeake Bay area. These modern day "Armies of the Potomac"—identified pejoratively as "Form 4 Firms"—were known for scouring the paper filings at SEC headquarters in Washington, D.C. for the purpose of filing 16(b) derivative actions. These specialty firms later yielded influence to attorneys nationwide, as the required submissions migrated to the E.D.G.A.R. system between 1993 and 2003[23] (and thus became available via the Internet to all interested parties).

2. Perennial Questions

Much has been made about the refusal of the 1934 Congress to go further when promulgating Section 16(b), both in terms of scope and penalty. Foremost among such concerns is the truth that the SEC itself has no cause of action under the provision. But the measure is nonetheless remarkable for its expansion of corporate fiduciary duties to include the duty to share inside information with stockholders, and, concurrently, to usher in new moralistic expectations of "insiders." As the Smolowe *court stated:*

> *The statute is broadly remedial. Recovery runs not to the stockholder, but to the corporation. We must suppose that the statute was intended to be*

---

22. In 2002, the Sarbanes-Oxley Act shortened the time lapse for such reporting to 2 business days. Pub.L. 107-204 (2002).

23. Born in the mid-1990s, the "E.D.G.A.R.," or Electronic Data Gathering Analysis and Retrieval, system allows any Internet user to access filings submitted to the Commission. The system presently boasts of over 20 million filings.

thorough-going, to squeeze all possible profits out of stock transactions, and thus to establish a standard so high as to prevent any conflict ...[24]

Since the 1948 decision cementing the private cause of action,[25] the provision itself has never truly been in danger of repeal or avoidance. The harsh scrutiny of insider transactions lives on and continues to strike fear into the hearts of officers and directors (the usual target of "swing trading" lawsuits). Over the years, SEC rulemaking has alternatively expanded or contracted the scope of 16(b) but its existence as a weapon has been cemented.[26]

Still, the private cause of action created by Section 16(b) may thus best be remembered for what it did not reach. An issuer's rank and file employees were not subject to the measure, nor the average investor in its stock. Tipping of inside information is unaddressed. Section 16(b) forever focused the Prohibition on *trading*,[27] while the ban left for the future interpretations which would reach those insiders who have others do their trading for them. Finally, not even all companies were contemplated—the issuer had to have a class of securities listed on a national stock exchange. Surprisingly, for a measure more often than not branded a weak compromise, relevant litigation has abounded. A 2012 Supreme Court decision refused to the extend its express 2-year statute of limitations.[28] A May 2015 decision clarified that "reporting groups" (i.e., affiliated entities/people satisfying the 10% threshold of the statute) should include shareholders forming a joint venture group, even in situations where voting power of the shares is delegated to others.[29]

It can safely be said Section 16(b) was a laudable attempt to wrest privilege from the insider. It was without precedent and without follow-up: No prior insider trading provision could boast of such dire consequences for potentially innocent trades, and no subsequent measure would again apply equally to

---

24. 136 F.2d at 239.

25. *Truncale v. Universal Pictures Co.*, 76 F. Supp. 465, 470 (S.D.N.Y. 1948) ("the stockholder's claim under § 16(b) is not, strictly speaking, derivative at all, but one possessing independent statutory origin").

26. *Compare* SEC Rule 16a-10, 17 C.F.R. § 240.16a-10 (1968) (eliminating § 16(b) liability where a transaction is exempted from reporting under § 16(a)), *with* SEC Rule 16a-1(f), 17 C.F.R. § 240.16a-1(f)(1991) (including "officers" in fact along with "officers" in title for purposes of 16(a) reporting).

27. As discussed later in Chapter XIII, some other nations (e.g., Germany) more pointedly address the mere act of spreading inside information in their own prohibitions.

28. *Credit Suisse*, 132 S. Ct. 1414.

29. *Greenberg v. Hudson Bay Master Fund Ltd.*, 2015 WL2212215 (S.D.N.Y. May 12, 2015).

corporate insider and outside investor. It remains the most statutorily grounded piece of the Prohibition. As admirable as it was that Congress offered the scant guidance that it did when first blaming corporate insiders with an informational advantage, as both a general and specific deterrent, its efforts were mixed. It would thus take some creative thinking to craft an application of the existing framework to both cover those with loose lips and to introduce the Commission to the fray; to be sure, discipline that went beyond checkbooks was also a necessity. The combination of those goals and a determined SEC Chair led to the famed *Cady, Roberts* decision, the first subject of the next Chapter.

Selected Bibliography

Hearings Before Senate Committee on Banking and Currency, 73rd Congress, 2d Session 6557 (1934) (testimony of Thomas G. Corcoran).

Herbert J. Deitz, *A Practical Look at Section 16(b) of the Securities Exchange Act*, 43 FORDHAM L. REV. 1 (1974).

SEC Release, *Changes to Exchange Act Registration Requirements to Implement Title V and Title VI of the JOBS Act* (May 24, 2016).

Gilbert King, *The Man Who Busted the "Banksters,"* smithsonian.com (November 29, 2011).

Paul Alexander Gusmorino, *The Main Causes of the Great Depression* (May 13, 1996), *available at* http://www.investorvillage.com.

SEC Release, *SEC Announces Charges Against Corporate Insiders for Violating Laws Requiring Prompt Reporting of Transactions and Holdings/Nearly Three Dozen Charged in Enforcement Initiative to Root Out Repeated Late Filers* (Sept. 10, 2014).

Client Memo, *Section 16 Reporting Requirements as amended by Sarbanes Oxley Act of 2002* (Feb. 27, 2003), *available at* http://www.olshanlaw.com/resources-alerts-111.html.

CHARLES R. GEISST, WALL STREET, A HISTORY 133–34 (Oxford University Press, Inc. 1997) (noting both that the U.S. Senate heard testimony from corporate leaders in 1913 about the use of inside information and that not until 1934 was the practice addressed again by the federal legislature).

Report of Special Study of the Securities Markets of the Securities and Exchange Commission—Part 1 (1963), as requested by H.J. Res. 438, 87th Cong., 1st Sess. (1961).

Chechele v. Morgan Stanley, 896 F. Supp. 2d 297 (S.D.N.Y. Sept. 26, 2012) (following *Credit Suisse* by dismissing a 16(b) complaint filed more than two years after the plaintiff "knew or reasonably should have known" the necessary facts).

Stock Exchange Practices, Introduction to the Pecora Committee Report No. 1455 (June 6, 1934), *available at* http://3197d6d14b5f19f2f440-5e13d29c4c01 6cf96cbbfd197c579b45.r81.cf1.rackcdn.com/collection/papers/1930/1934_ 06_06_Intro_to_Pecora_C.pdf.

Franklin D. Roosevelt: Campaigns and Elections/The Campaign of 1932, UVA Miller Center, https://millercenter.org/president/fdroosevelt/campaigns-and-elections.

JONATHAN MORELAND, PROFIT FROM LEGAL INSIDER TRADING/INVEST TODAY ON TOMORROW'S NEWS (Dearborn Press 2000), at 18 (also noting the confession by the 1934 Congress that not all insider trading could be identified; at pp. 13–14).

Federal Securities Law Reports, *Insider Reporting and Short-Swing Trading,* Report 1527 (November 5, 1992) (Part 2), at 69.

John E. Munter, *Section 16(b) of the Securities Exchange Act of 1934/An Alternative to Burning Down the Barn in Order to Kill the Rats,* 52 CORNELL. L. REV. 69 (Fall 1966).

JOHN KENNETH GALBRAITH, THE GREAT CRASH 1929, at 10, 22, 56 (Mariner Books, 7th ed. 1997). Galbraith, whom *Time* magazine called "one of the great intellectuals of our time," detailed an array of causes for the mammoth stock market decline, chief among which were over-speculation, latent economic flaws, foreign trade imbalance, and the listing of ill-understood investment trusts on the New York Stock Exchange in 1929. The reference to the brokerage house with the speakeasy "peephole" appears on p. 64.

Thomas G. Corcoran Obituary: https://www.washingtonpost.com/archive/local/ 1981/12/07/thomas-g-tommy-corcoran-lobbyist-of-new-deal-era-dies/e95 f174b-338e-4486-ab2c-eb11103b6190/?utm_term=.9b35e1644821.

Thomas G. Corcoran Obituary: http://www.nytimes.com/1981/12/07/ obituaries/thomas-g-corcoran-aide-to-roosevelt-dies.html.

Peter M. Dugre, *Securities Exchange Act Section 16(b): Fourth Circuit Harvests Some Kernels of Gold,* 42 FORDHAM L. REV. 852 (1974).

ROBERT W. HAMILTON, CORPORATIONS (Black Letter Series) (2d ed. 1986) ("Section 16(b) creates automatic liability ... 'Profits' are computed so as to squeeze out all possible profit (in favor of the corporation." at 348–349; "Most inadvertent violations probably are a result of the failure to appreciate how broadly the words 'purchase' and 'sale' are construed," at 351).

SEC, *Statement on Leon Cooperman Settling Insider Trading Charges* (May 18, 2017) (describing, among others, a $1 million penalty for "beneficial ownership reporting violations").

Fair to All People: The SEC and the Regulation of Insider Trading, http://www.
sechistorical.org/museum/galleries/it/fullDisclosure_a.php ("Instead of a
direct frontal attack on insider trading, the SEC [via the SEA] promoted
the values of full disclosure for investors to insure a high standard of
fairness and ethical business dealing in the securities industry.").

Chapter II

Fire Trucks and Alarms:
The Birth of Rule 10b-5

*It soon became clear that not only officers, directors, and large share-
holders enjoyed privilege. The '34 Act had promised an agency to enforce
rules controlling fraud. The resulting sword within the Prohibition was
Rule 10b-5, a generic measure adopted by a show of hands before agency
rulemaking was formalized and opened to the public. More secretive still
is the story of the paths not taken or trampled in the crafting of a brief
measure that would later justify the reallocation of fortunes.*

A. The People Behind the Rule

Addison Ward LaFrance, an American entrepreneur, was an ambitious man.
In the early 1900s, he interned with his uncle's New York company, "LaFrance
Manufacturing" (which made fire trucks and parts); by 1918, Addison had
launched his own rival company, "American Ward LaFrance." A trademark dispute nearly a century later noted that, in name and purpose, the two businesses
competed for over 50 years. But Addison's greater legal struggle may have taken
place in the 1940s, when the company bearing his name took hold as a closely-
held concern in Boston.

By 1942, Ward LaFrance had over 27,000 shares outstanding. Addison and
the company treasurer owned over 20,000 shares (i.e., 74%). That summer,
another ambitious man convinced Addison to embark on a stock buyback plan
in anticipation of a lucrative, private sale of the entire company. A stockbroker
was hired to purchase Ward LaFrance shares from shareholders, who knew not
the identity of the purchaser, nor of the company's dramatic upturn: During

the first 11 months of 1942, the government's wartime need for fire trucks had quietly increased net income eleven-fold, and jumped earnings per share nearly 500%. The 1941 financials—the only data available to shareholders—did not give any hint of the glaring 1942 profits.

The broker succeeded in quietly buying back over 2,300 shares, thus enhancing the control value of the shares owned by Addison and the treasurer. Whereas the selling shareholders could rely only on the 1941 financials, the company's planned buyer twice received updated financials disclosing the boom in Ward LaFrance profits. More importantly, all of the subject stock was bought back between $3 and $6 a share; Addison and the treasurer, in turn, sold all of their shares to the buyer at over $45 a share.

The sale of the company was completed in November 1942. Complaints by shareholders who had sold cheap were subsequently made to the SEC. But the Commission had already been watching.

1. Buybacks without Details

In the spring of 1942, both the Philadelphia and Boston offices of the SEC buzzed with tales of owners buying back company stock without disclosing company good fortunes. Records establishing the seminal case diverge, but it appears that the Ward LaFrance buyback was one example haunting the Commission. Apart from its obvious dishonesty, buyback fraud offended conscience for several reasons: 1) The sole anti-fraud provision within the Securities Act of 1933 nominally reached only *sales* (whereas buyback artists committed fraud in the *purchase*), 2) Section 16(b)—the only clean fit for an insider's personal use of confidential corporate information—did not grant the SEC a cause of action, and did not reach private companies, and 3) The SEC had been tasked 8 years earlier with effectuating the anti-fraud provision found in Section 10(b) of the '34 Act, and no rule had yet been adopted.

The SEC Commissioners—displaced to Philadelphia by the wartime crunch on D.C. office space—thus took immediate action against a beknighted practice and adopted Rule 10b-5. The populist recollection describes a yellow legal pad being passed around a table seating the handful of chieftains, who all agreed to the addition of a sole sentence to text borrowed from Section 17(a) of the '33 Act[1]. Therefore, the impromptu administrative act served to close the statutory loophole (i.e., since the '33 Act was adopted in response to crooked *sellers* on the New York Stock Exchange, there had not been cause nor

---

1. 15 U.S.C. §77q (2012).

time to address crooked *buyers* in the secondary market). Rule 10b-5, as adopted, thus expressly added purchasers to the mix:

> It shall be unlawful for any person, directly or indirectly, by the use of any means or instrumentality of interstate commerce, or of the mails or of any facility of any national securities exchange,
>
> (a) To employ any device, scheme, or artifice to defraud,
>
> (b) To make any untrue statement of a material fact or to omit to state a material fact necessary in order to make the statements made, in the light of the circumstances under which they were made, not misleading, or
>
> (c) To engage in any act, practice, or course of business which operates or would operate as a fraud or deceit upon any person,
> **in connection with the purchase or sale of any security.** (emphasis added)[2]

The populist view of Rule 10b-5's origin further opines that Section 17(a)'s failure to contemplate fraud on the *buy* side was merely Congressional myopia: The '33 Act targeting fraudulent issuance of securities, there was no cause to protect defrauded sellers. To be sure, Congress had become transfixed on the example of issuers and their agents pushing worthless securities on buyers.[3] But the statute itself renders that pedestrian history a bit superficial.

'33 Act Section 17(a)

First, taken as a whole, Securities Act Section 17(a) is intent neutral. It reaches conduct—even well meaning—that results in a fraud upon the investor. Conversely, as has become axiomatic, all three branches of SEC Rule 10b-5 require intent or extreme recklessness on the part of the defendant.

Second, by the SEC's own admission, Rule 10b-5 was necessary to expand the scope of the defendants subject to the Commission's anti-fraud measures. As the minutes of the famed May 1942 Commissioners meeting disclose:

---

2. At no time has the language of Rule 10b-5 mentioned "insider trading," although the term was added to related Section 10 of the '34 Act in 2010 (to make swap agreements amenable to prosecution).

3. One tale described the stock of "Banco Corporation" being listed on the Chicago Stock Exchange when its assets were falsely quadrupled. *See, e.g.,* 78 Cong. Rec. (1934), at 7077–7081. Of course, Congress concluded that, overall, "millions of shares" of questionable value had been issued in the 1920s. *See supra* p. 6.

> The Securities and Exchange Commission today announced the adoption of a rule prohibiting fraud by any person in connection with the purchase of securities. The previously existing rules against fraud in the purchase of securities applied only to brokers and dealers ...

Essentially, Section 10(b) of the '34 Act had expressly called upon the Commission to draft enabling rules, thus foretelling of an antifraud measure of some ilk at some juncture. When buyback fraud highlighted the threat caused by non-industry personnel, a broad measure was necessitated.

Finally, the drafters of Section 17(a) (the only anti-fraud measure granted the government by the '33 Act) must have contemplated that a sale would be accompanied by a purchase, rendering fraud in one-half of the transaction detrimental to the entire trade. In fact, section 17(a) of the '33 Act from its adoption has included such an elaboration in its definitional section:

> The terms "sale", "sell", "offer to sell", or "offer for sale" shall include every contract of sale or disposition of ... a security or interest in a security, for value ... *Any security given or delivered with, or as a bonus on account of any purchase of securities or any other thing, shall be conclusively presumed to constitute a part of the subject of such purchase and to have been sold for value* (emphasis added).

Accordingly, Section 17(a) arguably already reached the trades of buyback fraudsters, who provided ample opportunity for the Commission to strengthen its arsenal by reaching non-registrants (i.e., entities other than broker-dealers), the over-the-counter (i.e., non-exchange) market, and purchases without accompanying sales. Nonetheless, the perception of Rule 10b-5 as expedient stop-gap persisted. That simplicity was reinforced by the measure's title, which for years to come concluded with the words "by a Purchaser."[4] Yet the larger loophole to be closed centered on unfair transactions by corporate insiders with an informational advantage, a cause without name when considered by Congress in 1934.

Actual Goals?

In truth, while Rule 10b-5 nominally expanded Section 17(a) of the Securities Act to cover secondary trading under the Exchange Act, the measure actually exponentially enlarged the reach of the securities laws by freeing disciplinary cases from any meaningful statutory standard. Indeed, the 1942 Commission faced a conundrum not born of "loopholes," but rather one of granted

---

4. *See* Securities Exchange Act Release No. 3634 (August 1951).

wishes. To wit, having been given plenary powers by Congress, it was without adequate law: Section 17(a) of the '33 Act covered only those sizeable entities formally bringing securities to market, and Section 10(b) of the '34 Act served simply as a blank check for future cashing. It was as though the new sheriff, having been sworn in to eliminate Al Capone, knew not what to do when facing a teenage pickpocket, and thus was born a rule that would capture both.

Sans statutory or regulatory standard, that elastic rule required the Commission to simply fall upon a lawyer's sense of equity and looked to reasonable acts attending arms length transactions. Even the casual read discloses that *Ward LaFrance* was in shadow and effect a disclosure case, as the parties in issue were readily determined by the SEC to have bargained unfairly:

> There can be no question that the failure of LaFrance, [the Treasurer], and [the Buyer] to disclose the improved financial operating conditions of the Truck Corporation, the negotiations and deal arranged between them, and the identity of the purchasers of the outstanding shares, placed the stockholders at a distinct disadvantage in dealing with them.[5]

A spectator to a new genre of fraud, and effectively without Congressional guidance, the SEC employed *fairness* as the standard guiding the newest and most potent of the Commission's tools. As shall be demonstrated later on, *fairness* became the default standard for countless 10b-5/insider trading cases with unsympathetic defendants. Thus, it is perhaps more accurate to summarize that the adoption of Rule 10b-5 foremost empowered the Commission's arsenal to imaginatively reach unpredictable, unsavory market behavior and its equally unforeseeable perpetrators, a novel jurisdictional approach that would later be enhanced by doctrines, statutory amendments, and Supreme Court decisions. And of course, *fairness* dictated that, in 1943, Addison and his treasurer be punished.

2. The Result

In May 1943, nearly a year to the date after its adoption, incipient Rule 10b-5 was utilized by the SEC. In announcing formal discipline against Addison and the treasurer titled "Report on Investigation," the Commission tersely concluded that the buyback purchases had been "unaccompanied by appropriate disclosure," and that "adherence to the standards" of Rule 10b-5 would have

---

5. *In the b Matter of The Purchase and Retirement of Ward La France Truck Corporation Class "A" and Class "B" Stocks*, 13 S.E.C. 373, 378–79 (1943). In recognition of the Commission's investigative findings, Addison and the treasurer paid over $164,000 to shareholders who had sold back their shares prior to the sale of the company.

prevented the harm. Footnote 8 to the decision attempted to provide a statutory basis for the decision by adding:

> The standards adopted by the Commission in its rule [10B-5], it will be noted, make applicable to the purchase of securities, the same broad antifraud provisions which the Congress has imposed in Section 17(a) of the Securities Act of 1933, in connection with the sale of securities.[6]

Implicit in the *Ward LaFrance* report was a concept of **fairness** in dealing with shareholders. The decision did not address *insider trading* or its synonyms; however, the authoring Commissioners no doubt were mindful that Congress had implemented Section 16(b) of the '34 Act. Since Ward LaFrance was a private company, its officers could not be sued by investors under Section 16(b) (nor under Section 11 of the Securities Act). Section 17(a), warts and all, needed to be referenced.

The keen observer will further note that *Ward LaFrance* more accurately speaks to the discrepancies between private and public companies in terms of ensuring publicly available information. The company—not being registered—had no duty to update its 1941 financials until year end, perhaps prompting the November paperwork between Addison and the buyer, and undoubtedly shielding news of the company's upturn for most of 1942.[7] Such result was unquestionably unfair, as was the relevant agency's impotence.

Via *Ward LaFrance*, the war on *unfairness* was given limitless new weapons. The Commission at once expanded the scope of defendants (to include private companies), expanded the subject activity (to include secondary market transactions), and filled in the name of the federal regulator to be named later (the SEC). The famed piece of yellow legal pad thus did much more than add a sentence to a statutory provision; it added a second approach, and fulfilled a Congressional mandate in the process. If such monumental change behind administrative closed door seems fantastic, it bears noting that it would be another four years before Section 553 of the Administrative Procedure Act would require public notice and comment for similar rulemaking. If the expedient rulemaking seemed highhanded, it nonetheless served the most noble of causes: investor protection. As Milton Freeman and Mayer Newfield (two of the famed 1942 Commissioners) agreed, the impromptu adoption of the

---

6. 13 S.E.C. at 379 n.8.

7. The decision at footnote 4 notes a shallow proxy soliciting letter dated November 12, 1942. That proxy, coming after the necessary buybacks, again, was not subject to the requirements of Section 14 of the Securities Exchange Act (because LaFrance's securities were not registered).

Rule was punctuated by a declaration, "Well, gentlemen, we are all against fraud, aren't we?"

Non-registered individuals had indisputably come within reach of the SEC. Intent and something less than intent had been proven to suffice. Addison Ward LaFrance and other anonymous repurchasers had been defeated. Curiously, there are no additional reported SEC cases utilizing Rule 10b-5 in the immediate years after 1943. Nineteen years later, the war on *unfairness* was trotted out to target a new but more frequent enemy.

B. 1961, and the Birth of Unfair "Insider Trading"

William L. Cary was both an intellectual and a civil servant. After graduating from Yale University, he served in World War II as an officer with the predecessor to the Central Intelligence Agency. He subsequently taught as a Columbia University professor, and, in 1974, published the leading argument for the federal regulation of corporate charters. Between these stints, he was appointed SEC Chairman, a post he held from 1961–1964.

Early in his Commission stewardship, as legend has it, Cary was asked by President John F. Kennedy to make the markets more egalitarian. The request resonated with Cary, who throughout his Commission tenure opined loudly and often that corporate managers owed duties to the market. His most public screed against company greed was sounded in the Congressionally-mandated "Special Study" of the securities markets of 1963, which read in relevant part as follows:

> A renewal of investors' confidence in the exchange markets can be effected only by a clearer recognition upon the part of the corporate managers and companies whose securities are publicly held of their responsibilities as trustees of their corporations. Men charged with the administration of other people's money must not use inside information for their own advantage. Because it is difficult to draw a clear line as a matter of law between truly inside information and information generally known by the better-informed investors, the most potent weapon against the abuse of inside information is full and prompt publicity ...[8]

---

8. *Report of the Special Study of the Securities Markets of the Securities and Exchange Commission*, April 3, 1963, *available at* http:www/sechistorical.org/museum/papers/1960/page-2.php.

Sensing an immediate opportunity in 1961, Cary focused on a disciplinary case weighing the actions of two stockbrokers from a registered broker dealer called Cady, Roberts & Co. One of the brokerage's registered representatives (J. Cheever Cowdin) simultaneously served as a Director of Curtiss-Wright Aircraft. When a Board meeting at that public company revealed that a pattern of healthy dividends during the first three quarters of 1959 would cease, Cowdin immediately confided the news to his brokerage partner, Robert Gintel. Gintel acted fast (within 20 minutes) to decrease Curtiss-Wright positions in approximately 25 of their (discretionary) customer accounts. Subsequently, the news broke that the corporation's string of robust dividends had ended. The clients of the two brokers profited from the approximately 30-minute head start for the sales. A total of 7,000 shares were sold at a price roughly $5 higher than when the news of the decreased Curtiss-Wright dividend broke. Among Gintel's quick transactions was a short sale in his wife's account, but the broker did not otherwise trade for his own benefit.

The SEC investigation yielded these uncontested facts. Cowdin passed away during the inquiry, but Gintel and the broker-dealer Cady, Roberts were named in the resulting stipulation. That stipulation went before the five SEC Commissioners in November 1961 for a ruling on penalty. Four of the Commissioners agreed upon a 20-day suspension for Gintel and the concurrent recognition of a $3,000 fine which had been imposed by the New York Stock Exchange; the broker-dealer was deemed sanctioned by publicity of the decision.[9] A lone, dissenting Commissioner felt that harsher medicine was warranted.

Cady, Roberts Determinations

The administrative decision that explained these sanctions is forever cited in any Brief that must confirm the existence of the Prohibition. Though reading more like an egalitarian quest than a court ruling, the decision is nonetheless masterful in its amalgamation of support for a rule of law more intuitive than supportable.

First, the decision—in a footnote—endorsed the "special circumstances rule," blandly commenting that the Commission and the courts had "consistently held" that insiders must disclose pertinent facts to their counterparties at the time of the transaction. Gintel was thus found to have "at least" violated subdivision 3 of Rule 10b-5 (i.e., fraud/deception), thus rendering analysis of the first two subdivisions (scheme and misstatements) unnecessary.[10]

---

9. *In re Cady, Roberts & Co.*, 40 S.E.C. 907 (1961).
10. 40 S.E.C. at 911 n.13.

Second, having identified the fraud, the decision simply concluded that Gintel had fulfilled its usual characteristics. Gintel, who had testified to "accidentally" learning of the slashed dividend from a director (i.e., Cowdin), acted willfully when he entered trades for his customers' accounts because "he knew what he was doing." The slashed dividend information was "material" because Gintel and the stock price reacted quickly. And Cady, Roberts was implicated because, as employee, Gintel was the broker-dealer's agent.

In support of these determinations, the Commission cited a wide variety of sources including the "special need of regulation for the protection of investors," NYSE rules, private case law (from the years 1938 right up to 1960), and prior SEC rulings. Notably, such choices commenced with the Commission's declaration of the "the inherent **unfairness** involved where a party takes advantage of such information knowing it is unavailable to those with whom he is dealing." Some other quotes that still permeate pleadings today are listed below:

- "These anti-fraud provisions [Section 17(a) and Rule 10b-5] are not intended as a specification of particular acts or practices which constitute fraud, but rather are designed to encompass the infinite variety of devices by which undue advantage may be taken of investors and others."

- "It might be said of fraud that age cannot wither, nor custom state its infinite variety." [Footnote 12]

- "Failure to make disclosure in these circumstances constitutes a violation of the anti-fraud provisions. If, on the other hand, disclosure prior to effecting a purchase or sale would be improper or unrealistic under the circumstances, we believe the alternative is to forego (sic) the transaction."

The last of the above quotes inspired the language for the extracted "abstain or disclose" rule, a remedial obligation still subscribed to by the Commission.[11] Another doctrinal contribution (also not directly stated) is the parity of information theory, which asserts that all market participants deserve the same information.

Among the defenses rejected by the Commission was the argument that "an insider's responsibility is limited to existing shareholders." Such a "narrow" construction, held the decision, "ignores the plight of the investing public." Here is perhaps the greatest sleight of hand by the 1961 SEC: In extending the

---

11. Likewise, the decision does not use the words "tipper" and "tippee," although those were the roles played by, respectively, Cowdin and Gintel.

insider's duty to shareholders both existing (i.e., sellers) and new (i.e., buyers), the precedents that had rested the duty on a bond between a corporation and its owners were effectively amplified.[12] The Commissioners issuing the *Cady, Roberts* decision opined that to distinguish between defrauded buyers and sellers contravened the anti-fraud letter and spirit of the Acts. Further, the decision — in a footnote — added that the burden is upon the defendant to prove that the buyers of the subject stock were not already shareholders (a task not undertaken by Gintel or his employer, Cady, Roberts).

Lasting Effects

To be sure, the *Cady, Roberts* decision exhibited a number of Commission default arguments (e.g., protecting the inexperienced investor by majestically declaring that, "Intimacy demands restraint, lest the uninformed be exploited."). However, in mission and in purpose, the administrative decision employed *fairness* in creating a new species of wrong, namely, illegal trading by those close to the creation of corporate information. As many commentators have noted, prior to 1961, such opportunistic trading may have legally existed for centuries (and certainly blossomed on Wall Street both before and after FDR's federal regulation). But such advantage would now not only be frowned upon: It was illegal. Chairman Cary had effectuated the President's request, and satisfied his own hopes in the process. An SEC attorney who had worked on the case noted that the *Cady, Roberts* decision had served as the agency's primal attack on yet unlabeled "insider trading," a blow so monumental that Cary insisted on signing the decision personally.

The decision also set a precedent for Section 17(a) and Rule 10b-5 as the premises for a suspension from service and a monetary fine. Yet, *Cady, Roberts* added so much more to Commission lore. Having initially been used against a private company in *Ward LaFrance*, Rule 10b-5 found itself once again grounded in a statutory constraint aimed at public companies, namely the targeted practice of "unfair use of information" introduced in Section 16(b) of the Exchange Act. Further, the SEC commenced its now legendary pattern of testing theories in cases imposing only nominal penalties, a tactic that would seamlessly grow Commission powers in countless subsequent adjudications. Additionally, Commission anti-fraud measures now undoubtedly applied

---

12. For example, *Speed v. Transamerica*, 99 F. Supp. 808 (D. Del. 1951), which is cited by *Cady, Roberts* as a building block for the "special circumstances rule," had held that the duty under Rule 10b-5 existed between corporate management issuing a tender offer to existing shareholders.

equally to face-to-face and exchange-based transactions. Most importantly—as later defendants and their counsel would learn—*Cady, Roberts* birthed the "Classical" approach to liability for insider trading under Rule 10b-5, an application governing insiders that, once attached, is nearly impossible to defeat in court.[13]

C. The Trappings and the Fallout

Overall, taken together, *Cady, Roberts* and *Ward LaFrance* provided agency notice that Rule 10b-5[14] applied to companies both public and private, to defendants both professional and novice, and to behaviors both intentional or with unintended consequences. Continuing a trend made manifest in the adoption of the Acts, the private citizenry would be deputized in the fight against stock market fraud. The American insider trading prohibition was thus at once formalized and made without frontier. And the alarm had been sounded for officers, traders, and other professionals throughout the country.

The observant analysis notes that the Commission could have legislated an insider trading rule (just as it had legislated a fraud upon sellers rule in 1942 in drafting 10b-5). Further, Henry Manne wrote in his controversial 1966 book, *Insider Trading and the Stock Market,* that via litigation, 10b-5 had legislated what Congress had expressly refused to (i.e., a blanket prohibition against **unfairness** in securities transactions). Manne detailed a 1934 Congress that had failed to articulate a reason why insider trading was wrong, or how it could rationally alternate in focus between issuer, broker, and layman.

Manne proved to be not alone in his suspicion of detached lawmaking: A law professor's review of Manne's critical work noted the momentum behind the fledgling Prohibition, which had become "the majority view and the clear policy of the SEC." The same review ultimately found some strength in Manne's

---

13. The two major companion theories of Rule 10b-5 application (the "tippee theory" and the "misappropriation theory") are discussed in detail in Chapters V and VI, respectively.

14. Section 17(a) as a weapon against insider trading has gone in and out of style. Apart from its inapplicability to purchases, Section 17(a) was severed from Rule 10b-5 when the latter was unequivocally held by the Supreme Court to require scienter between 1978 and 1980 (discussed later herein). Those holdings led even the Second Circuit, which had previously found a private claim to exist, to change course, stating "[W]e can no longer justify the private cause of action under §17(a) on the ground that rule 10b-5 provides the same cause of action anyway." *Finkel v. Stratton Corp.*, 962 F.2d 169 (2d Cir. 1992).

arguments, which advanced insider trading as both a legitimate means of corporate compensation and as a means of promoting market stability.

Further, the attentive observer records that the specific deterrence aim of *Ward La France* (i.e., removing buyback artists from the market by taking away all gains) subtly yielded to the general deterrence aim of *Cady, Roberts* (i.e., imposing a mild penalty of a 20-day suspension but establishing discipline for a newly labeled fraud).

The two cases (from 1943 and 1961, respectively) demonstrated a fruitful pattern by which the SEC would provide disquieting facts, and the trier of those facts would supply/affirm the duty and its breach. Such pattern, which earns victory but obscures certainty, would play out repeatedly in administrative hearings and courts for decades to come.

Fast Forward

The Prohibition as stated by Rule 10b-5, a Rule which one former SEC Commissioner labeled "the most fruitful source of implied private remedies under all of federal statutory law,"[15] has grown to serve as statute, regulation, and moral boundary. In the 1980s, Congress twice convened to consider a definition of insider trading. On both occasions, a definition was rejected, but corresponding penalties ended up being expanded. The scope of the Prohibition grew in significance—laymen, analysts, and even a former department of defense undersecretary were charged. And the recovered monies proved fungible: Notorious investment banker Dennis Levine agreed in 1986 that $2 million of his $11 million SEC fine should go to pay back taxes.

In the late 1980s, the government imposed fines totaling $700,000 million against two defendants alone. Halfway through the ensuing decade, Congress and the Supreme Court had acted to diminish securities class actions. However, to any extent that securities fraud litigation diminished as a profitable enterprise, the financial crisis of 2007/2008 resurrected the cause.

To wit, in July 2010, Congress acquiesced to many of the White House's reforms in adopting the Dodd-Frank Investor Protection Act. "Whistleblowers" could now utilize Rule 10b-5 in applying for massive bounties. The U.S. Attorney for the Southern District of New York contemporaneously commenced scores of insider cases generating tens of millions of fines for the federal treasury. Predictably, additional regulators have sought to expand their reach,

---

15. ROBERTA S. KARMEL, REGULATION BY PROSECUTION/THE SECURITIES AND EXCHANGE COMMISSION VERSUS CORPORATE AMERICA 193 (1982).

arguing for broader powers to levy fines. And class actions tied solely to insider trading have grown to include shareholders aggrieved by scoops not shared, failed mergers, and just "bad information."

Clearly, the detection and prosecution of securities fraud has become big business, with a ledger numbering in the billions, attracting middlemen around the world to the crusade. A well-meaning judiciary played a key hand in expanding Rule 10b-5's reach, purpose, and penalties. As Milton Freeman later commented, "Myself, I tend to think that judges do not extend principles that do not appeal to their basic sense of **fairness** and equity." It would be a federal judge in 1946 who confirmed the existence of a private cause of action under Rule 10b-5; it would be the highest court in the land that confirmed in 1997 that the Prohibition extended to those *insiders* "outside" the corporation. In between, the SEC geared up for federal court approbation of its novel "abstain or disclose" requirement. The chance for such approval arose at the expense of some overly opportunistic mineralogists at the core of the 1968 *Texas Gulf Sulphur* case, the focus of the next Chapter.

Selected Bibliography

Wunami Bewaji, Insider Trading in Developing Jurisdictions: Achieving an Effective Regulatory Regime 48–49 (Routledge Press 2012) (noting the Supreme Court's refusal to acknowledge a duty of insiders in *SEC v. Chenery Corp.*, 318 U.S. 80 (1943)).

Book Review, *Insider Trading and the Stockmarket*, by Henry G. Manne, *available at* scholarship.law.duke.edu/cgi/viewcontent.cgi?article=2096&content=dlj.

Jennifer Bothamley, Dictionary of Theories 168 (defining the "efficient market hypothesis").

Congressional Record—House (May 22, 1933), at 3891–3892.

Christopher Matthews, *Why is insider trading even illegal?* (July 26, 2013), *available at* http://business.time.com/2013/07/26/why-is-insider-trading-even-illegal/ (noting that the goal of insider trading law is "to promote a fair stock market").

Bromberg, Securities Fraud/Fraud—SEC Rule 10b-5, at 63 (1973) ("Finally, the generality of 10b-5's language overruns neat boundaries. All that we can sensibly do is explore the territories it occupies or has under siege.").

Department of Justice web page, *Meet the U.S. Attorney—Preet Bharara*, https://www.justice.gov/usao-sdny/meet-us-attorney (last visited February 17, 2017).

Roni A. Elias, *The Legislative History of the Administrative Procedures Act*, 27 Fordham Envt'l L. Rev. 207 (2016).

Milton V. Freeman, *Administrative Procedures*, 22 Bus. Law. 891 (1966–67) (detailing the famed story of the adoption of Rule 10b-5 in response to the purchase "loophole" occasioned by Section 17 of the 1933 Act).

In the Matter of Albert Heglund, Jr. and Fred O. Paulsell, Jr., SEC Administrative Proceeding No. 3-3253 (March 11, 1974) (noting that the *Ward La France* decision was the first published use of Rule 10b-5; at FN 2).

In re Independent Media Marketing, Inc., No. 76411149 (Sept. 29, 2004), United States Patent and Trademark Office, Trademark Trial and Appeal Board, p. 8.

Note, *Section 17(a) of the '33 Act: Defining the Scope of Antifraud Protection*, 37 Wash. & Lee L. Rev. 859, 862 (1980) (explaining the Supreme Court's ruling in *United States v. Naftalin*, 441 U.S. 768 (1980), that the defendant, in effecting sales and offsetting purchase, engaged in a scheme, and that the three subsections of Section 17(a) make no distinction between initial issue or aftermarket trading).

Securities and Exchange Commission, Decision and Reports, Volumes 12–15, U.S. Government Printing Office.

SEC Press Release No. 3230 (May 21, 1942) (announcing the adoption of Rule 10b-5 to close a loophole in the protections against fraud).

Mark A. Ryan, "What Did Congress Really Want? An Implied Private Right of Action Under Section 17(a) of the 1933 Securities Act," 63 Indiana Law Journal 623 (1988).

SEC Press Release, *Whistleblower Earns $3.5 Million Award for Bolstering Ongoing Investigation* (May 13, 2016) ("Whistleblowers can receive an award not only when their tip initiates an investigation, but also when they provide new information or documentation that advances an existing inquiry."; statement of Director of Commission's Division of Enforcement).

SEC Press Release, *SEC Announces Insider Trading Changes in Case Involving Sports Gambler and Board Member* (May 19, 2016).

SEC Press Release, *Sean McKessy, Chief of Whistleblower Office, to Leave SEC* (July 8, 2016), *available at* https://www.sec.gov/pressrelease/2016-136.html (noting that, since its inception in February 2011, the Office had awarded more than $85 million to 32 whistleblowers).

U.S. Securities and Exchange Commission Response to Freedom of Information Act Request No. 16-03374-FOIA (May 13, 2016).

Chapter III

"Fairness" Takes Hold:
Major Cases and
Miner Defendants

The most common defendants in seminal Prohibition cases were, surprisingly, geologists. The commonality amuses and yet piques any serious observer's interest: Must an investor be an expert to understand confidential news?

A. The Company and Its People

Texas Gulf Sulphur [sic] ("TGS") was the world's largest supplier of sulfur by 1963. At that time, over 10 million of its shares were held by the public, with over 1.5 million shares residing in the company treasury. The stock was advertised for sale on both the New York Stock Exchange and the Midwest Stock Exchange, and the company's annual sales exceeded $62,000,000.

While the price of sulfur declined over 25% between 1956 and 1963, a subsequent market shortage spurred a $2 per ton increase in 1964. Indeed, TGS's gross sales for 1963 were the highest in four years when it lost a key transport vessel (the "SS Marine Sulphur Queen") and replaced the doomed ship in January 1964 with the world's largest super tanker. The next month, TGS announced its plans to increase Canadian mining production by 500 tons a day. Contemporaneously, the company both diversified (e.g., mining phosphate, potash, oil and gas) and acquired drilling properties from others.

An undeveloped area in Ontario, Canada had been identified as early as 1959 as a potential drilling site; in June 1963, variations in results of local conductivity tests prodded TGS engineers to purchase approximately 160 acres ("Kidd 55") in the region. A handful of specific Kidd 55 locations were drilled between November 8, 1963 and April 16, 1964. High concentrations prompted additional purchases of land and, gradually, deeper and more enlightening drilling. Ultimately, a 10 million ton ore strike was confirmed.

As test results became irrefutable, so too was their expected positive effect on company share price. Numerous TGS employees and officials (and their close relations) purchased stock and options for themselves and/or recommended purchases to others as the price climbed from approximately $17 a share in November 1963 to $58 per share in April 1964; along the way, the TGS countered newspaper reports of a huge ore find in a press release dated April 12, 1964. However, four days later, the company admitted via a second press release its vast ore find to the public.

In 1965, the SEC charged a dozen TGS employees with insider trading prior to the issuance of the second release under the "abstain or disclose" theory announced in *Cady, Roberts*. The migration of that theory from the SEC's halls to the federal courthouse depended heavily on which judge(s) heard the case.

Dudley B. Bonsal was born in 1907 and attended Harvard Law School during the roaring '20s. He was in his 50s when he came to the Bench as a federal judge in the Southern District of New York. Specifically, President Kennedy seated him via recess appointment in 1961 and then as a permanent appointment in 1962.

Judge Bonsal had spent years in private practice punctuated by work urging reform to federal civilian security programs started during wartime. His attendant Bar association report urged "a continuing appeal to the oppressed in every land." His 1995 obituary noted his 1970 application of "a new legal standard laid down by the Court of Appeals" aiming to protect the "reasonable investor." However, in actuality, he had opposed that SEC standard (and resulting extended Commission reach) more than any jurist of his time. Indeed, his poorly-timed failure to limit the scope of the securities laws ensured that Rule 10b-5 would expand to unforeseeable proportions for the ensuing half of a century.

B. A Common Claim in Common Law

The 1960s proved to be fertile ground for federal jurists to sow new Prohibition law. A mining case from a prior generation, *Goodwin v. Agassiz*,[1] had tested the

---

1. 186 N.E. 659 (Mass. 1933).

"majority rule" that shielded directors and officers from liability for their personal trading. In that pre-'33 Act state case, a geologist's prediction of a large ore find in Michigan sparked both company purchases of adjacent lands and employee purchases of company stock. The plaintiff was a seller of company stock without the benefit of the geologist's prognostication; the defendants were company directors who had bought with the inside information. The court held for the defendant but acknowledged that, in "appropriate circumstances," there could arise a duty of directors to disclose such information to the market. "Law in its sanctions is not coextensive with morality," the Massachusetts high court ruled.

A quarter of a century later, the Commission's victory in *Cady, Roberts*, while game-changing, was hardly comprehensive. The SEC's Special Study of the Securities Markets, released in 1963, had not even referenced the case, instead suggesting that the protections of Section 16(b) (i.e., the swing trading prohibition) be extended beyond companies listed on an exchange.[2]

Thus, throughout the 1960s, the Commission remained poised to widely legislate the new morality. SEC Chair Cary's dream of a far-reaching prohibition would come closer to reality with a federal court case confirming the nascent notion of abstain or disclose. In 1966, the Commission charged TGS and twelve of its employees (including the President, General Counsel, Secretary, and two Directors) with violations of Section 10(b) of the '34 Act and Rule 10b-5. The charges all related to stock and/or option trading between November 12, 1963 (i.e., the day of the first Kidd 55 drilling) and April 16, 1964 (i.e., the day of the second press release; collectively "the Releases"). The company's issuance of the first Release was also targeted as a misleading statement to the investing public.

The *TGS* Bench Trial[3]

The District Court bench trial lasted 17 days. The contest was dominated by expert testimony, and, consequentially, the subsequent written decision

---

2. The actual suggestion was phrased as follows:
> ... Another void in investor protection in the over-the-counter market relates to insider trading. An insider of a listed company must report his transactions in the company's stock; his short-swing trading profits in the stock are recoverable by the company; and he is prohibited from selling the stock short. The policies expressed in these sections should also be applicable in the over-the-counter market ...

Special Study, Transmittal Letter of William L. Cary, Chairman (April 3, 1963), at VII.

3. The TGS trial court decision and appellate decision are collectively hereinafter referred to as "the TGS Cases."

served as primer on the fundamentals of land drilling. With a scientist's eye, District Court Judge Bonsal detailed repetitive "geophysical surveys," variations in "conductivity," and the confirmations provided by "chemical assays." Perhaps more importantly, his granular recounting at times credited TGS suspension of drilling and contemporaneous internal order of confidentiality as "usual practice in the mining industry." Overall, the tale of was centered on the creation of initial drill holes in October 1963, supplemental land purchases, and "core drilling" in April 1964,[4] as well as attendant trading by employees, wives, and friends in November 1963 and April 1964. The story ended with the issuance of the second Release, which acknowledged a significant ore discovery on April 16, 1964, four days after the more lengthy communication with the public (i.e., the first Release) discounted the value of the company's Kidd 55 drilling.

The trial court decision commenced its legal analysis with reference to the preamble of the '34 Act. The survey of applicable law continued through four Act subsections speaking to agency authority, the public interest in fair prices, and the danger of stock manipulation.

The decision then offered as primary guidance Rule 10b-5, in conjunction with two Act subsections speaking to SEC jurisdiction.[5] The argument put forth by defendants that the Commission needed to satisfy "traditional" elements of common law fraud was rejected.[6] Likewise, the court dismissed the contention that '34 Act Section 16(b) limited the SEC's discretion when determining scope of defendants and penalties.[7] The decision then further centered on subsection (3) of Rule 10b-5 (i.e., a practice acting as a fraud).

Interestingly, the decision—by focusing on relationships and "**unfairness**"—held in short order that "insider" for purposes of evaluating inside information was a term contemplating all employees. This determination would be the lone dogmatic victory for the SEC at this level of the court proceedings.[8]

The District Court weighed heavily the question of *materiality*, holding that it was "obvious" that any employee would know more of a company's affairs than "an outside stockholder." The court ruled that such information must be subject to a conservative test, "particularly since many actions under Section

---

4. *SEC v. Texas Gulf Sulphur Co.*, 258 F. Supp. 262, 269–273 (S.D.N.Y. 1966).

5. Specifically, Sections 21 and 27, 15 U.S.C. §§78(u) and (aa).

6. 258 F. Supp. at 276–78.

7. 258 F. Supp. at 278.

8. Until the present, the TGS Cases stand for the proposition that "insiders" include all of a company's employees.

10(b) are brought on the basis of hindsight." Citing testimony by geologists and engineers that the results of a single drill hole could be insignificant, the court found trading before April 9, 1964, to be based upon information coined "remote." Further, the second Release was found to have accurately disclosed news once material, thus undermining the SEC's accusations that the first Release was misleading. In a bold rebuke of any trend towards the outlawing of information asymmetries, the District Court held

> ... It may be that the 'fairness' overtones of *Cady, Roberts* indicate a trend toward the elimination of all insider purchasing. But even were the court prepared to accept the proposition that all insider trading is unfair, a proposition of doubtful validity at best, it would be deterred by the admonition of Judge Learned Hand that it is not 'desirable for a lower court to embrace the exhilarating opportunity of anticipating a doctrine which may be in the womb of time, but whose birth is distant' (cites omitted).[9]

In sum, Judge Bonsal concluded as a matter of fact that material information did not surface until a point very late in the story, and as a matter of law, that most defendants had engaged in speculative trading at their own risk. Further, the District Court held that the core Rule 10b-5 element of *materiality* should be strictly construed, and that a broader test would "prevent some management trading that represents an abuse, but only at the cost of possibly exposing management to meritless litigation." Resultantly, the Commission charges against the company and 10 and 12 individual defendants were dismissed. Appeal was made, and ultimately an en banc decision speeded the womb of time, for both the SEC and corporate America.

Before the Second Circuit Court of Appeals

Adopting the Record wholly as determined by Judge Bonsal, the majority opinion spoke for no less than 9 Second Circuit jurists. The Second Circuit decision delivered at once a different take on Rule 10b-5 elements and the purposes of the securities laws; moreover, without much explanation, the appellate bench proclaimed that the nature of Rule 10b-5's required elements varied with the relief sought. The dismissals ordered by the District Court were reversed, and charges were reinstated against 9 TGS employees.[10]

---

9. 258 F. Supp. at 284.

10. *SEC v. Tex. Gulf Sulphur Co.*, 401 F.2d 833, 842–43 (2d Cir. 1968). After appeal, no TGS defendant was exonerated; several had their cases deemed moot because company stock options had been rescinded or canceled. *See id.* at 856–858.

The *TGS* appellate decision commenced with a salute to the mission of Rule 10b-5, which was described as "the implementation of the Congressional purpose that all investors should have equal access to the rewards of participation." The Rule was declared rightfully promulgated by the SEC, pursuant to '34 Act Section 10(b). The Act in general designed to "insure (sic) **fairness** in securities transactions," its egalitarian standard was said to be aimed at those coming upon information intended for a "corporate purpose." Such fortunate insiders—constructive or actual—were thus prohibited from taking advantage of the information "knowing that it is unavailable" to counterparties, a category expanded to include the investing public.

The authorities for this broad codification were an article by Commissioner Cary himself, as well as an article by his former assistant, a lawyer who published a Law Review piece titled "The Implications of the Texas Gulf Sulphur Proceedings." The latter article was released between the time the company was charged by the SEC and the time at which the District Court heard the first TGS Case. The Implications article had concluded that any uncertainty for insiders with such access would be naturally cured ("Good judgment and common sense as to what is **fair** will in general suffice as guidelines."). The article was relied upon twice by the appellate court in bridging logical gaps of the newly announced Prohibition.

Regarding *materiality*, the Second Circuit disagreed with the District Court's conclusion that the test must be "conservative." The second *TGS* decision avoided SEC Rule 405 (which contains the traditional definition of "material," to wit, "those matters to which there is a substantial likelihood that a reasonable investor[11] would "attach importance") by focusing on market impact. The court noted that a popular trade publication had characterized an early drill hole as significant. Additionally, the timing and nature of employee trading (e.g., first-time purchases of call options) supported the importance of the drilling information long before final test results in April. The inside information being rendered material, its possession implicated defendants of every ilk, and even parties outside of the corporation.

Further, the Second Circuit took the occasion to thwart an equally novel defense: That profits from insider trading served as a form of remuneration to corporate management. The chief proponent of this notion was Henry Manne, an outspoken critic of *Cady, Roberts*.[12] The court had little tolerance for the

---

11. 17 C.F.R. 230.405—Definitions of terms.

12. Manne, who would later become Dean of the George Mason University School of law, published his seminal *Insider Trading and the Stock Market* (1967) during the TGS Cases.

theme, refusing to dignify fears that "the elimination of insider trading benefits will deplete the ranks of capable corporate managers."

Additionally, the Second Circuit provided guidance as to when insiders could lawfully trade. The testimony of one defendant's desire to "beat the news" was criticized. Accordingly, market participants were advised to forestall insider trading activity "until the dissemination of a material news announcement." Here, again, the court directly countered the judicial restraint of the District Court, which had opined that any judge-made rule requiring insiders to wait until information was "absorbed" would lead to hopeless uncertainty.

Also, the final TGS precedent ultimately rejected a good faith defense to Rule 10b-5 charges. Three TGS employees had argued that they honestly believed the information regarding the ore strike had become public at the time they entered their purchase orders. The Second Circuit clarified that case law had previously established that specific intent was unnecessary, so that even "negligent insider conduct" was unlawful.

Finally, regarding the applicability of Rule 10b-5 to the first press Release, the Second Circuit holding loosened the requirements of the "in connection with" language at the end of the measure. The Circuit Court opined that legislative history and policy reasons supported a finding that "[t]here cannot be honest markets without honest publicity," thus dissolving the defense argument that the Release, because it was not a securities transaction, was outside the coverage of the Rule.

The Lessons of *TGS*

Writing on a clean slate, the TGS Cases cemented certain approaches to insider trading but also evidenced some fleeting notions that are not applied today. Foremost, the Commission's "abstain or disclose" requirement for those in possession of an informational advantage was effectively elevated by federal court to the law of the land. Such duty/admonition has persisted for decades; if quixotic, it is nonetheless consistently taught and repeated. While the class of persons subject to the requirement has occasionally been altered, the remedy remains the only legal option for those otherwise satisfying the case law definition of "insider trader."

On a semantic level, the Commission's war against insider trading took on some defined terms. "Tipper" and "tippee" — the monikers accorded, respectively, the source and recipient of insider information — were forever labeled, albeit in whimsical fashion. The Commission's landmark *Cady, Roberts* case had simply lumped together tipper (sans name) and tippee as "persons who [were] in a special relationship with a company and privy to its affairs." As subject information, categories of defendants, and other working parts in the challenging insider trading equation would change, the terms "tipper" and "tippee" have remained remarkably steadfast, at once bifurcating and anchoring attending analyses.[13]

In terms of the role of common law fraud, the TGS Cases labeled the Acts as an improvement. Judge Bonsal and the Circuit Court opinion agreed that traditional fraud elements had been superseded by the Acts. Future courts would not be so sure, often relying on the common law notion of fraud to support an interpretation.

Perhaps most importantly, an equation was offered for future judges tasked with determining *materiality*. The TGS Cases—flip sides of the coin on the issue—ultimately landed on the side of information that *might* influence market price ("might well have affected the price of TGS stock," directly counter to the District Court's emphasis on the more definite result, *would* have had a substantial market impact). This tilting of the equation against the defendant was never truly re-struck, although the Supreme Court did vary considerations 20 years later.[14]

To be sure, some notions extolled by the Second Circuit are now hopelessly outdated. Tipper/tippee cases are determined by a test created by the Supreme Court in 1983, and the concept that those possessing inside information owe duties to the entire market was expressly quashed three years earlier. The emphasis on harm to the market (over the trader's obligation or intent) was an idea that would come and go, depending on the specific theory offered at trial.

However, the TGS Cases first and foremost succeeded in imposing upon the corporate world the daunting principle that inequalities in trading information would not be tolerated, and the courts would not be rendered impotent in striking the balance. The Circuit Court expressly opposed the District Court's exercise of judicial restraint, energetically stating, "Such inequities based upon

---

13. *See, e.g., United States of America v. Salman*, 792 F.3d 1087, 1090 (9th Cir. 2015), *available at* http://www.scotusblog.com/wp-content/uploads/2016/01/14-10204.pdf, at 6 ("Salman [a tippee] then moved for a new trial pursuant to Rule 33 of the Federal Rules of Criminal Procedure, on the ground, inter alia, that there was no evidence that he knew that the disclosed confidential information was in exchange for a personal benefit.").

14. *See Basic, Inc. v. Levinson*, 485 U.S. 224 (1988) (finding preliminary merger negotiations material because a reasonable investor would consider them before trading, a standard harkening back to SEC Rule 405). That standard was re-affirmed by the Supreme Court in *Erica John Fund v. Halliburton*, 563 U.S. 804 (2011).

unequal access to knowledge should not be shrugged off as inevitable in our way of life, or, in view of the congressional concern in the area, remain uncorrected." The resulting "access to information" (a.k.a. "parity of information") theory would characterize the Prohibition for over a decade.

Finally, on a practical level, the TGS Cases added money as a sanction to be considered. At this point, damages were still compensatory. Indeed, despite the impressive analysis undertaken of the reimbursement due to the company from each liable defendant, none of the numbers exceeded the profit gained (and the Acts did not incorporate anything approaching punitive damages until granting the SEC treble recovery for insider trading in 1984[15]). Further, much private litigation money was on the table: While the District Court was weighing its decision, 49 private actions collectively seeking $77 million in punitive damages were pending against TGS.[16]

The SEC bargained for far less, obtaining only approximately $150,000 in "rescission" from the broad array of TGS defendants. But such recovery went beyond the suspension and recognition of a nominal stock exchange fine that resulted from *Cady, Roberts*. The addition by judges of the money factor as a bonus of active enforcement was sure to help expand the Prohibition, and to lure more plaintiffs to the cause.

C. The First Derivative Action:
Diamond v. Oreamuno

Meanwhile, the private Bar was pushing the envelope.

In early 1968, a state appellate panel considered the lower court's dismissal of a stockholder's derivative action against directors of a New York corporation. The suit had been filed by a shareholder who alleged that two Directors profited from trades using inside information, taking advantage of an approximately 6-week delay in releasing the news of poor quarterly financials. When the dour data was publicly shared, the stock price dropped from over $23 a share to $11.

The corporation's other Directors were blamed for ratifying the wrongful trades. The defendants collectively asserted a defense of failure to state a cause of action.

---

15. That grant of authority, part of the Insider Trading Sanctions Act, is discussed later in Chapter VIII.

16. 258 F. Supp. at 267, n.1.

At the time, a private cause of action under Rule 10b-5 had been found by a lower federal court in another Circuit;[17] later, in 1971, the implied cause of action would be summarily ratified by the Supreme Court.[18]

Citing agency law in general and New York law on Director duties in particular, the appellate court reversed the dismissal, stating, "[These fiduciaries] are being charged because they converted into money to their own use something belonging not to them but to their corporation — inside information."[19] The decision's concluding footnote also found support in Section 16(b) of the '34 Act, which the appellate panel — via the Congressional Record of 1934 — traced to the common law edict that an agent's profits inure to his principal.[20]

On appeal to the high court of New York in 1969, the reversal of the dismissal was upheld. That court found support for the shareholder derivative claim in the duties of fiduciaries, as well as Section 16(b), on the latter point stating:

> The remedy which the Federal statute provides in that situation is precisely the same as that sought in the present case under State law, namely, an action brought by the corporation or on its behalf to recover all profits derived from the transactions.
>
> In providing this remedy, Congress accomplished a dual purpose. It not only provided for an efficient and effective method of accomplishing its primary goal — the protection of the investing public from **unfair** treatment at the hands of corporate insiders — but extended to the corporation the right to secure for itself benefits derived by those insiders from their exploitation of their privileged position.[21]

Explaining that the sales in issue world escape the reach of 16(b) because of their timing (i.e., over 6 months apart), the New York high court acknowledged the broad, federal "regulatory scheme" and the role of Rule 10b-5, which had been held applicable to insider trading by the second TGS Case during the *Diamond* appeals. The fact that said regulatory scheme had yet failed to identify damages and their administration was secondary, accord-

---

17. *Kardon v. National Gypsum Co.*, 69 F. Supp. 512 (E.D. Pa. 1946). The *Kardon* court based the right on the Restatement of Torts, the "broad purpose [of the '34 Act] to regulate securities transactions of all kinds," and Section 29 of the '34 Act which, by declaring void all contracts contrary to the Act, simultaneously assumes a (money) remedy at law.

18. *Superintendent of Insurance v. Bankers Life & Cas. Co.*, 404 U.S. 6, 10 n.9 (1971).

19. *Diamond v. Oreamuno*, 29 A.D.2d 285, 288 (N.Y. App. 1st Div. 1968).

20. 29 A.D.2d at 289 n.4.

21. *Diamond v. Oreamuno*, 24 N.Y.2d 494, 500 (N.Y. 1969).

ing to the court, while "the desirability of creating an effective common-law remedy [was] manifest."

D. An Aftermath, and a Beginning

Thus, judges and geologists had combined to ensure that Rule 10b-5 would complement Section 16(b). Over time, corporate scientists would appear to have learned the lessons of *TGS* and *Diamond*, but some truisms about the Prohibition's molding during the period of 1966–1969 persist:

- The earliest private insider trading cases largely resemble the SEC case activating Rule 10b-5 in the federal courts (i.e., *Texas Gulf Sulphur*). An inordinate number of these seminal cases involved geologists. Perhaps this is more coincidence than phenomena, but the easily discernible fact patterns therein do suggest some triage choices concerning defendants who appreciate the advantage created by advance knowledge.

- At this point, only two subsections of Rule 10b-5 are deemed relevant (i.e., "a"—scheme, and/or "c"—deception/fraud). That would later change.

- Most conspicuously, the elements of Rule 10b-5 were largely supplied by the defenses raised by its early insider trading defendants. To that end, priorities set via written court decisions elevated federal judges in shaping the Prohibition. Indeed, the story of the evolving definitions and pleading requirements of the 4–6 elements required of insider trading parties in interest rivals the story of the fairness standard itself in both interest and import; accordingly, it is the subject of the next Chapter.

Selected Bibliography

"The SEC Takes Command/Texas Gulf Sulphur," www.sechistorical.org/ museum/galleries (last visited November 22, 2017).

Aaron v. Securities and Exchange Commission, 446 U.S. 680 (1980) (finding scienter to be a pleading requirement for SEC actions, and defining the element as "embracing the intent to deceive").

Eric Pace, *Dudley B. Bonsal Dies at 88; Was U.S. District Court Judge*, N.Y. Times (July 25, 1995).

Stephen M. Bainbridge, Securities Law/Insider Trading 16–20 (1999).

Arthur Fleischer, Jr., *Securities Trading and Corporate Information Practices: The Implications of the Texas Gulf Sulphur Proceeding*, 51 Va. Law R. 7 (Nov. 1965), pp. 1271–1305, 1305. This is the pivotal article referenced on p. 42.

Kurt A. Hohenstein, *Fair to All People: The SEC and the Regulation of Insider Trading*, *available at* http://www.sechistorical.org/museum/galleries/it/take Command_a.php (last visited November 17, 2016).

Irving M. Pollack, E-Mail of November 13, 2004. The decorated, former SEC official and longtime securities lawyer was an employee of the Commission for 34 years and its first Director of its Division of Enforcement in 1972. In the e-mail, he explained to the present author (then an adjunct professor) that *TGS* "expanded the group of individuals subject to insider trading beyond directors of a corporation and also established that federal law would supersede state law on the fiduciary duties of directors in this area."

Roger P. Kirman, *A Comparison of Insider Liability Under* Diamond v. Oreamuno *and Federal Securities Law*, 11 B.C. L. Rev. 499 (1970).

Ernst & Ernst v. Hochfelder, 425 U.S. 125 (1976) (finding scienter to be a pleading requirement for private actions, and defining the element as "embracing the intent to deceive").

Joel Seligman, The Transformation of Wall Street/A History of the Securities and Exchange Commission and Modern Corporate Finance 651–52 (3d ed. 1997).

Roberta S. Karmel, Regulation by Prosecution/The Securities & Exchange Commission Versus Corporate America (Simon & Schuster 1982).

Letter from Meyer U. Newfield to Milton V. Freeman, re. Rule 10b-5 (February 8, 1996) ("No one dreamed at that time of the avalanche of fraud litigation which followed."), *available at* the SEC Historical Society, www.sec historical.com/galleries.

Biography, Dudley Baldwin Bonsal, www.fjc.gov/history/judges/bonsal-dudley-baldwin.

Chapter IV (*Checkpoint #1*)

Elements from the Defense, Defenses in the Elements

*Between 1942 and 1968, Rule 10b-5's theoretical underpinnings had been crafted, re-crafted, and occasionally ignored (the decades that followed proved no less intellectually dishonest). Thus the resulting Prohibition, although a perennial paragon of SEC authority, frequently falters under a close scrutiny. Indeed, to speak of a discrete set of Rule 10b-5 elements is somewhat folly—the **definition** of insider trading contains one of several of its **elements**, and the list of primary requirements can vary with the plaintiff, or the court, or the relief requested. Nonetheless, since the defeat of an element of the overarching Rule poses the best possible defense to its application in a crime under its wing, the study of the parts of that crime to be pleaded is vital. Perhaps even more interesting is the story of their malleability—or outright disappearance—over time.*

A. Rule 10b-5's Initial Scope: Separating Fraud from Disturbances

As cases such as *Ward LaFrance; Cady, Roberts;* and *Texas Gulf Sulphur* make clear, the initial defenses proffered against the Commission were far ranging and often policy driven. The initial defendants[1] facing SEC discipline over the

---

1. The term "defendant" appears most often when the Commission sues an alleged violator in federal court (discussed further in Chapter V). For its own internal proceedings before an Administrative Law Judge, "respondent" is most often used. Further complicating the nomenclature are appeals, which sometimes substitute "appellant"/"appellee" for the original moniker. To simplify these terms, this Book—unless providing directly quoted language—uses the term "defendant."

new crime of insider trading proffered rationalities ranging from a lack of harm when profits are repaid to the pricing benefits of insider transactions. Additionally, as commentators have noted, *the definition* of material, nonpublic information often overlaps with *the duties* delineated under Rule 10b-5, creating a tautology that seems unsolvable.[2] Over time, obstacles posed by a very short list of four more conventional "elements,"[3] all contributed by defenses that had parsed the Rule's 81 words, were dignified by the courts. Overall, the four elements required of an SEC Rule 10b-5 action (most clearly stated by the Supreme Court in 2005[4]) have proven to be quite malleable—a series of cookie cutter pleading requirements dwarfed by a matter's notion of fairness. This handful of debatable topics are discussed in the context of their lead cases below.

1. Fraud/Deception (Subdivision "c" within Rule 10b-5)[5]

In *Santa Fe Industries v. Green*,[6] the defendant company impressed upon the Supreme Court the fact that it had complied with a state short-form merger statute in buying back stock from minority shareholders. The Court noted the lack of deception or misrepresentation, as well as the traditional relegation of such matters to state law. The plaintiffs lost, thus temporarily cabining Rule 10b-5 causes of action. Noteworthy is the fact that the plaintiffs had alleged a share price discrepancy of over 500% ($772 versus $150 per share), yet the Court majority—focusing on a legislative history that appeared centered on stock manipulation—concluded that "the **fairness** of the terms of the transaction is at most a tangential concern of the statute."[7]

---

2. *See, e.g.,* Donald C. Langevoort, *The Muddled Duty to Disclose Under Rule 10b-5*, 57 VAND. L. REV. 1639, 1643–44 (2004) (noting that in written opinions "it is often hard to determine whether the judge is basing her decision on materiality or duty").

3. Two additional elements are required of private Rule 10b-5 plaintiffs under *Dura Pharmaceuticals v. Broudo*, 544 U.S. 336 (2005), *infra* n. 4.

4. *Dura Pharmaceuticals v. Broudo*, 544 U.S. 336 (2005). *Broudo*, a case centering on the damage pleadings required in a class action, recognized two additional elements for the private plaintiff asserting Rule 10b-5: transaction causation (i.e., the fraud caused the plaintiff to enter into the transaction), and loss causation (i.e., that the transaction caused a loss to the plaintiff). Conversely, the SEC need not plead or prove any form of investor loss.

5. Violation of Rule 10b-5 is synonymous with "securities fraud," although the latter term is more inclusive than is the term "insider trading."

6. 430 U.S. 462 (1977).

7. *Id.* at 478.

However, 20 years later, the Supreme Court attenuated this analysis by ruling (for insider trading cases and others) that Rule 10b-5's fraud/deception requirement could be met by "feigned loyalty." The *O'Hagan* decision found no difficulty even in creating a new duty for an otherwise silent defendant, citing a 1952 Court decision for the premise that the "requirement of the presence of culpable intent" did not support the argument that finding the defendant guilty in his circumstances was "unjust."[8] Thus, the element of fraud/deception, initially acting as a brake upon burgeoning case law, now appears in the post-*O'Hagan* world to be a minor consideration inviting, at most, inventive application by the suing party utilizing the Prohibition.

2. Materiality (Subdivision "b" of Rule 10b-5)

In *Texas Gulf Sulphur* (discussed in Chapter III), the Second Circuit reversed the narrow reading of the element by the trial court. In so doing, "materiality" became divorced from SEC rulemaking, for Commission Rule 405 had weighed what any reasonable man would consider,[9] while *Texas Gulf Sulphur* added a balancing test that weighed "the indicated probability that the event will occur and the anticipated magnitude [on the market] of the event."[10]

In 1976, the Supreme Court returned to a Rule 405 standard for purposes of SEC Rule 14a-9 (regarding alleged fraud in the solicitation of shareholders of voting proxy by management). The Court held that a "material" fact was one that posed a substantial likelihood that a reasonable investor would consider it in deciding to vote.[11] However, the more direct precedent resides in *Basic v. Levinson*, a case that considered whether preliminary merger negotiations need to be revealed to investors.[12] In that 1988 case, the standard was

---

8. *United States v. O'Hagan,* 521 U.S 642, 666 (1997) (citing *Boyce Motor Lines v. United States,* 342 U.S. 337, 342 (1952)).

9. Specifically, Rule 405, 17 C.F.R. §240.405 (a '33 Act interpretive device), states as follows:

> *Material.* The term *material,* when used to qualify a requirement for the furnishing of information as to any subject, limits the information required to those matters to which there is a substantial likelihood that a reasonable investor would attach importance in determining whether to purchase the security registered.

10. *SEC v. Tex. Gulf Sulphur Co.,* 401 F.2d 833, 849 (2d Cir. 1968).

11. *TSC Industries, Inc. v. Northway, Inc.,* 426 U.S. 438 (1976).

12. *Basic Inc. v Levinson,* 485 U.S. 224 (1988). *Basic* is a fascinating study in recusal: Three judges abstained from voting; per custom, reasons for High Court recusal are not provided. Counsel for the defendant later asserted that the recused Justices would likely have voted to adopt the Sixth Circuit's bright line test (i.e., not requiring disclosure of negotiations until a formal agreement was reached).

slightly modified for Rule 10b-5 to examine whether the examined information altered the "total mix" of information to a prospective investor. The *Basic* "total mix" standard was recently reiterated in the *Halliburton* case of 2014.[13]

More significantly, as countless SEC cases attest, materiality for purposes of the Prohibition translates to news that once made public affected the stock price in an appreciable manner. As then-Third Circuit judge Samuel Alito wrote in the year 2000, in an "efficient" stock market "the concept of materiality translates into information that alters the price of the firm's stock."[14] Such a hindsight approach perhaps skirts the true import of the materiality determination, which, in SEC Rule and court holdings, examines decision making at the time of purchase.

Further, statutory changes such as the addition of a private insider trading cause of action in 1988 (discussed in Chapter X) all but eliminated the reliance requirement in Prohibition cases, simultaneously making evaluations of materiality obsolete (i.e., a plaintiff class was determined by the prior, criminal conviction of an insider trader, regardless of what he/she knew). The result is an element that is easily pleaded and rarely an obstacle, although, in theory, driving the distinction between the improperly advantaged and the rest of the market.

3. "In Connection With" (Parting Words of Rule 10b-5)

The "in connection with" language may be the most difficult element to isolate in insider trading cases. The words serve both as a barrier to the plaintiff's standing and as an element of the offense itself.

As an Element of the Rule

The parting words of Rule 10b-5 (which had been ceremoniously added to Section 17(a) in order to create the new rule) have been offered as a defense in numerous cases. The height of Commission embarrassment may have been in 1998, when a notorious fraudster defeated a Rule 10b-5 charge because his falsification of trading records, while enough to bankrupt a historical Wall

---

13. *Halliburton Co. v. Erica P. John Fund, Inc.*, 134 S. Ct. 2398 (2014) (re-affirming *Basic v. Levinson* in finding that plaintiffs are entitled to a rebuttable presumption of reliance at the class certification stage).

14. *Oran v. Stafford*, 226 F.3d 275 (3rd Cir. 2000).

Street firm, were determined by an SEC administrative law judge to not be in connection with securities transactions.[15]

In *Texas Gulf Sulphur,* the Second Circuit saw no difficulty in linking a flawed press release (i.e., a misstatement) to purchases/sales by investors, and such a connection was never seriously questioned thereafter. Regarding cases tying behavior to the requirement, the Court made clear that the connection need only be tenuous with the *Zandford* case of 2002.[16] In that year, the Justices took up the appeal of a Maryland securities broker who misappropriated over $400,000 from the discretionary joint account of an elderly man and his mentally challenged daughter. After the broker was indicted, the Commission brought suit; the defendant argued that his crimes did not equate with securities fraud. The Fourth Circuit agreed.

On appeal, the Supreme Court was not troubled by the lack of any securities purchases or sales as part of the fraud. Animating the intention of the Acts "to bar deceptive devices and contrivances," Zandford's illegal sales of existing securities in the joint account to provide cash for his theft were found to satisfy the "in connection with requirement."

All of which effectively relegates the "in connection with" requirement to mere formality, although such absolution has never been granted in writing by the Supreme Court.

As a Standing Requirement

However, in *Blue Chip Stamps v. Manor Drug Stores,*[17] the Court formalized the *Birnbaum*[18] Rule, an obligation that required plaintiffs seeking standing in Rule 10b-5 lawsuits to have actually purchased or sold a security. The Court not only limited access to the courts for categories of plaintiffs but also colorfully added to the Rule 10b-5 lexicon by stating that the related private cause of action was "a judicial oak which has grown from little more than a legislative acorn."[19]

---

15. *In the Matter of Orlando Joseph Jett,* Administrative Proceeding File No. 3-8919 (July 21, 1998). The ALJ ruled that the fictitiously paired transactions did not "touch" upon actual purchases/sales as in precedent cases. The defendant was found to have aided and abetted books and records violations by his brokerage firm employer and ordered to pay a disgorgement of his bonus of approximately $8.2 million, as well as a $200,000 fine.

16. *SEC v. Zandford,* 535 U.S. 813 (2002).

17. 421 U.S. 723 (1975).

18. *Birnbaum v. Newport Steel Corp.,* 193 F.2d 461 (2d Cir.), *cert denied,* 343 U.S. 956 (1952).

19. 421 U.S. at 737.

In *Blue Chip*, the issue centered on the propriety of the defendant's compliance with an antitrust decree. The government had ordered Manor Drugs to make stock available to its top customers; plaintiff had cried foul over efforts by the defendant to dissuade potential takers from the exchange. In finding for the defendant, the Court held that those who did not purchase had simply possessed no Rule 10b-5 cause of action. The Court reasoned that 1) actual trading is the most objectively reliable evidence of fraud, 2) broader language (i.e., "attempts at the purchase or sale") had previously been rejected by Congress in the late 1950s, and 3) that "vexatious litigation" would result in the lack of the *Birnbaum* requirement of standing.

Blue Chip thus set the standard for Rule 10b-5 litigation. The presumption is that the plaintiff will have purchased or sold the stock effected by artifice, misstatement, or fraud; this presumptive requirement is overcome by discreet circumstances, normally coined "intervening cause."

The Eleventh Circuit has opined that the "in connection with" element does not require any actual trade.[20] However, the Supreme Court has not gone that far, and, in fact, appeared skeptical of such reach in oral argument in the *Zandford* case:

> COURT: Well, do you say then that any fraud by a broker in connection with a customer is actionable by the SEC[?]
>
> SEC Counsel: That goes back to the question that Justice Scalia asked me, Your Honor. And under the theory that we are advocating here, and for the Court to rule for us here, you don't need to conclude that. The SEC does take that position.
>
> COURT: Does take what position?
>
> SEC Counsel: That any fraudulent conversion by a broker from a brokerage account is a violation of 10(b) because it's fraud and it's in connection with the purchase or sale of securities; because the very purpose of the brokerage account is to buy and sell securities. And the broker has access to the customer's assets —
>
> COURT: That's quite a leap —
>
> SEC Counsel: — for the purpose of —
>
> COURT: That's a leap from any case we've ever decided.[21]

---

20. *Grippo v. Perazzo*, 357 F.3d 1218 (11th Cir. 2004).

21. Transcript of Oral Argument at 5–6, *SEC v. Zandford*, 535 U.S. 813 (2002) (No. 01-147).

However, in early 2009, the grandest Ponzi schemer of all-time, Bernard Madoff, pleaded guilty to Rule 10b-5 violations for his multi-decade fraud. Subsequent investigation by the SEC and others confirmed that Madoff's illicit enterprise did not effect any purchases or sales for customers. Accordingly, it would seem that the promise of transactions in connection with securities are enough to utilize Rule 10b-5.

4. Scienter Requirement (Implied from "Device," "Scheme," "Artifice," and/or "Deceit")

In *Cady, Roberts*, the tippee (Cowdin) was said to have acted willfully because "he knew what he was doing" when trading quickly on the time-sensitive information he had "accidentally" received. Somewhere between those three relevant terms is a standard speaking to knowledgeable behavior.

In *Texas Gulf Sulphur*, the defendants' commitment to the trade was cited as proof of evil intent to do wrong; alas, that notion failed to catch on in subsequent cases. Overall, however, that failure was of little consequence. The landmark geologist case favored deterrence over legal niceties, observing:

> ... a review of other sections of the Act from which Rule 10b-5 seems to have been drawn suggests that the implementation of a standard of conduct that encompasses negligence as well as active fraud comports with the administrative and the legislative purposes underlying the Rule ... This [mental state] requirement, whether it be termed lack of diligence, constructive fraud, or unreasonable or negligent conduct, remains implicit in this standard, a standard that promotes the deterrence objective of the Rule.[22]

Negligence did not persist as the standard for Rule 10b-5 case law (the closest salvation of the concept comes from an employer's failure to supervise an employee or to implement procedures, both obligations coming from 1980s statutes discussed later in Chapter V). Regardless, between 1976 and 1980, the Supreme Court imposed a scienter requirement of proving the "intent to embrace a fraud" upon both the SEC and private plaintiffs.[23] Those cases did not, however, expressly exclude reckless as a means of satisfying the scienter requirement.

---

22. 401 F.2d at 855. In his Concurring Opinion, Justice Friendly took issue with the Majority's avoidance of a scienter requirement.

23. *Ernst & Ernst v. Hochfelder*, 425 U.S. 185 (1976); *Aaron v. SEC*, 446 U.S. 680 (1980).

By 2012, the dual requirement of either scienter or recklessness appeared etched in stone within the Circuit that most often hears Prohibition cases. As summarized in *SEC v. Obus*:

> Liability for securities fraud requires proof of scienter, defined as "a mental state embracing intent to deceive, manipulate, or defraud." *Ernst & Ernst v. Hochfelder* (cites omitted). Negligence is not a sufficiently culpable state of mind to support a section 10(b) civil violation. While the Supreme Court has yet to decide whether recklessness satisfies section 10(b)'s scienter requirement, see *Matrixx Initiatives, Inc. v. Siracusano*, 131 S.Ct. 1309, 1323 (2011), we have held that scienter "may be established through a showing of reckless disregard for the truth, that is, conduct which is highly unreasonable and which represents an extreme departure from the standards of ordinary care," *SEC v. McNulty*, 137 F.3d 732, 741 (2d Cir.1998) (internal citations and quotation marks omitted); see *SEC v. U.S. Envtl., Inc.*, 155 F.3d 107, 111 (2d Cir.1998) (recognizing that eleven circuits hold that recklessness satisfies the scienter requirement of section 10(b)).[24]

Indeed, in the past two decades, examples of scienter/recklessness have ranged from the most generic (i.e., "evil mind" intent, as the *O'Hagan* Court phrased it) to the most specific intent to evade SEC detection.[25]

The elements being interchangeable or simply on the wane, increasingly, successful battle lines are drawn around the procedural limitations upon the Rule, which can serve to ground the Prohibition.

B. Definitional and Procedural Considerations

The fungible nature of Rule 10b-5 has made it a proper fit for unforeseen violations. The most common applications include issuer misstatements, cor-

---

24. *SEC v. Obus*, 693 F.3d 276 (2d Cir. 2012) (reversing summary judgment for defendant tippees of inside information).

25. *See, e.g.,* Kevin McCoy, *Want to get away with insider trading? Don't do this*, USA TODAY ONLINE (July 12, 2017), *available at* https://www.usatoday.com/story/money/2017/07/12/want-get-away-insider-trading-dont-do-this/473496001/ ("[SEC] investigation of [defendant] Yan's computer activity showed he conducted 2016 Google searches for the phrases 'how sec detect unusual trade' and 'insider trading with international account,' the court complaint charged.").

porate malfeasance, broker misconduct,[26] market manipulation, Internet fraud, conflicted investment advice, and, of course, insider trading (since 1961).

The commonplace definition of insider trading is phrased in words akin to trading based upon material, non-public information obtained in violation of a duty. The description of the subject information is surprisingly uniform, although its two component parts have definitely not received equal attention. *Materiality* was discussed above; *non-public* is addressed below.

"Non-public information" normally precedes trumpet blasts about confidential sources or news. In both *Cady, Roberts* and *Texas Gulf Sulphur*, the press release disclosing the insider information was found to be the watershed event rendering the inside information public. Not all cases have included such grand pronouncements. Over time, the mere fact that a stock price had been impacted by investor trading after first public announcement of the inside information led to the legal conclusion that such news had been sufficiently confidential. By the time the Supreme Court heard *O'Hagan*, considerable stock movement alone was enough to render all preceding knowledge both material and confidential.

As a result, "non-public" has avoided serious debate and is defined more often by its remedy than its terms. In the 1970s, the SEC articulated in the *Faberge* case the "broad dissemination standard" that called for two steps to reparation after wrongful disclosure: 1) use of a means calculated to reach far and wide, and 2) time for the public to digest the broadly disseminated news.[27] In 2000, with the adoption of Regulation FD,[28] the Commission provided an express defense for issuer agents who immediately disclose the inside information through the company web site or a press conference. In 2014, in a report absolving a company of any blame, the SEC embraced Facebook as a means of broad dissemination, under certain circumstances.[29] Interestingly, whereas *Faberge* evaluated both the means of dissemination and the allowance

---

26. Such colorful application to intermediaries as "scalping" (i.e., an analyst using his following to boost the price of a security before his own sales); "churning" (i.e., effecting excessive trading in a customer's brokerage account, as in churning butter, over and over); and "painting the tape" (i.e., needlessly separating trades so as to create the illusion of trading activity in a stock).

27. *In re Faberge Inc.*, 45 S.E.C. 249, 256 (1973). The "S.E.C." reporter covered internal Commission decisions and stopped reporting in the 1970s; the cites are still valid and retrievable on most search engines.

28. Regulation FD is explained in detail in Chapter VIII.

29. SEC Release No. 69279 (April 2, 2013) (investigative report of Netflix, Inc. and Reed Hastings).

of time for the public to digest the news, that standard was effectively reduced to a sole factor of broad dissemination by *Netflix*.

The informal definitional requirements—like the Rule's elements—often proving interchangeable or simply extinct, the only means of thwarting a Rule 10b-5 claim may lie its procedural restraints, several of which are explained below.

1. Jurisdiction

The authority of Congress to adopt the Acts (and, in turn, the Commission to enforce them) derives from the Interstate Commerce Clause of the Constitution.[30] Further, Rule 10b-5 explicitly states that subject transactions must have been effected "by the use of any means or instrumentality of interstate commerce, or of the mails or of any facility of any national security exchange." Accordingly, a jurisdictional argument can be made by a defendant where the means of interstate commerce have not been satisfied (e.g., a face-to-face exchange of securities described orally).

However, such purely local transactions are few and far between. And prosecutors, regulators, and plaintiff attorneys have become exceedingly well versed in the varied ways in which the '34 Act's jurisdictional means are met.[31]

2. Presence of a Security

Often the threshold question as to the presence of the security subsumes any adjoining debate on fraud. For example, in *Hocking v. Dubois*, the Ninth Circuit was tasked with evaluating the sale of a Hawaiian condominium as an offending sale of a security. Specifically, the plaintiff alleged that he was motivated to purchase the unit by the developer's promise of an accompanying list of potential lessors, which would guarantee $2,000 to $3,000 a month in income. In reversing the lower court's summary judgment for the defendant, the court of appeals paved the way for an accompanying 10b-5(2) claim for misrepresentation, despite the SEC's amicus brief urging the court to ignore a 1973 Commission release equating condominium sales with securities under certain circumstances.[32] In that case, the Ninth Circuit

---

30. U.S. Const., Art. I, sect. 8(3).

31. *See, e.g.*, SEC Litigation Release No. 34-78996, *In the Matter of Mason D. Newman* (Sept. 29, 2016), *available at* https://www.sec.gov/litigation/admin/2016/34-78996.pdf (noting violations effected "through the use of telephone and/or email"). *See also infra*, p. 146, n. 15.

32. *Hocking v. Dubois*, 885 F.2d 1449 (9th Cir. 1989).

ultimately relied upon the Supreme Court's landmark 1946 decision that established a four-part test gauging the presence of a security in the form of an "investment contract."[33] As both student and scholar can affirm, the *Howey* test quite generously finds the presence of a security both intended or not; nonetheless, a security (either purchased or sold) must be found for Rule 10b-5 to apply.

3. Aiding and Abetting Lability

In 1994, the Supreme Court eradicated "aiding and abetting" liability in private lawsuits alleging Rule 10b-5 violations.[34] The SEC's authority to bring such lawsuits was never really threatened; still, Congress subsequently affirmed the Commission's continued ability to bring actions against secondary actors.[35]

4. Statute of Limitations

One of the major challenges in interpreting Rule 10b-5 over the years has been its extra-statutory origin. A *regulation* created by an agency sets forth the standard by which an offense is defined, while *a cause of action* created by statute can additionally outline both remedy and procedure. To be sure, such distinction is fraught with difficulties. Further, a non-statutory cause of action (such as 10b-5) goes through countless permutations. The question thus persisted in litigation of what statute of limitations applied to the private Rule 10b-5 action.

In 1991, the Supreme Court—borrowing from a statute of limitations expressly pertaining to investor suits under the '33 Act—created a 1 year/3 year rule for 10b-5 cases (i.e., 1 year from discovery, tolled to a maximum of 3 years from the transaction).[36]

In 2002, in response to accounting irregularities and ensuing scandals, Congress passed the Sarbanes-Oxley Act. Section 804 of that law created an extended 2 year/5 year rule for private plaintiffs alleging "fraud, deceit, manipulation, or contrivance." However, Section 804 does not expressly reference Rule 10b-5. It would thus seem that equally compelling arguments could be

---

33. *SEC v. W.J. Howey Co.*, 328 U.S. 293 (1946).

34. *Central Bank of Denver v. First Interstate Bank of Denver*, 511 U.S. 164 (1994).

35. *See, e.g.*, The Private Securities Litigation Act of 1995, Pub.L. No. 104-67 (amending Section 20 of the '34 Act).

36. *Lampf v. Gilbertson*, 501 U.S. 350 (1991) (utilizing Section 13 of the '33 Act).

made for both a 1 year/3 year rule and a 2 year/5 year rule when timing Rule 10b-5 actions.

In terms of tolling, SEC Enforcement actions when seeking fines, injunction or penalty are normally subject to the general five-year statute of limitations for government actions.[37] For many years, the SEC enjoyed boundless time for suits seeking only disgorgement as a remedy. The rationale that recovering investor monies invited a different scrutiny was approved by the courts.[38] However, in early 2017, the "disgorgement exception" was abolished by the Supreme Court, thus ensuring that the 5-year statute of limitations applies to all actions brought by the Commission.[39]

More to the point, the '34 Act expressly limits insider trading actions to a 5-year statute of limitations for both the SEC and private plaintiffs.[40] The time period is measured from the last purchase/sale covered by the allegations.

C. Ubiquitous and Growing

Procedural hurdles notwithstanding, Rule 10b-5 remains the tool of choice for the SEC, regulators, prosecutors, and plaintiffs. Adopted eight years after the statute that enables it (i.e., Section 10b), the provision has inspired a massive body of precedent that, in turn, has more often than not allowed recovery where unfair play is shown. The measure's inherent advantages are many:

- Unlike state remedies for fraud, recklessness can suffice, and proof of loss is not necessary when the SEC is the plaintiff.

- Unlike the express statutory claims created by the Acts (e.g., Sections 11 and 12 of the '33 Act), no limit on plaintiffs/defendants is contemplated. Celebrities, corporate officials, former government employees, townships, unincorporated entities and minors have all been sued by the Commission.

- Unlike foreign prohibitions, which often emanated from the rules of large stock exchanges, Rule 10b-5 applies equally to private and public companies.

---

37. 28 U.S.C. § 2462 (2016) (specifically covering fines, penalties, and forfeitures).
38. *See, e.g., SEC v. Rind*, 991 F.2d 1486 (9th Cir. 1993)
39. *Kokesh v. SEC*, 137 S. Ct. 1635 (2017).
40. *See* Section 21A(d)(5) *and* Section 20A(4).

- Its private cause of action was adopted without Congressional intervention, and without much judicial deliberation.[41]

- Its jurisdictional means are readily met (internet, stock exchange transactions, federal chartered bank checks, telephones). Further, the '34 Act provides for nationwide service of process and a wide choice of venues.

- Case law has shown the remedy to be cumulative, allowing Rule 10b-5 claims to be freely joined with state cases and other violations under the Acts. Further, the DOJ often charges securities fraud in conjunction with mail and wire fraud, two provisions that have proven far less vexing over the years.

Nonetheless, Rule 10b-5 actions are not without limit. Some restrictions are highlighted below.

- The Rule does not apply to inaction—a purchase or sale is nominally required. Further, a defendant's duty to speak arises only in the presence of a fiduciary duty or its equivalent.

- The "interstate means" requirement translates to the Rule's inapplicability to oral, intrastate fraud.

- There remains some questionable application to exotic instruments (e.g., Credit Default Swaps). The '34 Act in large part defers to agreements between the SEC and the Commodity Futures Trading Commission.[42]

- Rule 10b-5 does not cover outright theft. But it is nonetheless frequently applied to Ponzi schemes (wherein the defendant often settles).

- "Tolling" of the Rule's statute of limitations been on the wane.[43]

The key that unlocks the door is the location of a fiduciary duty to act, speak, or remain silent. The inability of the Prohibition to adhere to a clear, consistent notion of duty spelled its glaring defeat on numerous occasions in the years 1980–1997, the subject of the next part of the Book.

---

41. Namely, by *Kardon v. National Gypsum,* 69 F. Supp. 512 (E.D. Pa. 1946) (discussed *supra* in Chapter III). The private claim was later tersely ratified by the Supreme Court in a footnote within *Superintendent of Insurance v. Bankers Life,* 404 U.S. 6 (1971).

42. Created in 1974 by the Commodity Futures Trading Commission Act, the CFTC enforces the laws governing the derivatives markets. Interestingly, in the wake of the credit crisis of 2008, the agency has often received a much higher annual budgetary increase (on a percentage scale) than the SEC.

43. *See Gabelli v. SEC,* 133 S. Ct. 1216 (2013) (refusing to prolong the "discovery rule" exception to the applicable statute of limitations).

Selected Bibliography

J. Scott Colesanti, *We'll Know When We Can't Hear it: A Call for a Non-Pornography Test Approach to Recognizing Non-Public Information*, 35 Hofstra L. Rev. 539 (2006).

Allen Ferrell and Andrew H. Roper, *Price Impact, Materiality and Halliburton II* (2016), *available at* https://corpgov.law.harvard.edu/2016/09/01/price-impact-materiality-and-halliburton-ii/.

Jill E. Fisch, *As Time Goes By: New Questions About the Statute of Limitations for Rule 10b-5*, 61 Ford. L. Rev. 101 (1993).

Paul Weiss Client Memorandum, *U.S. Supreme Court Holds Materiality Is Not a Prerequisite to Class Certification in Fraud-on-the-Market Cases* (February 28, 2013) *available at* https://www.paulweiss.com/media/1521304/28feb13amgen.pdf.

Ray J. Grzebielski, *Why Martha Stewart Did Not Violate Rule 10b-5: On Tipping, Piggybacking, Front-Running and the Fiduciary Duties of Securities Brokers*, 40 Akron L. Rev. 55 (2007).

Donald C. Langevoort, *Reflections on Scienter (and the Securities Fraud Case Against Martha Stewart that Never Happened)*, 10 Lewis & Clark L. Rev. 1 (2006)

Note, *Rule 10b-5: The Rejection of the* Birnbaum *Doctrine by* Eason v. General Motors Acceptance Corp. *and the Need For a New Limitation on Damages* (1974), *available at* scholarship.law.duke.edu/cgi/viewcontent.gi?article=2493&content-dlj.

Allana M. Grinshteyn, *Horseshoes and Handgrenades: The Dodd-Frank Act's (Almost) Attack on Credit Rating Agencies*, 39 Hofstra L. Rev. 1 (2011) (discussing loss causation).

J. Scott Colesanti, *Why Materiality May Someday Become Immaterial*, LexisNexis Expert Commentary (July 2008).

SEC v. Great American Industries, Inc., 259 F. Supp. 99 (S.D.N.Y. 1966).

In the Matter of Orlando Joseph Jett, SEC Administrative Proceeding File No. 3-8919 (July 21, 1998).

SEC v. Zandford, 535 U.S. 813 (2002).

C. Edward Fletcher, III, *The "In Connection With" Requirement of Rule 10b-5*, 16 Pepp. L. Rev. 4 (1989).

Daniel A. McLaughlin & Mark Taticchi, *Corporate Scienter Under Section 10(b) and Rule 10b-5*, 46 Securities Regulation & Law Report 875 (May 5, 2014) (discussing, among other cases, the Second Circuit's 2008 decision in *Teamsters Local 445 Freight Div. Pension Fund v. Dynex Capital Inc.*).

Part Two

The Journey Towards
Judicial Empathy

Chapter V

The End of Parity of Information

The initial Commission successes at punishing insider trading (1961–1980) were accomplished at indeterminate times by varied approaches. Indeed, there was often little commonality of target, penalty, and underlying theory. With the Prohibition's first significant defeat came a name for those glory years: The parity of information[1] period, defined by a largely unquestioned approach positing that all investors could receive all the material news at the same time. That noble goal served as the end justifying all means, leading to conflicting dogma and alternating victims. Fairness truly had no opposition, until the Supreme Court intervened.

A. The People Who Halted the March

Warren Burger, the 15th Chief Justice of the Supreme Court, was the right sheriff at the right time. The quintessential self-made man, Burger sold newspapers as a boy in Minnesota while his large family struggled to make ends meet. He put himself through night college by selling life insurance during the day, but he perhaps found a quicker means of progress when he joined the local Republican Party. In 1948, he met then Congressman Richard Nixon at the Republican National Convention; four years later, Burger was instrumental in securing the Presidential nomination of Dwight Eisenhower. Burger subsequently served as an Assistant Attorney General within the Department of Jus-

---

1. "Parity of information" is also referred to as "access to information," "information," or "equal access" theory by commentators and the courts. See *supra* Chapter III.

tice, afterwards receiving an appointment to the United States Court of Appeals for the D.C. Circuit in 1956. Burger often played the role of dissenter on the liberal D.C. bench.

In 1968, Nixon was elected President on a law and order platform. The 37th President had quoted Burger in a campaign speech, extolling his thoughts that criminal trials were too often delayed at the start and likewise too frequently succeeded by appeals. While seeking a new Chief Justice for the Supreme Court, Nixon met with Burger and was impressed with his views on judicial efficiency. Burger subsequently became Court chief in May 1969, and a loud voice for conservative values thereafter.

The *Chiarella* appeal, a seminal business law case, was taken up the Court in 1980. A District Court jury had convicted the printer on 17 counts of securities fraud (i.e., Rule 10b-5 violations), and the Second Circuit had upheld the conviction. The Supreme Court viewed the case differently; in turn, Burger resorted to his dissenting ways, inspiring the Commission as no other dissenter has since.

Vincent Chiarella was an opportunistic "markup man" within a printer's shop. The company served a Wall Street niche by preparing (and secreting) the documents used in public company mergers and acquisitions. Although the names of the companies were kept off the documents until the last possible stages, Chiarella learned how to translate such coded titles into actual entities, and, in turn, how to turn his advance information of industry deals into trading profits.

Over a period of 14 months, Chiarella made approximately $30,000 by effecting purchases before news broke on a total of 5 merger/takeover targets. The SEC then brought suit and disgorged the $30,000 in profits; Chiarella's employer fired him on the day his consent decree was announced. But Chiarella's troubles were far from over.

Chiarella was indicted by the Department of Justice in the first criminal case concerning insider trading as covered by Rule 10b-5. After a jury trial, he was found guilty and sentenced to a year in prison. The Second Circuit Court of Appeals upheld the conviction, during which the DOJ slightly modified its approach. Chiarella's ensuing Supreme Court appeal in 1980 focused on his connection (or lack thereof) to the target companies whose stock he traded. The renowned *Chiarella* opinion sided with the printer, by a tally of six Justices to three. While the DOJ was dealing with the *Chiarella* appeals, the SEC was engaged with a resurgent insider trading defendant of their own.

Raymond Dirks was the perfect regulatory target. An outspoken securities analyst, he broke rank with all in the industry by publically exalting his own methodology over the contemporaneous myopia of his fellow investment professionals. Witness the blunt language of his 1979 book explaining his investment theory:

> … Most of Wall Street's theories are little more than excuses to justify the purchase of overvalued securities. Without such purchases, brokers couldn't stay in business. But the real problem with Wall Street is more than a matter of its theories. It's a matter of Wall Street's own economics—which preclude the very kind of analysis and underwriting effort that would most benefit the small investor …

On the topic of inside information, Dirks was even more pointed:

Wall Street's Cardinal Sin (emphasis is original)

> The name of the game in investing is 'information.' Find a profitable company before the crowd does. Buy shares in the company for your clients and yourself. Then spread the word, and watch the price go up as other investors come in.[2]

Dirks was in name and fact a breed apart. As the saga of the SEC trials against him (1975–1983) revealed, a "whistleblower" at a public company chose to confide to the analyst in March 1973. The whistleblower imparted seemingly fantastic details of pervasive fraud within Equity Funding, a successful NYSE stock. Skeptical of the insider's revelation, Dirks sought to corroborate the tale of a massive scheme; his investigation entailed, among other things, sharing the whistleblower's conversation with *The Wall Street Journal* (who refused to print a story).

The accounts diverge at this point. Dirks claimed that he never contacted the SEC because Secrist had informed him that the Commission was already aware of the accusations. The Commission stated it never received any detailed word of Dirks' unique information until it contacted him after the information went public. When the news broke that Equity Funding was in fact a massive fraud, its stock price tumbled from $26 a share to $15 a share. However, Dirks' clients avoided the bloodbath, as he had warned them of the suspected foul play at the company.

Dirks cooperated with the SEC's investigation. The Commission thanked him for his assistance but nonetheless imposed a minor penalty upon him (for using the inside information to the advantage of his clients). Dirks fought for

---

2. Ray Dirks, Heads You Win Tails You Win/The Dirks Investment Formula 33–34 (1979).

years to clear his name, in battles that started within the four walls of the Commission and ended before the nation's highest court at a time when the Bench was growing accustomed to quelling storms.

————————

Lewis F. Powell, Jr., Associate Justice of the Supreme Court, was born in Virginia in 1907. His storied career listed stints as a Major in the U.S. Air Force, as a student with Felix Frankfurter, as a partner of a prestigious law firm, as American Bar Association President, and as a champion of local business. He came to the Court in 1972 and is normally recalled for his soft spoken Southern accent and temperate views, a moderate force on the High Bench during a time of cases centering on desegregation, prisoner rights, and abortion.

In 1983, Justice Powell authored the written opinion in *Dirks v. SEC*,[3] the second time the Supreme Court had heard an insider trading case in four years. Dirks won, and avoided a penalty of a censure.[4] In somewhat stinging terms, Powell reminded the Commission that something more than the possession and use of inside information was necessary to trigger Rule 10b-5. Nonetheless, true to his compromising approach, Powell offered in the *Dirks* decision a 4-part test by which other facts might satisfy the Rule, the standard for adjudging "tippers" and "tippees" until today.

Collectively, Burger, Chiarella, Dirks and Powell served to remind the government of the Prohibition's limitations and opportunities. Indeed, the entire decade of the 1980s can be said to have given and taken from the application of Rule 10b-5 to insider trading while never quite elaborating on the specific point of how far the Prohibition should reach.

————————

3. 463 U.S. 646 (1983).

4. Penalties in securities cases brought by the SEC or other civil securities regulator normally run the gamut from censure (i.e., public reprimand) to monetary fine, up to bar from the industry. The censure is often viewed as the slightest of sanctions; however, this view is belied by its history (dating back to the announcement at the Opening Bell of the New York Stock Exchange). The storied sounding of the Bell communicated the start of daily news, including a public warning to the Trading Floor to proceed cautiously in transactions with disciplined stock exchange participants. Regardless of the import of a censure, Dirks' refusal to settle for the reprimand during a decade-long battle with the SEC was seen as somewhat of a testament to his sincere belief in his innocence.

B. Defendants Stand Up, and Congress Takes a Seat

As the Prohibition progressed through the 1980s, it struggled against growing numbers of litigants, jurists, and skeptics. The non-statutory rule of law was increasingly seen as subject to unfettered SEC discretion. Such disputes were largely academic, until jail time was in the mix.

1. The First True Setback

In *Chiarella*,[5] the printer availing himself of the news deciphered from draft documents faced criminal charges for insider trading under Rule 10b-5, even as the proper victim of such misdeed was left open for debate. Was it Chiarella's employer, or the companies who were the subject of the confidential takeover? Was Chiarella hurting those who did not share his privileged access to information, or the American stock market in general?

At trial, the DOJ, offered as victim sellers in the market. The DOJ later emphasized in its appellate Brief that Chiarella had also defrauded his employer's customers. The change in strategy seemed to inspire more confusion than comfort with a rule that was aggressively expanding targets. Not surprisingly, the government solicitor had his hands full at the Supreme Court.

a. The Supreme Court Oral Argument

A discussion with the High Court about a common law restriction is bound to be far-ranging and, at times, unpredictable. The *Chiarella* Oral Argument was surprisingly prescient in terms of the debates that would haunt the expanse of the Prohibition for years.

From the outset, counsel for Chiarella emphasized that a "market insider rule" had previously been negated by the Court. While acknowledging that Chiarella was part of a relationship of some sort with the printer's customers, counsel argued, "Simply put, there has been no deception, no manipulation here within [Section 10(b)]."

The Court asked whether *Texas Gulf Sulphur* readily resolved the instant case, with counsel retorting that the famed geologist case centered on insiders and their tippees (i.e., not a primary violator who was an outsider, such as

---

5. *Chiarella v. United States*, 445 U.S. 222 (1980).

Chiarella). Concurrently, counsel used the term "remote tippee" to describe the printer; that term would later serve to cabin the Prohibition in 2014. Interestingly, in handling the Bench's questions on Classical Theory, counsel glossed over the question of whether the insider's "duty of loyalty" runs to the corporation or its selling shareholders, a query that has persisted in insider trading debates since 1961.

In the main, Chiarella's counsel asserted that his client had owed no duty to selling shareholders of target companies, with whom he shared no privity. To the extent Chiarella wronged his printing press employer, such was "no more than a state fiduciary duty." Additionally, to the extent that Rule 10b-5 should arguably stretch to cover new victims, counsel urged that such new theory had not been supported by sufficient trial evidence.[6]

For his part, the government Solicitor was forced by prior case law into attempting to maintain some irreconcilable positions. The oralist ably stressed precedent supporting a trader's duty to the market and that subdivision (c) of Rule 10b-5 reached fraud practiced upon "any person." The Court's initial questions pondered whether the Williams Act, which resulted in modifications to Section 14 of the '34 Act, in effect permitted the offeror company to withhold information from sellers while buying back stock until the 5% threshold was reached; in such case, Chiarella was being held to a standard higher than that governing the printer's clients. The Solicitor responded that Chiarella had harmed both the clients and the selling shareholders, a repetition not uncommon in SEC consent decrees distributing disgorged funds.

The High Court eerily presaged future hypotheticals in asking whether a cleaning woman or "office boy" happening upon material, non-public information violates Rule 10b-5 (the Solicitor blandly opined that parties knowing they are acting improperly would be covered by the duty being proposed for Chiarella). The Solicitor also steadfastly maintained that the government need not establish harm/injury in insider trading cases, and that there had been "20 to 30" criminal 10b-5 cases before that of Chiarella (but no criminal cases for insider trading). Overall, the government position creatively drew from its own precedent, private case law, cases utilizing Rule 10b-5 or Section 17(a), and even prior Supreme Court holdings. But the Prohibition had simply grown too wide to garner intellectual support.

In reversing the Second Circuit, the Court's ultimate thrust was two-fold:

---

6. The entire *Chiarella* Oral Argument is available at https://www.oyez.org/cases/1979/78-1202.

1) The troublesome fact that if Chiarella had disclosed his breach of company policy (i.e., using information learned on the job to personal gain), he might have avoided breaking the law but nonetheless would not have helped selling shareholders, and

2) The equally troubling notion that the criminalization of employee confidentiality policies seemed endless.

On this latter point, Justice Rehnquist—commenting on a hypothetical involving a company official selective disclosing news to a favored analyst—asked, "Are you saying ... that whether there was a duty on the part of the CEO or the corporate President not to disclose to the analyst would depend upon the law of the fifty states?" At that point alone, the cause may have been lost, for it would seem incontrovertible that the Acts had sought to federalize and harmonize securities regulation.

b. The Resulting Written Decision

The Supreme Court, in essence, boiled down the case to one word: Duty. Chiarella not possessing a duty to "absolute strangers," he could not be guilty. In fact, specific duty had not even been discussed at trial or during appeal, as the Court clarified:

> In effect, the trial court instructed the jury that petitioner owed a duty to everyone; to all sellers, indeed to the market as a whole. The jury simply was told to decide whether petitioner used material, nonpublic information at a time when "he knew other people trading in the securities market did not have access to the same information." ... The Court of Appeals, like the trial court, failed to identify a relationship between petitioner and the sellers that could give rise to a duty ... [Its] reasoning suffers from two defects. First, not every instance of financial **unfairness** constitutes fraudulent activity under § 10(b). Second, the element required to make silence fraudulent—a duty to disclose—is absent in this case ...[7]

In sum, the Court saw no evidence of Congress or the Commission creating a "parity-of-information" rule; further, the Court would not create such duty. Additionally, the High Court offered some truisms that pepper the Briefs of litigants until today, such as:

---

7. 445 U.S. at 231–32.

- "Section 10(b) is aptly described as a catchall, but what it catches must be fraud."[8]
- "We hold that a duty to disclose under 10(b) does not arise from the mere possession of nonpublic market information."[9]
- "We cannot affirm petitioner's conviction without recognizing a general duty between all participants in market transactions to forgo actions based on material, nonpublic information. Formulation of such a broad duty ... should not be undertaken absent some explicit evidence of congressional intent."[10]
- "[Chiarella] was, in fact, a complete stranger who dealt with the sellers only through impersonal market transactions."[11]

And yet, the *Chiarella* opinion also served to diplomatically enhance prior SEC victories. The *Cady, Roberts* administrative decision was characterized as chiefly reliant upon a 1951 Delaware court decision finding the "necessity of preventing a corporate insider from ... tak[ing] **unfair** advantage of the uninformed minority stockholders."[12] And the Court's *Affiliated Ute* decision of 1972[13] was maximized for the premise that silence could possibly constitute fraud, if a duty to disclose were present.

Additionally, *Chiarella* gifted the Commission with some sub-holdings that drew little space or attention. For example, "market" information (i.e., facts concerning the intention of third parties to purchase stock, as opposed to facts about the public company itself) was evaluated as inside information without question. Further, SEC rulemaking was placed on a par with legislative debate and enactment (thus reinforcing the deference emphasized by *Chenery II*[14] in 1947).

After all is said and done, the *Chiarella* case first and foremost distinguished insider from outsider, leaving the Commission at a loss for a theory to apply Rule 10b-5 to the latter. That still hypothetical reach was subsequently enabled by the guidance of the dissent by Chief Justice Burger. Indeed, without giving the theory a name, the dissent nonetheless spelled out a game plan for the Commission by which "outsiders" could be brought within Rule 10b-5's reach:

---

8. *Id.* at 234–35.

9. *Id.* at 235.

10. *Id.* at 233.

11. *Id.* at 232–33.

12. *Speed v. Transamerica Corp.*, 99 F. Supp. 808, 829 (Del. 1951).

13. *Affiliated Ute Citizens of Utah v. United States*, 406 U.S. 128 (1972).

14. *SEC v. Chenery Corp.*, 332 U.S. 194 (1947). In that little-known decision, the Supreme Court (upon rehearing) had deferred to the SEC, which had decided that company officers and directors were under a duty not to trade during a reorganization.

I believe that the jury instructions in this case properly charged a violation of § 10(b) and Rule 10b-5, and I would affirm the conviction. As a general rule, neither party to an arm's length business transaction has an obligation to disclose information to the other unless the parties stand in some confidential or fiduciary relation. *See* W. Prosser, Law of Torts § 106 (2d ed.1955). This rule permits a businessman to capitalize on his experience and skill in securing and evaluating relevant information; it provides incentive for hard work, careful analysis, and astute forecasting. But the policies that underlie the rule also should limit its scope. In particular, the rule should give way when an informational advantage is obtained not by superior experience, foresight, or industry, but by some unlawful means.[15]

The Chief Justice, again ensuring law and order, had explained in clear terms that (nondescript) unlawful behavior could trigger 10b-5; in implied language, the Court's leader had advised the Commission to look harder for a direct victim from the defendant's conduct. Justice Burger had reminded all that Rule 10b-5 derives from the law of torts, and that theft of property is a crime.[16] Taken together, the dissent's musings informed the theory that the Commission would modify, perfect, and offer repeatedly to the Second Circuit and other courts throughout the 1980s and 1990s (*i.e.*, the "Misappropriation Theory" or "Theory"). However, the Supreme Court would first issue a reminder of the depth of its indifference towards theories that reached everyone in the market and branded possession of inside information a crime.

2. The *Dirks* Echo

As in *Chiarella*, in *Dirks* (1983)[17] the Supreme Court held that something more than receipt of inside information was needed to trigger a duty to abstain or disclose. The case likely presented the most unique facts of any insider trading investigation imaginable. Once again, the holding gifted the SEC both a loss and a platform for untold future victories.

Dirks was an analyst specializing in the stocks of insurance companies. A former employee turned whistleblower (Ronald Secrist) of Equity Funding, a publicly-traded insurance company, disclosed to him on two occasions in

---

15. 445 U.S. at 240.

16. Black's Law Dictionary defines misappropriation as "The application of another's property or money dishonestly to one's use. See EMBEZZLEMENT." (emphasis in original).

17. 463 U.S. 646 (1983).

March 1973 that Equity was essentially a Ponzi scheme relying on phony insurance policies. The second such conversation between Dirks and Secrist lasted over three hours. Dirks next proceeded to inform the *Wall Street Journal*, who found the story too fantastic to publish. Dirks followed up by interviewing Equity officials and six former company employees. During his investigation, Dirks began to feel that Secrist's story was corroborated, and so advised numerous institutional clients and others to sell Equity stock.

The SEC sued Dirks (a registered analyst) in an internal hearing,[18] and an internal Commission judge imposed the sanctions of a censure and a fine. On appeal, the fine was dropped, but the liability for aiding and abetting violations remained. True to maverick form, Dirks fought on, and the Supreme Court granted certiorari.

a. The Oral Argument

At oral argument,[19] counsel for Dirks was first asked why the analyst did not immediately report Secrist's disclosures to the SEC; counsel disagreed that such was Dirk's duty, particularly in light of the fact that Secrist had stated to Dirks that the matter had been disclosed to the SEC years prior in 1971. Counsel also stated that Dirks "told literally a hundred people" about Secrist's disclosure, but neither Dirks or his firm had traded on the information, and the firm had received but one "indirect commission" from trades related to the disclosures. It was also disclosed that some of Dirks' tippees had been disciplined by the SEC, and that Dirks himself had been subjected to (unsuccessful) class action litigation once his Commission discipline had become known.

Tellingly, counsel for Dirks was asked how, if at all, the present case was any different from *Chiarella* (i.e., in which the nature of the communication and the resulting profits were deemed irrelevant because no duty to disclose could be located). "I do not know why you are afraid to make [that] argument," Justice Stevens commented.

The tougher questions seemed reserved for the SEC, counsel for which was asked whether anyone at the Commission had been "censured" (as Dirks had been) for failing to act sooner on the fraud at Equity Funding. The government

---

18. Since its inception 1934, the SEC has been empowered to seek redress for violations in both its own administrative courts and in federal court. The internal route is largely reserved for SEC registrants (e.g., investment advisers, and stockbrokers). *See* Sections 20 and 21 of the '33 Act and '34 Act, respectively.

19. The full oral argument of counsel for Dirks and the Commission is available at https://www.oyez.org/cases/1982/82-276.

Solicitor was also queried as to how Dirks' actions differed from the expectation of any analyst, who, as a matter of job function, evaluates rumors and possibilities. The attorney responded as such:

> The Commission said a line has to be drawn between the usual functions of analysts and their trading on inside information that would not be available to anyone. The line is between what might be called **fairness**, as far as is possible to do so, on the one hand, as against the role that analysts play on the other hand.

That line, the Solicitor argued, favored the SEC where, as in the *Dirks* case, "devastatingly important information" had come into the analyst's possession.

Further questioning of the government Solicitor elicited the absolute yet incomplete nature of the Commission's "abstain or disclose" interpretation of the Prohibition. Counsel asserted that the case was "not about confidentiality," but rather the duty to all market participants. In the Commission's view, even proper disclosure through a wire service or newspaper still precluded trading by the tippee, and, regardless, Dirks was ultimately liable for the $17 million in losses avoided by his five customers (who were similarly charged with violating 10b-5). Moreover, a "never ending chain" of tippees could occur, as long as each tippee could be shown to have known that the inside information was confidential.

The Solicitor drew laughter from the packed Court chamber by maintaining that Dirks had a duty to inform buyers of Equity shares, "This is a bad stock." Counsel likewise steadfastly maintained that Dirks would not have been free to trade on the information even if he had called the SEC or New York Stock Exchange—such disclosure was still not broad enough to ensure that the news was adequately shared. Most importantly, the SEC was unable to articulate the nature of the duty borne by Secrist/Dirks: Such duty ran either to existing Equity shareholders, new purchasers who bought while Dirks' tippees sold, or both. Additionally, the Commission was not clear on how that amorphous duty could be discharged, in general, or could have been met by Dirks, in particular. Commission counsel's attempt to rely on the 1971 internal precedent of *Investors Management* turned out to be more of a battle squeak than battle cry,[20] as the Court was seemingly not interested in the dated, internal SEC decision.

---

20. *In the Matters on Investors Management Co.*, 44 SEC 633, 639 (July 29, 1971). In that case, the SEC, in an administrative decision, readily concluded that investment bankers tipping other outsiders violated registration sections of the '34 Act because "The maintenance of **fair** and honest markets in securities and the prevention of inequitable and **unfair** practices in such markets are primary objectives of the federal securities laws."

Overall, some of the finer points of "abstain or disclose" were altogether un-addressed. The Commission could not state whether an avoidance of a loss was the same as an insider trading profit (a point clarified by statute in 1984). Also, SEC counsel acknowledged that any monies paid to Dirks' firm were im-material, that the Commission did not charge Secrist (although arguing that both he and Dirks shared the same duty), and—to the seeming chagrin of the bench—that there existed no authority for the notion that criminal activities must be reported to the Commission. The height of the Bench's skepticism may have come when Justice Powell asked rhetorically, "Is it a fact that *The Wall Street Journal* was nominated for the Pulitzer Prize [for its article on the Equity Funding scandal] and Dirks was prosecuted?"

On rebuttal, counsel for Dirks poked fun at the Commission's draconian answers on the abstain-or-disclose theory, which, given the present circum-stances, seemed to impose a duty on Secrist to remain silent about a massive, continuing fraud. In counsel's estimation, such duty was readily distinguishable from the duty to keep confidential news of an impending dividend (as in *Cady, Roberts*) or the duty to keep confidential the news of a large ore find (as in *Texas Gulf Sulphur*). Secrist possessing no duty, there was no obligation for Dirks to inherit, and no violation of Rule 10b-5.

b. The Written Decision

Justice Powell and the majority agreed. The decision largely reiterated the Court's holding three years prior:

> As we emphasized in *Chiarella*, mere possession of non-public infor-mation does not give rise to a duty to disclose or abstain; only a specific relationship does that. And we do not believe that the mere receipt of information from an insider creates such a special relation-ship between the tippee and the corporation's shareholders.[21]

However, Justice Powell—who had asked the government during oral argument, "How far does the [tippee] chain go?"—resumed his role as pragmatist and took the occasion to articulate two tests by which outsiders (or "strangers") could be charged. The first test looked for, in turn, an original duty owed by the insider, and, next, a benefit to be gleaned from the tip. The second test evaluated, in turn, whether the tippee could inherit the insider's duty, and, next, whether the tippee had reason to know of the insider's breach of his duty. Thus, the conse-quential *Dirks* test, to this day, asks the following four questions:

---

21. 463 U.S. at 656, n.15.

1. Did the tipper possess a duty?
2. In tipping, did the tipper obtain a benefit?
3. Could the tippee be said to have inherited the tipper's duty?
4. Did the tippee know that a duty had been breached by the tipper?[22]

The "never ending chain" feared by Justice Powell seemed legally unsupportable in the *Dirks* case. Moreover, Justice Steven's adherence to *Chiarella* proved to be fatal to the SEC's efforts at such support. Dirks received no censure, and the Prohibition weathered its second Supreme Court defeat in four terms.

The *Dirks* decision was not without controversy. The three dissenting Justices noted that, "even on the extraordinary facts" of the case, the limitation upon the protections of the '34 Act was not justified.[23] Additionally, the dissent minimized the role of Dirks in detecting the fraud while highlighting the selective disclosure by Dirks to his institutional clients. Such disclosure was said to enable them to "shift the losses that were inevitable due to the Equity Funding fraud from themselves to uninformed market participants."[24]

Subsequently, even when not primarily relied upon, *Dirks* had quick impact. In the famed "eavesdropper" decision of 1984, a celebrated football coach was exonerated for acting on a tip he claimed was overheard (from a friend) at a college track meet. The District Court decision found, inter alia, that the defendant—an outsider—would have to inherit a *Cady, Roberts* (i.e., insider) duty to be found liable; additionally, the defendant was absolved because *Dirks*, which was decided by the Supreme Court a year before, had clarified that the tippee's duty to abstain or disclose must be derivative of the tipper (i.e., the tipper must have breached a duty for the tippee to be found to have breached a duty).[25]

However, the *Dirks* loss provided the Commission with not one but two fully baked theories by which new classes of defendants could be readily reached. Justice Powell's dual 2-part tests established the means by which tippees could come within Rule 10b-5. Meanwhile, famed footnote 14 of the *Dirks* decision supplied the SEC with a tool to identify that discrete category of non-employees temporarily sharing the insider's fiduciary duty:

> Under certain circumstances, such as where corporate information is revealed legitimately to an underwriter, accountant, lawyer, or con-

---

22. As discussed in Chapter XI, the Second Circuit's decision in *United States v. Newman*, 773 F.3d 438 (2d Cir. 2014), for a time, heightened this requirement.
23. 463 U.S. at 668.
24. *Id.* at 670.
25. *SEC v. Switzer*, 590 F. Supp. 756, 765–66 (W.D. Okl. 1984).

sultant working for the corporation, these outsiders may become fiduciaries of the shareholders. The basis for recognizing this fiduciary duty is not simply that such persons acquired nonpublic corporate information, but rather that they have entered into a special confidential relationship in the conduct of the business of the enterprise and are given access to information solely for corporate purposes (citations omitted).

The irony of storied footnote number 14 should not be discounted. First, the rule appears in a footnote, instead of the text, underscoring its ultimate importance. Second, the rule relies in part on the *Monarch Fund* case,[26] which actually exonerated a fund trader because of a finding of no duty on recipients of information to ensure that it was public. Third, substantively, the rule may simple re-articulate the conclusions of the Classic or Misappropriation theories in that employees (contractual or otherwise) have duties to shareholders, and that theft of such information for trading purposes is prohibited.

Perhaps more interestingly, the *Dirks* dissent questioned the addition of improper motive to the equation: Since Secrist, as whistleblower, was found to not have been acting for personal gain, he received no benefit, and there consequentially attached no liability for him or his tippee (Dirks). But such a focus on the incentive for the tipper disregards the effect on counterparties in the market, who overpaid for Equity stock regardless. Although the dissent does not state it, such a focus on the market would appear to be much more in line with Congressional intent—at the time the strict liability Section 16(b) was adopted, at the time of *Texas Gulf Sulphur* cases, and at the time of the 1988 amendment of the '34 Act (discussed *infra*).

3. Other Speed Bumps for the Commission

Even before the losses in *Chiarella* and *Dirks*, notice had been taken of the Commission's concurrent aggressive enforcement of the Prohibition and its inherent vagaries. The inconsistencies revealed by the doctrine's frequent use were beginning to single out certain professionals for rough treatment. As the Second Circuit opined in *Bausch and Lomb*,[27] a case centering on a CEO's disclosure of negative earnings to a limited number of analysts:

---

26. *SEC v. Monarch Fund*, 608 F.2d 938 (2d Cir. 1979).

27. 565 F.2d 8 (2d Cir. 1977). Because the court found that the likelihood of recidivism was low, the SEC request for an injunction against Bausch & Lomb and its CEO was denied.

[S]ince the importance of a particular piece of information depends on the context in which it is given, materiality has become one of the most unpredictable and elusive concepts of the federal securities laws. The SEC itself has despaired of providing written guidelines to advise wary corporate management of the distinctions between material and non-material information, and instead has chosen to rely on an after-the-fact, case-by-case approach, seeking injunctive relief when it believes that the appropriate boundaries have been breached.

Spurred by judicial mistrust, the cries of uncertainty in the Prohibition grew. A 1983 defeat for the plaintiffs in a Second Circuit class action seemed to undo a holding about the proper scope of defendants from nine years earlier.[28] Twice during the 1980s, Congress convened to address codification of the violation of insider trading. On each occasion, with SEC support, the federal legislature avoided the task, rewarding what one Commission official would term favoring the minefield for the roadblock. The two Congressional measures are discussed in turn below.

a. The Insider Trading Sanctions Act

In 1984, the SEC proposed the idea of a statutory definition of insider trading, but then retreated from the notion. Congress thus took up a bill addressing insider trading obligations but ultimately (and resolutely) decided against definition therein. In the main, the Insider Trading Sanctions Act ("ITSA") provided the SEC with the authority to seek treble damages, increased criminal fines from $10,000 to $100,000, and extended the Prohibition to cover commodities and its brokers. While noting that insider trading had become so pervasive that two former government officials had been charged with the offense, one of the law's sponsors concurrently stated:

Although some commentators recommended that the legislation define the conduct which would be subject to the penalty action, both Houses of the Congress have determined not to adopt a statutory definition of insider trading. By the use of the language '[w]henever it shall appear to the Commission that any person has violated any provision of this title or the rules or regulations thereunder by purchasing or selling a security while in possession of material nonpublic information' the Congress intends that the civil penalty shall apply to any violation under the Securities Exchange Act that entails the commu-

---

28. Specifically, *Moss v. Morgan Stanley*, 719 F.2d 5 (2d Cir. 1983), and *Shapiro v. Merrill Lynch*, 495 F.2d 228 (2d Cir. 1974). Both cases are discussed in Chapter X.

nication of, or the purchase or sale of a security while in possession of, material nonpublic information ...

Such description of the final statute was idealistic for several reasons. First, communications alone are definitely not punishable under Rule 10b-5 (a trade is needed). Second, the characterization of the "civil penalty" may have been an understatement: The Acts in general prohibit punitive damages, and, as later cases show, the treble limit could be exceeded by the government in parallel DOJ actions. Finally, the conclusory assertion that possession alone could trigger a violation preceded a lengthy, litigated debate over whether the insider trading defendant must actually "use" the information of which he was alleged to possess; that debate was not resolved by the resulting law.

More idealistic still was the notion that SEC staff—past and present—supported ITSA. The Commission Chairman had hedged when asked during Congressional testimony whether a statutory Prohibition was necessary; in related correspondence, the Chairman wrote only that such a definition would be problematic. Noteworthy is that Milton Freeman, one of the drafters of Rule 10b-5, opposed the inclusion of a statutory definition for a unique reason. The storied former SEC official strongly believed in 1983 that the Prohibition should be limited to corporate information, and not the dual categories of company and market information being accepted:

> There is no question that as a result of the adoption of the [Prohibition], for over 40 years purchasing on inside information has been illegal. Such conduct has been subject to criminal penalties and to the right of the shareholder to impose recovery of civil damages. The law on this subject is clear, it requires no clarification or amendment. Indeed the SEC's concern in connection with the proposed bill is not principally and perhaps not at all with such insider trading.
>
> The Commission instead has made a proposal that is concerned more with the recent phenomenon of tender offers for the stock of companies in which an opportunity exists for **unfair** use of information to make profits. This is an entirely different matter. In my judgment the Commission has made a major error in trying to treat **unfair** use of information by outsiders such as tender offerors on the same basis as insider trading by corporation officials dealing with their own shareholders.
>
> It is my belief that the two types of transactions are in practice and in legal theory entirely different and require separate treatment. Thus it is fundamentally false labeling to call the proposal an Insider Trading Sanctions Act when its purpose is in fact to deal principally with **unfair**

use of information by outsiders. It is just as inappropriate to use tools designed for insider trading to apply to tender offer outsider trading as it would be to use indoor house paint for the outside of a house.[29]

When the debate was over, ITSA did not create new law or jurisdiction, but it greatly enhanced sanctions. Whereas prior to 1984, the Commission could seek only an injunction and disgorgement from the non-registrant (e.g., the layman in the tippee chain discussed during the *Dirks* oral argument), the arsenal of remedies was now summarily increased—and their bounties, per statute,[30] payable directly to the United States Treasury.

Curiously, while SEC penalties for stock exchange transactions were uniquely expanded to treble damages,[31] private face-to-face transactions were exempted. Such exception appears incongruous, as Rule 10b-5 lore commenced in 1943 upon application to the actions in the stock of a private company, namely, Ward LaFrance.

b. The Insider Trading Securities Fraud Enforcement Act

In 1988, Congress deliberated two Bills before adopting the Insider Trading Securities Fraud Enforcement Act ("ITSFEA"). The second of these, proposed by the SEC, would have codified the Prohibition as follows:

> It shall be unlawful for any person, directly or indirectly, to purchase, sell, or cause the purchase or sale of, any security while in possession of material nonpublic information concerning the issuer or its securities, if such person knows or recklessly disregards that such information has been obtained wrongfully or that such purchase or sale would constitute a wrongful use of such information.

Such proposal attempted to incorporate all existing theories of Rule 10b-5 applicability at the time (i.e., Classic, Misappropriation, tipper/tippee, and even constructive insider). The proposal begged the question of whom exactly was subject to such a possession standard. It was accompanied by a robust explanatory list that included people ranging from employees of the issuer to financial professionals, to "any other person who obtains such information as

---

29. Statement of Milton V. Freeman Before the House Telecommunications, Consumer Protection and Finance Subcommittee of the United States House of Representatives' Energy and Commerce Committee Scheduled for April 13, 1983, *reprinted in* BERNARD D. REAMS, JR., INSIDER TRADING SANCTIONS ACT OF 1984: A LEGISLATIVE HISTORY 163–64 (1989).

30. Namely, Section 21(d)(1) of the '34 Act.

31. In name, the Acts do not provide for "punitive" damages. The SEC's authority to seek treble damages in insider trading cases stands alone.

a result of a direct or indirect confidential relationship" with previously referenced individuals.

Both the proposed definitions of Congress and the SEC were ultimately rejected, likely because (again) the Commission Chairman had testified that a statutory definition was not necessary. Perhaps the lack of a definition was the prudent move: The proposed definitions seemed to echo SEC Rule 14e-3's emphasis on takeover transgressions, while the data indicates that modern insider trading is more often tied to less dramatic events (e.g., earnings forecasts).

Supporters of change did also succeed in increasing criminal sanctions, creating a 10% bounty for whistleblowers, and in imposing liability upon aiders and abettors, as well as "controlling persons" of primary violators.[32] Further, a statutory defense rewarding written preventative steps ensured that compliance departments all over Wall Street would be implementing/modifying procedures. Regulators other than the SEC and DOJ took heed, and the failure to prevent insider trading itself became a concern.[33]

Most importantly, ITSFEA added to the '34 Act new section 20A,[34] which codified a private cause of action for all "contemporaneous traders" (i.e., all those on the other side of the market) of a buyer/seller found to have violated the Prohibition. Such recovery was subject to a cap that considered SEC penalties for the same transaction; still, the provision proved to be a very effective in terrorem measure.

C. Voids and Promises

The Supreme Court rulings in 1980 and 1983 effectively ended the belief that use of material, non-public information by itself was a violation. In

---

32. The Acts, at Sections 15 and 20, respectively, impose liability upon employers per the industry title of "controlling persons," who are determined pursuant to factors such as the ability to direct the management or policies of a company. Thus, the *respondeat superior* doctrine is not relevant, and the liability of a manager is largely determined by reference to case law.

33. *See, e.g.*, New York Stock Exchange Disciplinary Action 89-50, *The First Boston Corporation* (June 5, 1989) (imposing a censure and a $60,000 fine in conjunction with the defendant firm's consent to findings of two supervisory violations premised upon 1) the failure to "provide for appropriate supervisory control to assure that material non-public information was not improperly disseminated within the firm," and 2) the failure to provide a system of follow up and review to assure compliance with various internal procedures).

34. The Section 20A cause of action is discussed further in Chapter X.

essence, "insider information" had grown between *Cady, Roberts* and *Chiarella* to approach the level of contraband: As a possession, it mattered little how it was obtained. The High Court's repeated emphasis on the need for a duty to be breached thus ensured that Rule 10b-5—essentially a business tort—would forever be tied to a corresponding duty.

The Commission's response to the loss in *Chiarella* was three-fold. First, the SEC adopted Rule 14e-3, which outlaws trading while aware of a tender offer in a company. Nicknamed "the other guy's tender offer rule,"[35] the Rule salvaged a small portion of the Parity Theory in that mere communication of inside information was outlawed. However, such wrongful dissemination was still tied to an eventual trade, much like tipper liability under the *Dirks* test.

Second, the Commission heeded the advice from Justice Burger on perfecting the Misappropriation Theory, which went through several permutations for years. The Theory punishes those who obtain information by unlawful means. In 1981, the DOJ indicted an investment banker named James Newman and four of his tippees for their sharing confidential news of takeovers learned from a client. The decision refusing to dismiss that indictment, albeit brief, gave formal rise to the Theory.[36]

Third, using its new weapon, in 1983, the SEC brought essentially the same case as *Chiarella* against a printer named Anthony Materia. A jury found Materia liable on 4 of 5 charges based upon the theory of a duty to his employer (the breach of which injured its reputation as a financial publisher).[37]

Nonetheless, despite several victories, the Theory invited attack upon the Prohibition like never before. The Supreme Court had refused it, and only a handful of Circuits employed it. Even the friendly Second Circuit had questions.

Penalties and Consequences

As for damages, the squelching of the Parity of Information Theory did result in a much more colorul palette of remedies, albeit arbitrary. Chiarella (a laymen) had paid with disgorgement and prison time. Dirks, a registered analyst subject to a Commission administrative hearing, had received a public censure. Newman was the subject of a criminal indictment, while Materia (an SEC defendant) received an injunction and an order to disgorge approximately $100,000. Thus, the Commission, although hesitant in the seminal applications

---

35. Rule 14e-3 is also discussed in Chapter VIII.
36. *United States v. Newman*, 664 F.2d 12 (2d Cir. 1981).
37. *SEC v. Materia*, 745 F.2d 197 (2d Cir. 1984).

to outsiders to ramp up the penalties, was quite comfortable referring matters to the Department of Justice while relegating some cases for less serious disposition.[38] Concurrently, the practice of holding civil (e.g., SEC) matters in abeyance until the resolution of the criminal charges grew into full bloom.

The twin cases indicating Supreme Court chagrin over SEC zealousness nonetheless provided the Commission with a number of predicates that would never again be seriously questioned. To wit:

- The Congressional amendments of 1984 and 1988 added color but acknowledged and relied upon the common law for the substance of the Prohibition. Since that time, Congress has not seriously considered codifying the Prohibition, although it seems that each decade highlights the calls of prosecutors or judges for direct definition.

- After *Chiarella*, the type of information at the center of the dispute need not be related to the subject corporation. For example, knowledge of a large institutional investor's planned trade (which would move the market price) could be "inside" information, even though it neither emanated from the company nor assisted with appraisal of its fortunes.

- After *Dirks*, tipper/tippee liability had a name and a test.

- Together, the two cases missed an enormous opportunity. If ancillary players could be separated from primary violators, over-reaching theories would have been more palatable. But by equating the liability of tippers (who could be liable even when not trading) with that of tippees (who must trade to be liable but could exist well outside the corporation), the incentive for both to abstain and cooperate with investigators was squashed.[39]

Thus, despite the pragmatism of Justices Burger and Powell, the Prohibition was far from settled. The concept that anyone possessing inside information could be liable to anyone who did not had proven unworkable. Given that, in

---

38. Since their inception, both of the Acts have expressly (albeit tersely) permitted SEC referral to the DOJ when investigations warrant. *See* Section 20(b) of the '33 Act, and parallel Section 21(d) of the '34 Act ("The Commission may transmit such evidence as may be available concerning such acts or practices as may constitute a violation of any provision of this title or the rules or regulations thereunder to the Attorney General, who may, in his discretion, institute the necessary criminal proceedings under this title.").

39. An alternative world of sliding accountability is more than just theory: Since 1994, Germany has distinguished between the administrative fine (for those solely disseminating information) and more serious penalties (including incarceration) for those who trade and profit. The alternative is discussed more fully in Chapter XIII.

the government's eyes, responsibility appeared joint and several (and sanction ran the gamut), it was uncertain that any replacement concept created by the SEC would ultimately be as effective or as fair. The Prohibition thus edged forward and back on an intellectual sea of to and fro for nearly two decades.

Selected Bibliography

Sarah S. Gold & Richard L. Spinogatti, *Consequences of Justice Powell's Slippery Slope in Dirk*, NEW YORK LAW JOURNAL (October 15, 2015).

MATT TAIBBI, THE DIVIDE 256 (Spiegel & Grau 2014) ("While the rest of America understood Michael Douglas's iconic Gordon Gekko character as a villain, and saw his famed 'greed is good' speech as incisive satire, many aspiring Wall Street traders sincerely thought—and still think—that Gekko was the movie's hero.").

BOB WOODWARD & SCOTT ARMSTRONG, THE BRETHREN/INSIDE THE SUPREME COURT 5–9 (1979).

Judge Calls on Congress to Pass Insider Trading Law, NEW YORK LAW JOURNAL (October 23, 2015) (quoting Southern District of New York Judge Paul Engelmeyer on the need for Congress to "reconsider the rules of liability").

Printer is Punished in Insider Case, N.Y. TIMES (Dec. 6, 1983).

BERNARD D. REAMS, JR., INSIDER TRADING AND THE LAW: A LEGISLATIVE HISTORY OF THE INSIDER TRADING SANCTIONS ACT OF 1984 (William S. Hein & Co., Inc. 1989).

Chiarella v. United States, 445 U.S. 222 (1980).

Dirks v. SEC, 21 S.E.C. Docket 17 (February 3, 1981).

Dirks v. SEC, 463 U.S. 646 (1983).

SEC v. Materia, 1983–84 Transfer Binder, Fed. Sec. L. Rep. (CCH), ¶ 99,526 (S.D.N.Y. 1983).

United States v. Newman, 664 F.2d 12 (2d Cir. 1981), *cert. denied*, 104 S. Ct. 193 (1983).

RALPH C. FERRARA, DONNA M. NAGY & HERBERT THOMAS, FERRARA ON INSIDER TRADING AND THE WALL (Law Journal Press; 2011 version) ("ITSA increased potential liability for insider trading but did not shed statutory light on the substantive limits of Section 10(b) ...").

Supreme Court Resources/Warren E. Burger, Oyez, *available at* https://www.oyez.org/justices/warren_e_burger ("Nixon appointed Burger in the hope that his deference to 'law and order' would rein in what many conservatives saw as liberal judicial activism.").

Lewis F. Powell, Jr., Oyez, https://www.oyez.org/justices/lewis_f_powell_jr (last visited June 19, 2017).

Bernard Schwartz, Super Chief: Earl Warren and His Supreme Court — A Judicial Biography (NYU Press 1983).

Linda Greenhouse, *Dirks Gets His Day in Court*, N.Y. Times (March 22, 1983) ("One unusual aspect of the case is that the Justice Department has refused to support the S.E.C.'s views on insider trading. The department urged the Justices to hear Mr. Dirks's appeal over the commission's objections, and it filed a strongly worded brief on his behalf.").

Malcolm A. Tripp, *Access, Efficiency, and Fairness in Dirks v. SEC*, 60 Ind. L.J. 535 (Summer 1985), *available at* http://www.repository.law.indiana.edu/ilj/vol60/iss3/5.

Donna M. Nagy, *Beyond* Dirks: *Gratuitous Tipping and Insider Trading*, 42 J. Corp. Law 1 (Fall 2016).

Congressional Record — House of Representatives (July 25, 1984), at 20969.

Gregory A. Robb, *S.E.C., in a Reversal, Offers Definition of Insider Trading* (August 8, 1987) (noting that "The word misappropriation does not appear in the S.E.C. proposal, though the agency maintains that the concept is there."). The article also noted that there was an incentive to delay adoption of a definition until the Supreme Court had issued its opinion in *United States v. Carpenter* in the Spring Term of 1988.

Insider Trading Sanctions Act of 1984, Pub.L. No. 98-376, 98 Stat. 1264.

Insider Trading Securities Fraud Enforcement Act of 1988, Pub.L. 100-704, 102 Stat. 4677.

Elkind v. Liggett & Myers, Inc., 635 F.2d 156 (2d Cir. 1980).

Bruce A. Hiler, *Dirks v. SEC — A Study in Cause and Effect*, 43 Md. L. Rev. 2932 (1984) *available at* http://digitalcommons.law.umaryland.edu/cgi/viewcontent.cgi?article=2553&context=mlr.

"Investors Management": *Institutional Investors as Tippees*, 119 Univ. Pa. L. Rev. 502 (Jan. 1971).

Chapter VI

The Prohibition's Period of Uncertainty

The frontier had closed. The pioneers had come home. The boundless reach of the Prohibition had met its end. Yet, as the 1980s came to pass, insider trading seemed to migrate from the financial pages to primetime news and culture. The Supreme Court heard the lurid tale of a Wall Street Journal reporter who accepted cash in return for advance news of his stories. The more earthen New York newspapers were fronted by pictures of alleged insider traders being led away in handcuffs (although their indictments seemed to later crumble under their own weight). A best-selling book detailed the intricacies of the offshore insider trading of New York investment banker Dennis Levine. Meanwhile, a mainstream movie providing faces to insider trading, "Wall Street," won an Academy Award for a popular actor.

The authority of the SEC (and private plaintiffs) had indubitably increased, and a deterrent to employer willful blindness had been implemented. But the central question of how far the Prohibition should extend was still unsettled. Even the Second Circuit had confessed that analysts were absolved when "piec[ing] seemingly inconsequential data together with public information into a mosaic which reveals material non-public information."[1] More generally, outsiders were somewhat reached by Section 16(b) (if 10% beneficial owners) and Rule 14e-3 (if acting upon news of a tender offer), thus lessening the need for broad remedy to the law. Additionally, any attempts at furthering the grasp of "securities fraud" inevitably raised the practical question of why the conduct was

---

1. *Elkind v. Liggett & Myers, Inc.*, 635 F.2d 156, 165 (2d Cir. 1980).

not already reachable under the wire fraud and mail fraud statutes, both of which are readily proven by patently deceptive conduct.

Courts and observers remained hesitant on the issue of embracing the legal fiction of the Misappropriation Theory. Would Chiarella have lost if the nascent doctrine had been presented to a Southern District of New York jury? Was Dirks wrong for advising his clients of an impending corporate collapse? Should everyday outsiders fear the Prohibition? Such questions proliferated for most of the 1990s, but not for lack of effort by the SEC. And those efforts—along with the those of the DOJ—began to inspire antagonism towards a theory that the SEC and supportive jurists believed simply sought fairness. Three cases between 1987 and 1994 highlighted the difficulty in relying on a proposed doctrine indifferent to the nature of the confidential duty or the penalty sought.

A. The *Carpenter* Case: The Dangerously Entrepreneurial Reporter

R. Foster Winans was a reporter for *The Wall Street Journal*. In the very early1980s, his daily "Heard on the Street" column (co-authored with another Journal reporter; hereinafter "Heard") was growing in reputation. Rumor had it that the prognostications therein themselves moved markets. In one of the most sordid fact patterns attending insider trading legal disputes, Winans was said to have conspired with two stockbrokers and two intermediaries to repeatedly exchange for cash the contents of Heard one day prior to publication.

A total of 27 Heard columns were leaked in advance between October 1983 and February 1984, and the scheme grossed nearly $700,000 in trading profits. Profits were split via deposits to joint accounts with misleading names; occasionally, a check with a false notation in the memo line conveyed a direct payment. Winans' roommate and co-worker, David Carpenter, helped the scheme by communicating trades/information and delivering documents between Winans and the stockbrokers. On one occasion, the brokerage contact forwarded to Winans a check for $15,000 (as an "advance" on the scheme) hidden in a research report.

The brokerage house employing the co-conspirators noted the parallel between Heard prognostications and its brokers' trades. In early March 1984, the SEC commenced an investigation. The five schemers began to align their explanations and to bicker on defensive tactics. Carpenter and Winans went to the Commission later that month and voluntarily disclosed the entire plot.

All five individuals faced justice; Winans, Carpenter, and one of the stock-brokers were criminally tried as co-defendants. The government initially accused Winans of defrauding *Journal* customers, but that approach was superseded by the assertion at trial that he had defrauded his employer. After a 20-day bench trial in the Summer of 1985, all three defendants were convicted, with Winans being found guilty of securities fraud (for violating Rule 10b-5), mail and wire fraud, conspiracy, and obstruction of justice. Winans was sentenced to 18 months in prison, after having separately concluded the related SEC action against him with a payment of a $4,500 fine. Carpenter was found guilty of aiding and abetting Rule 10b-5 violations, but he was, overall, said to have not understood the details of the scheme and accorded a sentence of three years of probation.

The written opinion of the District Court[2] clarified that inside "corporate" information was not at issue. Rather, the timing and content of the Heard column was sold in contrivance of a specific conflicts of interest policy that had been distributed by the *Journal* to its employees. The court dismissed the defense that not all trades were profitable and likewise the assertion that the defendants had no notice of the illegality of their actions.[3] The argument that the government's allegation of theft left the *Journal* free to trade on the subject information (i.e., the Heard column) did not persuade the court. Noting that Congress depended on the judiciary to interpret "broadly stated principles," the opinion bluntly found, "The **fairness** and integrity of conduct within the securities markets is a concern of utmost significance for the proper functioning of our securities laws."

On appeal, the Second Circuit was faced with a new type of dilemma. Aside from the Misappropriation Theory remaining a work in progress (it included language at this time regarding the requirement of a defendant's trading "advantage"), the preceding post-*Dirks* decisions had all included defendants privy to confidential stock market information: *Newman*[4] (investment banker), *Musella*[5] (law firm office manager), and *Materia*[6] (printer). Further, the Second

---

2. *United States v. Winans*, 612 F. Supp. 827 (S.D.N.Y. 1985). As an appeal lodged by several parties, the case later took the name "Carpenter" from Winans' roommate, who, as intermediary in the scheme, was convicted of lesser charges.

3. Section 32 of the '34 Act, which authorizes criminal penalties for any *willful* violation of the Title, concludes with the limitation that "no person shall be subject to imprisonment under this section for the violation of any rule or regulation if he proves that he had no knowledge of such rule or regulation." The requisite knowledge of illegality has always been interpreted most broadly, as is discussed in Chapter XI.

4. *United States v. Newman*, 664 F.2d 12 (2d Cir. 1981).

5. *SEC v. Musella*, 578 F. Supp. 425 (S.D.N.Y. 1984).

6. *SEC v. Materia*, 745 F.2d 197 (2d Cir. 1984).

Circuit had posed a setback for the Theory just two years earlier in *Moss v. Morgan Stanley, Co.*,[7] the civil, class action counterpart suit to the criminal *Newman* decision. That dissonance from *Newman* was troublesome for two reasons: 1) It was unclear—even in the Circuit most embracing the Theory—that the same standard applied to civil and administrative claims, and 2) It was equally unclear whether the same standard applied to criminal and all other cases.

The appellate court majority in *Carpenter*, while acknowledging that "not every instance of financial **unfairness** constitutes fraudulent activity under section 10(b)," noted that the stolen *Journal* information was of no value other than to the scheming defendants. Interestingly, in a footnote, the majority opinion added that "The general tort of breach of a duty of confidentiality to an employer is, of course, well settled"; while *Chiarella* had likened Rule 10b-5 to a tort, the comparison is not consistently made by litigants or the judiciary (i.e., Rule 10b-5 is its own administrative creation).

In turn, the dissent opined that a special relationship needed to be proven to apply the Theory, and that to focus on the "publication schedule" of the *Journal* was to "extend the sweep of section 10(b) and Rule 10b-5 beyond all reasonable bounds." In the end, the Second Circuit held in 1986 that there was little to distinguish *Carpenter* from prior Misappropriation Theory holdings in *Newman* (1983) and *Materia* (1984). However, the Second Circuit's discrepancies and questions would be resurrected at the High Court level.

The *Carpenter* Supreme Court Oral Argument

The Supreme Court was not as easily sold on the notion that fairness warranted adoption of a possible legal fiction. At Oral Argument, counsel for Winans (and his two co-defendants) first argued that securities fraud requires a victim who has purchased securities: "It is not something that can be committed upon a newspaper or a private employer that has not participated in the securities transaction ..." Counsel added that a company's internal policy

---

7. 719 F.2d 5 (2d Cir. 1983). In *Moss*, the shareholders of a target company who sold their stock sued the purchasers who had the benefit of inside information obtained from the investment adviser to the acquirer (Morgan Stanley). Oddly, although *Newman* had upheld the Theory the same year, the *Moss* panel—citing a prior Morgan Stanley case [*Walton v. Morgan & Stanley & Co.*, 623 F.2d 796 (2d Cir. 1980)]—focused on the duty to the client, and found none to exist when the investment adviser's agent works for the *acquiring* party but relays information on the *target* company. Further, the *Moss* panel bluntly stated, "We find that plaintiff's 'misappropriation' theory clearly contradicts the Supreme Court's holding in both *Chiarella* and *Dirks* and therefore conclude that the complaint fails to state a valid section 10(b) or rule 10b-5 cause of action."

does not "have the force of criminal law"; the *Journal*'s harm, if any, was to its reputation. When asked whether the case would be different had the government pleaded resulting injury to market participants, counsel still denied any securities fraud, "because a market participant must be defrauded in that capacity as a market participant, and that that is the reach of the securities laws." Justice Stevens asked whether there were any "judicial remedy" for Winans' behavior. Counsel stated that the remedy lied in the *Journal*'s public firing of Winans, which "effectively drummed him out of the profession."

When asked whether the *Journal* had a property interest in Winan's column, counsel for Winans maintained that the insider information only had value in comparison to rival newspapers. Interestingly, Justice Scalia posed a hypothetical in which Winans' premature disclosure of his column decreased the price rise in a stock; counsel mooted the question by responding that the government at trial had expressly disavowed the column's role as provider of investment advice on the market.

Finally, counsel for Winans pointedly proclaimed that upholding the convictions was tantamount to elevating "every employee ethical breach into a federal crime." The oralist closed by emphasizing that Rule 10b-5 when properly utilized protects "hoodwinked" investors, and he likewise warned that the *Journal* essentially had adopted an internal policy (by which Winans was fired) which imposed a requirement that employees observe the Parity of Information Theory (which had been rejected by the Court in *Dirks*, five years prior).

In responding for the government, the Solicitor had three obstacles to overcome. First, the Court had most recently found a narrow reading of the mail and wire fraud statutes in the *McNally* case.[8] Second, the lower courts had decided that Winan's theft injured both the reputational and property interests of the *Journal*, but not investors. Third (and paramount), the Theory, which still existed in various forms, was not universally embraced among the Circuits.

The Solicitor focused on the theft of information, clarifying that the "timing and content" of the Heard on the Street column had been stolen. The Justices were briefly troubled by the alleged misappropriation of *facts*, leading the Solicitor to argue that prior trade secret cases had held that employees could not freely disseminate either facts or opinions.

---

8. In *United States v. McNally*—issued during the spring 1987 term, just months the *Carpenter* Oral Argument—the Supreme Court had held that the mail fraud statute does not reach "schemes to defraud citizens of their intangible rights to honest and impartial government." 483 U.S. 350, 355 (1987).

Strangely, the Solicitor urged that, in enacting Section 10(b), "Congress assumed the ordinary common law meaning" of fraud (the government in *TGS* and other cases had asserted that the Acts went beyond the common law definition of fraud[9]). The Court interposed that some elements may draw from the common law. The government's position was further fleshed out as exceeding the requirements of embezzlement: Winans' fraud was not in simply stealing the inside information from his employer, but in trading on it or tipping it for trading purposes.

Justice Scalia expressed skepticism at the assertion that potential reputational harm could warrant criminal charges, drawing laughter from the Court chambers in the process:

> I must say that the concept of putting something at risk as harm sufficient to support a criminal charge is, it seems to me, rather strange. It is not even harm sufficient to support a tort action, or we would have a lot of tort suits for near misses instead of even fender benders.

Subsequently, the discussion of the mail and wire fraud charges triggered competing legal analyses of *McNally*. There ensued lively debate over the nature of fraud by deprivation, including the Solicitor's repeat offering of the example of the theft of a car, and references even to trespass upon (without damage to) a neighbor's land.[10] The Solicitor focused the Court on the government's belief that the *Journal* work rule was irrelevant to a finding of fraud while highlighting that Rule 10b-5 prohibits fraud "upon any person"—and that close to $700,000 had been netted by the defendants.

On rebuttal, Winans' counsel urged the Court to refrain from stretching statutes too far so as to impose a "limiting principle of **fairness**" on the market.

The *Carpenter* Written Decision

The Court partially agreed with Winans' version of fairness. Although unanimously upholding the mail and wire fraud convictions, the High Court was split 4–4 on the securities fraud conviction, thus elevating the Second Circuit holding to the final say on the matter.

---

9. *See, e.g., SEC v. Capital Gains Research Bureau*, 375 U.S. 180 (1963) (finding that the common law notion of fraud had been "adapted" by Congress in adopting the Investment Advisers Act, and granting an injunction against an adviser who purchased stocks, touted them, and then sold them for gain).

10. The entire *Carpenter* oral argument can be heard at https://www.oyez.org/cases/1987/86-422.

Regarding the non-securities charges, the decision rejected Winans' contentions that inside information did not rise to the level of *property* and that his theft merely violated a workplace rule. The Court readily concluded that the Heard column was *Journal* property and that Winans knew of the need for it to remain confidential; accordingly, the theft of the column's timing and content satisfied both the "scheme to defraud" and "fraudulent pretenses" language of, respectively, the mail and wire fraud statutes.

Regarding Rule 10b-5, the *Carpenter* decision said nothing other than that the Second Circuit decision was affirmed. In the end, Winans was criminally convicted, and inside information was incontrovertibly found to be "property" for purposes of the mail and wire fraud statutes. However, as of 1988, the Misappropriation Theory had not yet found approval with a court more authoritative than the Second Circuit.

B. The *Chestman* Case:
Excluding Government from Pillow Talk

Robert Chestman was a stockbroker. In November 1986, he received a tip from a client, Keith Loeb, that the public company Waldbaums was to be acquired within two months by rival food seller A & P. Loeb, an in-law of the family controlling Waldbaums, said the tip came from inside the corporation and asked Chestman whether he should purchase Waldbaums stock. Chestman, who had purchased Waldbaum stock for Loeb and others prior to 1986, later stated that he repeatedly refused to advise on Loeb's contemplated purchases but nonetheless bought Waldbaums shares for himself and his customers.

When the news of the Waldbaums-A&P merger broke, the stock jumped almost 50%, netting a sizeable profit for Chestman and his clients. Subsequent SEC/FINRA[11] investigation learned that the tip had traveled through several layers of the Waldbaum family, at each juncture accompanied with the admonition not to trade. The Commission and DOJ thus proceeded on a Misappropriation Theory that each family member had stolen the information from his/her source. The chart below details the flow of the "theft" of the merger information, per the case law:

---

11. Founded in 2007, FINRA ("Financial Industry Regulatory Authority") joined the New York Stock Exchange Division of Enforcement and the NASD Division of Enforcement to create the largest regulator of securities industry broker-dealers, all of whom are required to register with the self-regulatory organization under Section 15 of the '34 Act.

Main Players in the *Chestman* Informational Chain

Source of news	1st generation misappropriator	2nd generation misappropriator	3rd generation misappropriator	4th generation misappropriator	Tippee
Julia W. → told brother Ira not to trade	*Ira W.* → told daughter Shirley not to trade				
		Shirley W. → told daughter Susan not to trade			
			Susan Loeb → told husband Keith not to trade	*Keith Loeb* → discussed tip with his stockbroker, Chestman	
					Chestman *criminal defendant

Numerous parties "up the chain" from Chestman settled with the SEC; Keith Loeb disgorged $25,000 in profits and paid a fine of equal amount. However, Chestman, a licensed stockbroker at the end of the informational chain and the only "tippee," faced a criminal case. He went to trial, where he argued that he had purchased Waldbaums stock based upon his research. A federal jury found him guilty on all 31 charged counts (10 counts each of Rule 10b-5, Rule 14e-3, and mail fraud; 1 count of perjury).

On appeal, a Second Circuit panel reversed all of the guilty findings, dignifying Chestman's claims of insufficient evidence and Commission overreach.[12] The following year, the case was reheard en banc. In that decision, the Second Circuit issued two holdings: 1) The SEC had not exceeded its rulemaking authority in promulgating Rule 14e-3, and 2) Loeb could not have

---

12. 903 F.2d 75 (2d Cir. 1990).

misappropriated the subject inside information from his wife because marriage alone does not establish the requisite relationship.

Specifically, on the argument that the SEC had exceeded its rulemaking authority in promulgating Rule 14e-3, the court cited *Chevron* deference to administrative rulemaking,[13] as the court did not wish to second guess Commission authority to effectuate Section 10(b)'s generically stated desire that the SEC draft rules outlawing proxy fraud.[14] Further, the court held that Congressional activity during and after the SEC's adoption of Rule 14e-3 indicated legislative acquiescence to the SEC's interpretive rulemaking pursuant to Section 14 of the '34 Act. Finally, the court found that there is no need for information exchanged between tipper and tippee to be expressly labeled "confidential" for Rule 14e-3 to apply.

On the argument that Chestman did not violate Rule 10b-5 (or aid and abet Rule violations), the court agreed. Introducing the analysis as one of requisite fraud, the Second Circuit utilized the definition of a misappropriator that had worked in the Commission's favor in the *Materia*[15] case: "one who misappropriates nonpublic information in breach of a fiduciary duty and trades on that information to his own advantage." The court thus concluded that all family members who had relayed the information of the impending supermarket merger had deliberately disobeyed the immediately disclosing party (i.e., Shirley W. had defied Ira W, and, in turn was defied by Susan, whose instructions not to trade were ignored by husband Keith). But in order for the duty to run all the way down the informational chain, each relationship had to be characterized as fiduciary in nature—one cannot *misappropriate* (i.e., steal) information unless owing a duty of trust to the owner of that information.

---

13. *Chevron U.S.A., Inc. v. Natural Resources Defense Council, Inc.*, 467 U.S. 837 (1984). In *Chevron*, the Supreme Court announced a standard by which the decisions of agencies should be deferred to when the enabling statute is ambiguous or has not addressed an issue and the agency decision constitutes a final legal ruling and is not irrational.

14. Section 10(b) of the '34 Act prohibits, among other things, acts or practices "in contravention of such rules and regulations as the Commission may prescribe as necessary or appropriate in the public interest or for the protection of investors." 15 U.S.C. § 78j(b).

15. In *Materia*, the court imposed the sanctions of an injunction and disgorgement of approximately $100,000. Subsequently, Judge Kaufman's written decision for the Second Circuit upheld the finding and sanction, commencing in timely and poetic fashion: "Our era aptly has been styled, and well may be remembered as, the 'age of information.' Francis Bacon recognized nearly 400 years ago that 'knowledge is power,' but only in the last generation has it risen to the equivalent of the coin of the realm. Nowhere is this commodity more valuable or volatile than in the world of high finance, where facts worth fortunes while secret may be rendered worthless once revealed." 745 F.2d at 198.

The court concentrated its analysis on defining the required duty, a study that had two parts.

First, the court reminded that *Chiarella* and its progeny had established that the mere receipt of inside information did not create the duty required for application of the Theory.

Second, the court examined examples of fiduciary relationships and extracted, among others, the standard of "reliance and dominance." The prime example of the attorney-client privilege was noted; the husband-wife relationship was not. There being no fiduciary relationship occasioned by marriage (nor evidence that Keith Loeb was part of the "inner circle" of Waldbaum family matters), there was no confidence to betray, and no misappropriation. In turn, Chestman (as tippee, under the *Dirks* test) could not inherit a duty that did not exist, and he had to be acquitted.

Contemporaneously, the Second Circuit found two nullities in the search for the predicate relationship, memorialized in quotes normally used from the decision:

- "First, a fiduciary duty cannot be imposed unilaterally by entrusting a person with confidential information."
- "Second, marriage does not, without more, create a fiduciary relationship. '[M]ere kinship does not of itself establish a confidential relation.' ..."

In sum, while the *Chestman* court's fiduciary analysis entailed review of everything from Supreme Court precedent to treatises on fiduciaries, to Black's Law Dictionary, it foremost weighed the state common law of the relevant forum. Avoidance of state peculiarities—one of the paramount goals of federalizing the securities law—was subverted. The Prohibition thus encountered a new obstacle, namely, an unpredictable limit to the type of underlying relationships that would readily be deemed "fiduciary" in nature by the courts. Further, the list of relevant authorities was endless, as courts would review everything from state statutes to the Federal Rule of Evidence on privilege[16] in order to evaluate the legitimacy of a proffered fiduciary relationship supporting an allegation of theft by a trader.

Interestingly, scienter—likely the element spurring the criminal authority to initiate a case against Chestman, a stockbroker who should have known better— was not evaluated by the court. In response to the Prohibition's curtailment in

---

16. Federal Rule of Evidence 501 permits objections to evidence premised upon "[t]he common law—as interpreted by United States courts in the light of reason and experience."

Chestman, the SEC adopted Rule 10b5-2, but that was years later (the year 2000). In the mid-1990s, there still was time for the Theory's foes to grow in strength.

C. The *Bryan* Case: Outright Hostility Towards Legal Rationales

Elton "Butch" Bryan was the director of the West Virginia state lottery in 1991. It was alleged that, in that role, he was in charge of the process by which vendors were to be chosen for a lucrative video lottery terminal agreement and a $2.8 million advertising contract. Bryan learned to delay, "rig" and/or excessively formalize the process by which approval of vendor contracts was granted and communicated. By thus manipulating contracts and timing his personal trades in the bidding companies, he was ultimately alleged to have profited handsomely.

After a 1993 jury trial, Bryan was convicted of perjury (before the grand jury), manipulating two government contracts, insider trading, wire fraud and mail fraud. Bryan was sentenced to 51 months in prison.

On appeal, the Fourth Circuit Court of Appeals upheld all convictions save for insider trading. In issuing the most damning screed against the Theory by any judiciary to date, the *Bryan* court analyzed what it termed the Misappropriation Theory as upheld by a number of Circuits, which stated that a defendant

> (1) misappropriates material nonpublic information (2) by breaching a duty arising out of a relationship of trust and confidence and (3) uses that information in a securities transaction, (4) regardless of whether he owed any duties to the shareholders of the traded stock.[17]

The court readily conceded that Bryan's activities would violate the Theory as stated; however, the Theory itself was found to be "irreconcilable" with prior Supreme Court rulings. In the view of the Fourth Circuit, chief among the departures from Supreme Court holdings in cases such as *Sante Fe Industries*[18] and *Blue Chip Stamps*[19] was the Theory's abolition of the requirement that the alleged fraud victimize "a person in some way connected with or having a stake

---

17. *United States v. Bryan*, 58 F.3d 933, 944 (4th Cir. 1995) (citing *SEC v. Clark*, 915 F.2d 439 (9th Cir. 1990)).

18. *Santa Fe Industries v. Green*, 430 U.S. 462 (1977).

19. *Blue Chip Stamps v. Manor Drug Stores*, 421 U.S. 723 (1975).

in an actual or proposed purchase or sale of securities."[20] Bryan's victim being his employer, his securities fraud conviction was untenable. The court expressed its rejection of the Theory in clear terms:

> In contravention of this established principle, the misappropriation theory authorizes criminal conviction for simple breaches of fiduciary duty and similar relationships of trust and confidence, whether or not the breaches entail deception within the meaning of section 10(b) and whether or not the parties wronged by the breaches were purchasers or sellers of securities, or otherwise connected with or interested in the purchase or sale of securities. Finding no authority for such an expansion of securities fraud liability—indeed, finding the theory irreconcilable with applicable Supreme Court precedent—we reject application of the theory in this circuit.[21]

Further, the court took the occasion to assail SEC decision-making:

> Absent clearly defined rules, investors find themselves the targets of ad hoc decisionmaking or pawns in an overall litigation strategy known only to the SEC. See Central Bank of Denver, 511 U.S. at ___, 114 S.Ct. at 1454 (noting "undesirab[ility] ... of decisions 'made on an ad hoc basis'" (citation omitted)); Dirks, 463 U.S. at 664 n. 24, 103 S.Ct. at 3266–67 n. 24 (investor reliance upon the reasonableness of SEC's litigation strategy "can be hazardous").[22]

Finally, the Bryan decision took aim at holdings within the Second Circuit, noting that the seminal Newman decision itself lacked clarity as to what role Newman played in the tipping chain: "In truth, it is difficult to determine from the opinion in Newman the precise basis upon which Newman's conviction was affirmed."[23]

The appellate court found suitable alternative to the Theory in the mail and wire fraud statutes, tersely concluding, "Those who trade on purloined information but who do not come within the Chiarella/Dirks definition of 'insider' are still almost certain to be subject to criminal liability for federal mail or wire fraud."[24]

Therefore, in the eyes of the Fourth Circuit, Bryan's activities were subject to harsh charges and penalties—but he was not an insider trader, and the gov-

---

20. *Bryan*, 58 F.3d 933 at 949.
21. Bryan, 58 F.3d at 944.
22. 58 F.3d at 951.
23. 58 F.3d at 954, n.19.
24. 58 F.3d at 953.

ernment's hard fought victories for the Theory carried no weight in the region. An SEC official speaking to a group of student interns at the New York Stock Exchange a year later had an expedient (and possibly half-joking) solution, publicly declaring, "It's simple. We won't bring insider cases in the Fourth Circuit." On a more serious note, at least six Prohibition vagaries persisted by 1995:

D. A Half-Dozen Takeaways

Court opinions issued between 1986 and 1995 made manifest a half-dozen problems besetting the Prohibition:

1. The role of common law fraud is unclear.

In enacting Section 10(b) of the '34 Act, did Congress mean to supersede common law fraud, improve upon it, or sidestep it altogether? The three cases described above leave that question unresolved.

2. Price impact as dispositive proof of materiality is never questioned.

While the definition of "materiality" was up for grabs in the 1960s, by the 1980s, courts had seemingly settled upon the non-legal, price impact doctrine (i.e., if the stock price jumps after disclosure, the news was important) as the foremost proof of materiality. Price impact was more than a subtle SEC creation. The practical notion enjoyed the support of jurists.[25] Given that every modern Prohibition action relies at least in part on price impact to establish the element of materiality, such holdings may be the most significant contribution of private case law to SEC enforcement actions. For better or worse, that approach has never been altered.

3. No distinction is ever drawn between primary and secondary liability.

Carpenter received a lesser sentence because he was found to have not fully understood the significance of his actions, nor the overall workings of the larger scheme. However, the proof required for an aiding and abetting charge continued (as it had in *Dirks*) to be equated with the substantive Rule 10b-5 violation, a blurring that could only hinder settlement negotiation and deterrent effect.

Likewise, Chestman—who had been charged as both a primary violator and an aider/abettor—had his convictions altogether eradicated by the

---

25. *See supra* p. 50. *See also In re Burlington Coat Factory Sec. Litig.*, 114 F.3d 1410 (3rd Cir. 1997) (holding that in an "efficient market" the concept of materiality translates into information altering stock price).

majority opinion's finding that, "Absent a predicate act of fraud by Keith Loeb, the alleged misappropriator, Chestman, could not be derivatively liable as Loeb's tippee or as an aider and abettor."

4. The criminal-civil divide is never clarified.

Upon reflection, it appears that Chestman faced criminal charges because he was a stockbroker who should have known better.

Carpenter seemed to have damaged the reputation of Wall Street's premier publication.

Bryan can be said to have netted a provocative profit from a government job.

However, neither experience nor profits nor injury to reputation could account for the 1985 criminal charges at the heart of *United States v. Reed*.[26] In that case, the opinion detailed the option purchases by the son of a public company Board member but never stated the amount of profit after the news became public. Indeed, the trial appears to have been primarily motivated by the government's desire to bring a case against a non-cooperating outsider in the wake of the *Chiarella* and *Dirks* losses (1980 and 1983, respectively).

As a result, by 1995, the thought started to take hold within the industry that the factors leading to criminal prosecution were simply indiscernible.

5. Overall, much comes from the judges, sua sponte.

The debates over the Misappropriation Theory invited widely scattered commentary, upon topics ranging from criminal deterrence to tort law. The law of theft (a generality) was linked to the law of securities (a specialty). Theoretical approaches to duty and damages changed during appeals, often belying the severity of the sanctions sought. The academic bickering, while intellectually entertaining, collectively reinforced the criticism of securities law in general and Prohibition law in particular as being outcome-determinative.

6. Mail and wire fraud charges, routinely included as certain victories, had become a liability.

The *Bryan* decision, if not for the first time at least for the most noticeable occasion, indicated that multiple federal charges could work against the government. The scathing majority opinion openly queried why the deplorable conduct of the government official could not simply be covered by the mail

---

26. 601 F. Supp. 685 (S.D.N.Y. 1985) (finding that the existence of a fiduciary relationship "is ultimately a question of fact, the resolution of which rests on the particulars of the interactions between the parties and the texture of their specific relationship").

and wire fraud statutes without inviting the hallmark debates over the proper reach of the securities laws.

––––––––––

Despite Congress' amplifying sanctions, Justice Powell's pragmatism in *Dirks,* and the Commission's repeated refinements to the Theory, the Prohibition was at an impasse. Its victims were not always clear, and its very wording was still subject to ad hoc determinations. By itself, *fairness* as an incantation could be dwarfed by judicial fears of unanswerable hypotheticals, unforgiving SEC trading restrictions, inexplicable legal fictions distinguishing between victim and harm, and unmitigated criminal penalty. Further, the Theory, although dubious and limitless, had been the joint contribution of the SEC and the courts after decades and decades of effort and was thus very hard to discard. The answer, it would seem, would be to present the Supreme Court with a case posing a clear duty, a choice of victims, and a superfluous penalty.

By the mid 1990s, there thus circulated in regulatory circles the hope that a case of such egregious behavior would compel the Supreme Court to adopt the Theory in toto. Such a case wound its way through the Eighth Circuit to shocking result. The case involved a sole violator, previously imprisoned (making the scheme easier to comprehend and eliminating questions of relative culpability and sanction). Most importantly, it included such alarming facts and unquestionable duty as to readily tip the balance back in favor of the prosecution. The name of the case was *O'Hagan.*

Selected Bibliography

Donna M. Nagy, *Reframing the Misappropriation Theory of Insider Trading Liability: A Post-*O'Hagan *Suggestion* (1998), *available at* http://www.repository.law.indiana.edu/cgi/viewcontent.cgi?article=1617&context=facpub.

Howard J. Kaplan et al., *The Law of Insider Trading* (ABA Presentation of April 18–20, 2012), *available at* https://www.americanbar.org/content/dam/aba/administrative/litigation/materials/sac_2012/29-2_the_law_of_insider_trading.authcheckdam.pdf.

Timothy J. Horman, *In Defense of* United States v. Bryan: *Why the Misappropriation Theory is Indefensible,* 64 Ford. L. Rev. 2455 (1996).

SEC Speech, *Is the Sky Really Falling? The State of Insider Trading Law After the Winans Decision*" (January 26, 1988), *available at* https://www.sec.gov/news/speech/1988/012688grundfest.pdf.

DOUGLAS FRANTZ. LEVINE & CO./WALL STREET'S INSIDER TRADING SCANDAL (1987).

Moss v. Morgan Stanley Inc., 719 F.2d 5 (2d Cir. 1983).

United States v. Carpenter, 791 F.2d 1024 (2d Cir. 1986).

Carpenter v. United States, 484 U.S. 19 (1987).

United States v. Newman, 664 F.2d 12 (2d Cir. 1981) ("*Newman I*").

Jill E. Fisch, *Start Making Sense: An Analysis and Proposal for Insider Trading Regulation*, 26 GA. L. REV. 179 (1991).

Tamar Lewin, *Winans Conviction Upheld*, N.Y. TIMES (May 28, 1986), *available at* http://www.nytimes.com/1986/05/28/business/winans-conviction-upheld.html.

Sean P. Leuba, *The Fourth Circuit Breaks Ranks in United States v. Bryan: Finally, a Repudiation of the Misappropriation Theory*, 53 WASH. & LEE L. REV. 1143 (1996).

United States v. Chestman, 947 F.2d 551 (2d Cir. 1991) (*en banc*).

Barbara Bader Aldave, *The Misappropriation Theory: Carpenter and Its Aftermath*, 49 OHIO ST. L.J. 373 (1988), *available at* https://kb.osu.edu/dspace/bitstream/handle/1811/64417/OSLJ_V49N2_0373.pdf.

SEC News Digest, 85–204, *Permanent Injunctions Entered Against R. Foster Winans, Jr. and David J. Carpenter* (October 22, 1985), *available at* https://www.sec.gov/news/digest/1985/dig102285.pdf (describing the SEC settlement, which imposed injunctions against Winans and Carpenter and ordered disgorgement of $4,502). The Insider Trading Sanctions Act (which permits treble damages against insider traders) had not yet taken effect when the SEC charges against Winans were filed in 1984.

Christine Neylon O'Brien, *The Insider Trading Sanctions Act of 1984*, CPA JOURNAL (December 1986), *available at* https://dlib.bc.edu/islandora/object/bc-ir:100231/datastream/PDF/view ("The potential for multiple payments under ITSA also poses other problems. Extensive liability imposed against ITSA defendants may violate fundamental principles of **fairness** to the extent that such liability is too severe in relation to the activity to which it applies. Assessment of multiple damages in unreasonable amounts may have the undesirable effect of discouraging legitimate trading conduct of a creative or novel nature.").

William Globerson, *3 Leading Brokers Seized on Charges of Insider Trading; U.S. Inquiry Widens*, N.Y. TIMES (February 13, 1987).

Chapter VII

Paradise Regained:
The Supreme Court Approves
the Misappropriation Theory

Between 1980 and 1997, the Commission struggled mightily to find court approval for its Misappropriation Theory. As was the case before, the journey relied foremost on judges deciding a question of fairness. Fairness seemed to tilt in only one direction when the defendant, previously convicted for embezzlement and disbarred, used client secrets to make over $4 million. The Prohibition just needed some bold individuals who never let definition or procedure stand in the way of a just cause.

A. The People Standing in the Crossroads

James O'Hagan was a star defense lawyer and a partner of a prestigious Minneapolis firm. His personal legal troubles placed him on several battlefields at once in the late 1980s. His alleged transgressions included "borrowing" money from client accounts and later engaging in illegal securities trading to make repayment. The case was said to startle the staid Minnesota milieu, both for its magnitude and brazen nature. Ultimately, O'Hagan was disbarred, imprisoned via state court charges of embezzlement, subject to mammoth SEC fines, and convicted of federal crimes ranging from mail fraud to money laundering.

As part of the federal case against him, O'Hagan was accused of violating both Rule 10b-5 and Rule 14e-3 by using information learned at work for personal trading. The securities law case was almost a moot point: O'Hagan, already serving a 30-month sentence, had been fired from his firm and stripped of his law license. But the facts and attendant legal questions were somewhat unique—to wit, should an outsider who received no tip and committed no overt act of defiance nonetheless be held to the abstain or disclose requirement? Courts at the time had strong opinions on the subject.

———————

United States Deputy Solicitor General Michael Dreeben is one of only two oralists in the past century to argue 100 cases before the Supreme Court. Known for his diligent and practical approach, he confesses to rehearsing theories before laymen and friends. His storied resume includes stints investigating white collar fraud and serving as circuit court law clerk before first appearing before the High Court in 1989; in that case, he unsuccessfully argued against Double Jeopardy in multiple disciplinary actions premised upon Medicare fraud.[1] He won his next argument and many times thereafter, arguing before the Supreme Court every year between 1989 and 2016, when he hit the hundred mark as chief of the criminal docket before the High Court. Later that year, he successfully argued the *United States v. Salman*[2] appeal, skillfully scaling back the government's position on tipping liability. However, his Oral Argument of 1997—again a textbook adaption to the mood of the Court— may be the most influential of his career.

———————

Supreme Court Justice Ruth Bader Ginsburg has had a storied career punctuated by battles for equality. In law school, she was one of nine female students in a 500-person Harvard class, and the first female member of the institution's esteemed Law Review. She would later serve as the first female tenured professor at Columbia Law School.

Her work years graduated from displaying an expertise in civil procedure to her heading the influential ACLU Women's Rights Project in the 1970s. She continually championed the cause of those discriminated against in her six appearances before the Supreme Court in as many years. After 13 years on the District of Columbia Court of Appeals, she became the second female Justice on the Supreme Court in 1993. Three years later, she there authored the majority decision ordering the stoic Virginia Military Institute to admit qualifying women.[3]

———————

1. *United States v. Halper*, 490 U.S. 435 (1989). Interestingly, Dreeben's oral argument adversary in that case was future Chief Justice John Roberts, before whom he has appeared on many occasions.

2. 137 S. Ct. 420 (2016). The *Salman* decision defines "benefit" for purposes of the *Dirks* test (under certain circumstances) and is thus discussed in Chapter XI.

3. *United States v. Virginia*, 518 U.S. 515 (1996).

In a 2013 interview, a career advocate in the battle between civil rights and established procedure, Justice Ginsburg spoke of the role of secondary authority in informing judicial decisions:

> There's nothing a judge appreciates more than a good law review article on the topic. But sometimes we have the sense that the law faculties frankly are more interested in talking to each other and regard the courts as unimportant or obsolete, so they don't speak the language the court relates to ... But I would like to emphasize that there really is nothing better than a good unbiased law review article in a field, and if we have that, we're served better than we are by the lawyers' briefs.[4]

In her autobiography. Justice Ginsburg reprinted a 1992 article titled, "Speaking in a Judicial Voice." In that article, the seasoned jurist subscribed to the dictum that "Judges do and must legislate," with moderation. In 1997, a case pitting thievery against undecided law reached the Supreme Court, where Justice Ginsburg had been sitting for four years. If *fairness* were to have a champion, it need look no further than the judge who succeeded at every level in finding rationality without pause. If that rationality needed a boost more from Law Review articles than case law, so be it.

B. Vindication at Last—
The New (Common) Law

1. The *O'Hagan* Facts

As a partner in the Minneapolis headquarters of Dorsey & Whitney, O'Hagan learned in the summer of 1988 that his law firm had been retained by Grand Met, a British company seeking to acquire Pillsbury, a hometown enterprise. In August, the lawyer commenced purchasing Pillsbury "call options," a strategy that maximizes profits.[5] By the end of September, O'Hagan, in addition to own-

---

4. *A Conversation with Justice Ruth Bader Ginsburg*, Symposium Issue, 25 COLUMBIA J. GENDER & L. 6, 20 (2013). In the same interview, Justice Ginsburg spoke of the challenges presented by a multi-judge appellate bench, and of the concurrent need to accommodate requests from colleagues in order to form a majority.

5. A "call option" entitles its owner to purchase 100 shares of the underlying stock, usually within a finite, 3-month period. Since the option can be much cheaper than the share itself, its purchase leverages the investment money. For example, if the stock is trading at $40 per share, and the investor has $1,000 and believes the stock price will double (a very

ing 5,000 shares of Pillsbury stock, owned 2,500 Pillsbury options, entitling him to 250,000 shares should he decide to exercise the contracts.

In early October 1988, Grand Met (which had ceased being a Dorsey & Whitney client in early September) publically announced its tender offer for Pillsbury. The stock price jumped from $39 to $60 per share. O'Hagan exercised his Pillsbury contracts and made a profit exceeding $4 million. The SEC commenced an investigation into the trading activities of O'Hagan and others who had bet heavily on a Pillsbury stock rise.[6] O'Hagan was subsequently indicted on 57 counts (20 counts of mail fraud, 17 counts of securities fraud (i.e., Rule 10b-5 violations), 17 counts of violating Rule 14e-3, and 3 counts of money laundering).

At federal trial, the jury was charged with the instruction that O'Hagan owed a duty to both his employer law firm and its client, Grand Met. O'Hagan unsuccessfully urged that he owed no duty to Pillsbury shareholders.[7] He was convicted on all 57 counts. He was sentenced to 41 months in prison, and he appealed.

By majority decision, the Eighth Circuit Court of Appeals reversed. Declaring its focus to be the fraud/deception element of Rule 10b-5 (and relying on, among other things, private case law), the Circuit cited the Fourth Circuit's *Bryan* case in defining the Misappropriation Theory. That Circuit's version of the Theory would impose Rule 10b-5 liability upon a defendant who steals material, nonpublic information in breach of a confidential duty "regardless of whether he owed any duties to the shareholders of the traded stock."[8]

In language bordering on derisive, the court found the Theory as stated to be "without concern as to whether a party who did care about the securities transaction was defrauded."[9] Noting that it was adopting the entirety of the analysis of *Bryan*, the Eighth Circuit declared in similar vein that:

> In essence, the courts which recognize the Misappropriation Theory
> seem to have validated it on the basis of the assumed **unfairness** of al-

---

unlikely event), he can purchase hundreds of call options, whereas he would only be able to afford 25 shares.

6. *See United States v. O'Hagan*, 92 F.3d 612 (8th Cir. 1996).

7. O'Hagan's position was not completely absurd: Recall that approximately 14 years earlier in *Moss v. Morgan Stanley*, the Second Circuit had refused to impose liability where the defendant's use of information learned from an *acquiring* company affected the share price paid by shareholders of the *target* company.

8. *Bryan*, 58 F.3d at 944.

9. 92 F.3d at 617.

lowing an individual to trade securities on the basis of information which is not available to other traders (*citing Carpenter*) (misappropriation theory permissible to give "legal effect to the commonsensical view that trading on the basis of improperly obtained information is fundamentally **unfair** ...") ...[10]

Additionally, relying on the Supreme Court's emphases on breach of duty as stated in *Chiarella* and on actual misrepresentation as stated in *Central Bank of Denver*,[11] the Circuit rejected the Theory as conflicting with the High Court's desires. Further, for separate reasons, the appellate court held that SEC Rule 14e-3 exceeded the Commission's rulemaking authority. Finding the securities fraud to not exist, the court concurrently reversed the overlaying mail fraud, wire fraud and money laundering convictions as well.

2. The Supreme Court Case

The Supreme Court granted cert, and a number of amicus briefs were filed. Most significantly, Milton Freeman—the same Milton Freeman who helped draft Rule 10b-5—signed on for the National Association of Criminal Defense Lawyers in urging affirmance of the Eighth Circuit's decision.

a. The Oral Argument

Unlike the *Dirks* oral argument, this time the government had fully baked its theory. The government Solicitor consistently maintained that the inside information was "property," a notion that had caused problems nine years earlier during the *Carpenter* appeals. The exchange with the Chief Justice on breach of duty, albeit based on a novel concept, was nonetheless clear and direct:

> SOLICITOR DREEBEN: There are forms of improper conduct that section 10(b) does not reach, and the reason why section 10(b) does not reach them is it is a statute that is framed to reach fraudulent deceptive activity in connection with securities trading.

---

10. 92 F. 3d at 621.

11. *Central Bank of Denver v. First Interstate Bank of Denver,* 511 U.S. 164 (1994), effectively ended private litigation that utilized Rule 10b-5 against aiders and abettors. Therein, the Supreme Court took the occasion to pronounce several statements on the proper scope of Rule 10b-5 liability.

CHIEF JUSTICE: Well, ... the thing that bothers me about the case here is, where is the connection between the deceptive device and the purchase or sale of the security?

SOLICITOR DREEBEN: The connection, Chief Justice Rehnquist, lies in the fact that the misappropriation does not occur until the lawyer uses the information as the basis for his trades. It is that very information which drives his participation in the market and allows the profits to be ... reaped by him.

CHIEF JUSTICE: But he didn't deceive anyone who sold him securities.

SOLICITOR DREEBEN: That is true. The misappropriation theory doesn't rely on the notion that he owed a duty of disclosure to the shareholders on the other side of the transaction, but it does satisfy the requisite connection between the fraud and the securities trading, because it is only in the trading that the fraud is consummated.

CHIEF JUSTICE: But you think of fraud being practiced on a person who is damaged by it.

SOLICITOR DREEBEN: I think that under the common law view of fraud, Chief Justice Rehnquist, that is an accurate statement, but the securities laws are not framed to pick up only those violations that are covered by common law fraud. Congress did not pass a statute that says, it is unlawful to commit fraud on the purchaser or seller of securities.

Congress did not pass a law even that said it is unlawful to commit fraud in a securities transaction. It passed a law with a broader phrase, in connection with a securities transaction, because the very aim of this section was to pick up unforeseen, cunning, deceptive devices that people might cleverly use in the securities markets—

––––––––––––

To be sure, the government proffered an argument that invited question, namely, that O'Hagan committed securities fraud by his failure to disclose his trading to his employer. The argument was fraught with conflicting positions, such as asserting that the common law definition of fraud was not applicable, but its notion of deception was clear and digestible. Further, the government argued that, under the Misappropriation Theory, not every breach violated Rule 10b-5, but O'Hagan's was in a "core relationship" with his employer.

Meanwhile, counsel for O'Hagan sought to brand the inside information as public as of August 1988, while labeling the government's Rule 10b-5 theory confusing. The Bench reminded counsel that the jury had found the information motivating O'Hagan's purchases to be non-public. Regardless, the thrust of O'Hagan's argument sought to persuade that Rule 10b-5, as a "unitary concept," could not be parsed into, among others, elements of fraud and connection to security purchases. Counsel stated, "What's wrong with the government's theory is it doesn't have anything to do with **unfair** advantage being taken of a participant in the marketplace." Counsel added that theft is not fraud. Justice Kennedy pointed out that Rule 10b-5 reads fraud "upon any person," thus not requiring that the deceived party be the securities purchaser/seller.[12]

The eventual Supreme Court announcement of its opinion in June 1997[13] focused on a duty of "loyalty" and "deception by nondisclosure" satisfying Rule 10b-5. Justice Ginsburg's summary explained that, in light of the purpose of the securities laws, it would make "scant sense" to hold O'Hagan liable had he been employed by Pillsbury but not liable by nature of being employed by Grand Met (and thus covered by more traditional approaches).

b. The Supreme Court Opinion

Justice Ginsburg wrote for a 6–3 majority. Finding that the Court's *Chiarella* decision of 1980 had expressly left open the question of the Theory, the decision emphasized the government's satisfaction of two elements of Rule 10b-5, the fraud element and the "in connection with" element.

Regarding fraud, the opinion acknowledged the hurdle of inaction. While Rule 10b-5 had consistently been interpreted as requiring speech/action of those with a fiduciary duty, O'Hagan had no such duty to Pillsbury shareholders. Regardless, the majority opinion cited the 1987 *Carpenter* case for the premise that O'Hagan as employee owed a duty to both his employer and its client as his "principal." The Court continued its reasoning by noting that O'Hagan violated this duty by "feigning fidelity" to his employer (i.e., not disclosing his trading to co-workers). In short, the duty of loyalty to employer

---

12. The full oral argument is available at https://www.oyez.org/cases/1996/96-842. The second issue concerned whether the SEC exceeded its rulemaking authority in adopting Rule 14e-3. O'Hagan maintained that the SEC "redefined fraud" in drafting the rule, but the Justices repeatedly countered that the Rule merely effectuated a broad delegation of authority enabled by Section 14 of the '34 Act.

13. *United States v. O'Hagan*, 521 U.S. 642 (1997).

that had grown via *Cady, Roberts* to the duty to shareholders (old and new) had become interchangeable with the duty to the source of information.

Further, the question of whether fraud upon one party could be practiced to the detriment of a third party was expediently resolved via reference to a 1984 Law Review article,[14] which, in turn, had quoted a case from 1902.

Regarding the "in connection with" requirement, the decision needed to contend with the points raised during oral argument (and dwelled upon by the Dissenters) serving to blend the Misappropriation Theory with garden variety theft. Specifically, if information as property could be stolen and put to other use (e.g., sold on the market), what would distinguish the Prohibition from embezzlement?

Justice Ginsburg found that under the Theory, the fraud is consummated when—unbeknownst to the source of the information (i.e., Dorsey & Whitney or Grand Met[15])—securities are purchased/sold by the defendant. Likewise, it appeared to the Majority that to label the Theory overbroad because it theoretically captures a fraudulent bank loan used to buy securities was much more of a stretch than to fit the theft of inside information within the '34 Act. In sum, the Majority, often relying on secondary commentary, expanded the reach of Rule 10b-5 without critique of its chief opponent (i.e., the Fourth Circuit), but most definitely to the satisfaction of those seeking fairness in the marketplace.

Court Silence

Correspondingly, a number of non-choices by the Court are also worth noting. First, the Court declined to distinguish the case on the basis of information type: O'Hagan had learned of Grand Met's planned takeover of Pillsbury, and thus really learned of *market* information (as opposed to *inside* information, which would have emanated from and concerned the actions of Pillsbury).

---

14. Barbara Aldave, *Misappropriation: A General Theory of Liability for Trading on Nonpublic Information*, 13 HOFSTRA L. REV. 101, 119 (1984). The Adave article is cited as support for various holdings in the majority opinion.

15. In terms of the source of the information and thus the party to whom a duty is owed, the government did not offer (and the majority opinion did not delineate) any distinction between the firm or its client, as clarified by footnote 7:

"Where, however, a person trading on the basis of material, nonpublic information owes a duty of loyalty and confidentiality to two entities or persons— for example, a law firm and its client—but makes disclosure to only one, the trader may still be liable under the misappropriation theory."

Second, the case failed to provide guidance on when matters elevate to a criminal nature. The Justices seemed content to note that O'Hagan would be able to present other defenses not addressed by the decision on remand, and that the safeguards found in Section 32 of the '34 Act were sufficient for criminal defendants. On this last note, it apparently was of little consequence that the section ensures that a defendant to be incarcerated must have knowledge of the violation and the Misappropriation Theory effectively (and newly) expanded that violation.

Third, it is not at all clear why O'Hagan, as employee of the law firm confidentially retained by Grand Met, was not simply classified a temporary insider (per *Dirks* footnote 14), particularly in light of the majority's express reference to that sub-theory:

> The classical theory applies not only to officers, directors, and other permanent insiders of a corporation, but also to attorneys, accountants, consultants, and others who temporarily become fiduciaries of a corporation.[16]

Perhaps the dearth of a temporary insider analysis was due solely to the government's litigation choices. Still, it seems odd that O'Hagan, as a temporary insider attorney, is not even mentioned as a category of defendant previously contemplated by the Court in 1983.

Finally, in delineating Classical theory, there was no distinction drawn between current and new shareholders; stated otherwise, insiders theoretically owe a duty to both shareholders who sell and shareholders who buy, whereas ITSFEA created a private cause of action only for the latter grouping. Concomitantly, Justice Ginsburg pointed out during oral argument that a refusal to adopt the Misappropriation Theory might leave the statutory rules for the private cause of action "in shambles." Once again, the Justice had found the rationality of a decision to outweigh procedural obstacles.

Silences aside, *O'Hagan* stands till today as the most recent Supreme Court definition of the complementary Rule 10b-5 theories comprising the Prohibition. Some oft-cited, noteworthy language appears below:

- "Although informational disparity is inevitable in the securities markets, investors likely would hesitate to venture their capital in a market where trading based on misappropriated nonpublic information is unchecked by law ..."[17]

---

16. *O'Hagan*, 521 U.S. at 652.
17. 521 U.S. at 658.

- "... full disclosure forecloses liability under the misappropriation theory."[18]

- "[Rule 10b-5], as written, does not confine its coverage to deception of a purchaser or seller of securities [cite to *Newman*]; rather, the statute reaches any deceptive device used 'in connection with the purchase or sale of any security.'"[19]

c. The Counterpoints

The *O'Hagan* dissents each centered on a counter-theory that undermined expansion of the securities laws to outsiders. Justice Thomas took issue with the fungibility of the inside information, which he hypothesized could be misappropriated for purposes other than securities trading. The Majority opinion labeled such concern an "extremity" that is overridden with the intent of the '34 Act "to insure the maintenance of **fair** and honest markets."[20] To same end, the Majority rationalized that the labeling of the Misappropriation Theory a "partial antidote"[21] to the problem of fraud (because disclosure to the source removes the violation) should not effect the issue of whether the theory comes with the authority conveyed by Section 10(b). Chief Justice Rehnquist joined Justice Thomas' dissent from the securities law convictions because of concern over inconsistencies within the Theory, particularly when confronting actions seeming more akin to embezzlement than securities fraud.[22]

Separately, Justice Scalia dissented from the findings on Rule 10b-5 because he believed that the Majority position did not comport with the "principle of lenity we apply to criminal statutes": Section 10(b) demanding "manipulative" or "deceptive" mechanisms, a party to a securities transaction must be offered by the government as victim.

However, such concerns ultimately only retained force among academics. Likewise, O'Hagan's parallel criminal conviction, the lack of primary au-

---

18. 521 U.S. at 655.

19. 521 U.S. at 651.

20. Securities and Exchange Act Preamble, "Necessity for Regulation," 15 U.S.C. §78b (2016).

21. *O'Hagan*, 521 U.S. at 659.

22. On remand, the Eighth Circuit ruled, among other things, that the Rule 10b-5 and Rule 14e-3 convictions should be reinstated, but affirmed its prior reversal of the mail and wire fraud convictions. *United States v. O'Hagan*, 139 F.3d 641 (8th Cir. 1998).

thority on point, and even the opposition of Rule 10b-5's creator could not stem the tide. The Misappropriation Theory had finally been elevated to the law of the land.

C. The New World Order

1. The Political Aftermath

With the Supreme Court approval of the Misappropriation Theory, the Pro-hibition had been exponentially expanded via an argument deftly combining attributes of common law, statute, case law, and fairness. Within weeks of the Supreme Court decision, the SEC Chairman, in an oft-quoted speech, addressed both the continuing prioritization of (and legal vagaries attending) the Prohibition:

> Our markets are a success precisely because they enjoy the world's highest level of confidence. Investors put their capital to work—and put their fortunes at risk—because they trust that the marketplace is honest. They know that our securities laws require free, fair, and open transactions ... But if there is a perception of **unfairness**, there'll be no investor confidence—and precious little investment ... Just this week, we heard the disappointing news of the arrest of eight floor bro-kers and others at the New York Stock Exchange, who are charged with unfairly using their position to make more than $11 million in illegal trading profits.[23] News like this creates the appearance that exchange insiders may be profiting at the expense of ordinary investors. Such headlines shake the confidence of average investors in the **fairness** of our markets ... (emphasis added)[24]

In the same speech, the popular Chairman extolled the "straightforward approach—recognizing the common sense distinction between right and wrong" embodied in the *O'Hagan* decision. As the agency's chief

---

23. A sizeable group of Independent Floor Brokers were found by the SEC to have illegally shared in customer profits in violation of Section 11 of the '34 Act between 1993 and 1997. The NYSE itself received a censure for failing to adequately enforce relevant com-pliance procedures. SEA Rel. No. 41574 (June 28, 1999).

24. *A Question of Integrity: Promoting Investor Confidence by Fighting Insider Trading*, Remarks by Chairman Arthur Levitt, U.S. Securities and Exchange Commission (February 27, 1998), *available at* https://www.sec.gov/news/speech/speecharchive/1998/spch202.txt.

transparently confessed, "From this non-lawyer's point of view, Justice Ginsburg's opinion is an excellent summary of why we must take [insider trading] so seriously."

2. The Everyday Practicalities

The recognition by the country's preeminent Bench that stock trades could land one in prison regardless of occupation had far-reaching effects.

On a practitioner level, the *O'Hagan* decision became the written standard for the Prohibition's four enabling theories, addressing, separately, the duties of 1) insider (including temporary insider), 2) outsider, and 3) tippee of either insider or outsider. As such, the opinion provides great utility as a touchstone, and, accordingly, has been cited in over 1,500 cases to date.

On an investigative level, options surveillance became the preferred tool to uncover insider trading schemes, as the allure of riskless, leveraged trading had been publicized as a means to quick profits.

On an academic level, the Supreme Court's announcement evidenced a tortured path for the notion of duty. Since 1961, the obligations imposed by Rule 10b-5 spread haphazardly among individuals inside and outside the corporation, as the excerpts from key cases (and one statute) below exemplify:

1. *CADY, ROBERTS* (1961): *Duty to market, akin to duty of loyalty*

   Finding "[a]n affirmative duty to disclose material information, which has been traditionally imposed on corporate 'insiders,' particularly officers, directors, or controlling stockholders. We and the courts have consistently held that insiders must disclose material facts which are known to them by virtue of their position but which are not known to persons with whom they deal and which, if known, would affect their investment judgment."

2. *TEXAS GULF SULPHUR* (1968): *Duty to market, created by circumstance*

   "An insider's duty to disclose information or his duty to abstain from dealing in his company's securities arises only in 'those situations which are essentially extraordinary in nature and which are reasonably certain to have a substantial effect on the market price of the security if (the extraordinary situation is) disclosed.'"

3. *CHIARELLA* (1980): *No duty to "strangers" in the market*

   "[Rule 10b-5] liability is premised upon a duty to disclose arising from a relationship of trust and confidence between parties to a transaction. Application of a duty to disclose prior to trading guarantees that corporate insiders, who have an obligation to place the shareholder's welfare before their own, will not benefit personally through fraudulent use of material, nonpublic information."

4. *CHIARELLA* (dissent): *Proposed duty to source of information created by theft*

   "[A] person who has misappropriated nonpublic information has an absolute duty to disclose that information or to refrain from trading."

5. *DIRKS* (1983): *Reinforced non-duty to market*

   "... *Chiarella* made it explicitly clear that there is no general duty to forgo market transactions 'based on material, nonpublic information.' Such a duty would 'depar[t] radically from the established doctrine that duty arises from a specific relationship between two parties.'"

6. *BRYAN* (1995): *No duty to strangers in the market*

   "[The Misappropriation Theory authorizes] criminal conviction for simple breaches of fiduciary duty and similar relationships of trust and confidence, whether or not the breach entails deception within the meaning of section 10(b) and whether or not the parties wronged by the breaches were purchasers or sellers of securities, or otherwise connected with or interested in the purchase or sale of securities."

7. *O'HAGAN* (1997): *Duty to source of information*

   "A misappropriator who trades on the basis of material, nonpublic information, in short, gains his advantageous market position through deception; he deceives the source of the information and simultaneously harms members of the investing public ..."

8. S.T.O.C.K. ACT[25] (2013): *Duty to all Americans*

   "IN GENERAL—Subject to the rule of construction under section 10 of the STOCK Act and solely for purposes of the insider trading prohibitions arising under this Act, including section 10(b), and Rule 10b-5 thereunder, each executive branch employee, each judicial officer, and each judicial employee owes a duty arising from a relationship of trust and confidence *to the United States Government and the citizens of the United States* with respect to material, nonpublic information derived from such person's position

---

25. Pub. L. No. 112-105 (2012). Although rarely invoked, the S.T.O.C.K. Act is theoretically part of the Prohibition and thus is discussed later in Chapter VIII.

as an executive branch employee, judicial officer, or judicial employee or gained from the performance of such person's official responsibilities" (emphasis added).

Apart from the legal flux, *O'Hagan* effectively re-prioritized the Prohibition. Cases against insiders were easy pickings—Classical theory applications had abounded unchecked since *Cady, Roberts* in 1961, and a generic duty of corporations to shareholders dates back to the middle ages. But a duty to an informational source with a resulting harm to strangers in the market provided plenty of grey area (i.e., settlement would not be so quick). Court battles would heretofore center on outsiders; penalties tend to rise when prosecutors are forced to trial. And civil litigation would entropy as the "in connection with" requirement had been reduced to an exhortation by the Supreme Court.[26]

Separately, on an employer relations level, immediate changes were implemented by human resource departments at financial service providers and public companies. With the Supreme Court's recognition that inside information was property capable of theft, managers, employees, interns and contractors were uniformly asked to sign agreements expressly advising them of the need for confidentiality and the avoidance of informational larceny from the corporation.

Some Examples

On a litigation level, the Commission was now free to join all of the Prohibition's theories in a sole case, greatly expanding the outcome of an investigation.[27] While the number of insider trading enforcement actions remained consistent (10%), the nature of them changed dramatically. For example, in the highly publicized UBS case of 2007, 15 defendants at three different employers involved in two alleged schemes were alleged to be insiders, outsiders, and/or tippees. Such bureaucratic tallying is not a rare occurrence: The SEC's annual performance report for years highlighted cases that branched to include

---

26. *See, e.g., Merrill Lynch v. Dabit*, 395 F.3d 25 (2006) (removing a 10b-5 case centering on "holders" *who had not sold* their securities for the purpose of effectuating the clear Congressional policy of removing state securities fraud suits to federal court under the Securities Litigation Uniform Standards Act of 1998).

27. *See, e.g.,* Complaint, *SEC v. Guttenberg et al., available at* https://www.sec.gov/litigation/complaints/2007/comp20022.pdf.

an eye-catching number of defendants, as evidenced by the excerpt from the 1999 summary below:

> *SEC v. Cassano, et al.* The complaint alleging insider trading violations by 25 individuals in advance of the IBM takeover of Lotus Development Corporation named the largest single group of insider traders in the SEC's history. After an initial tip by Lorraine K. Cassano, a former IBM secretary, to her husband, material, nonpublic information about the proposed takeover spread rapidly through a network or relatives, friends, co-workers and business associates. Illegal trading by the defendants generated profits of more than $1.3 million ...[28]

With its stamp of approval from *O'Hagan*, the Prohibition became poised to at once cover insider, outsider, and tippee. "Tippee" chain cases now enjoyed the corroboration of two Supreme Court rulings, 14 years apart (i.e., *Dirks* and *O'Hagan*). Rule 10b-5 defendants became more numerous. Witness an example from 1999, where no less than eight tippees were named in a sole case:

> The SEC alleges that Sekhri, the source of the inside information, was an investment banking associate at Salomon at the time of the trading. Salomon provided investment banking services in each of the relevant corporate transactions and Sekhri worked specifically on at least one of those transactions. Sekhri tipped Dow, Sekhri's former college roommate. Dow then tipped Cochrane and Thifault, all three of whom collectively purchased common stock and/or call options ... in advance of six different public announcements of significant mergers involving these companies.

> The complaint alleges that Sekhri also tipped Sehgal, his father-in-law, in advance of at least four of these announcements; Rajan, his friend, in advance of at least three of these announcements; Kapoor, his friend and then a broker at Merrill Lynch, Pierce, Fenner & Smith, Inc. in San Jose, California, in advance of six of these announcements; and Sharma, Kapoor's wife, in advance of at least four of these announcements. The complaint also seeks disgorgement from relief defendants Mahendar and Sharda Sekhri, Arjun Sekhri's parents, of assets transferred to them by the defendants ...[29]

---

28. 1999 Annual Report of the U.S. Securities and Exchange Commission (Enforcement Section), available at https://www.sec.gov/pdf/annrep99/enforce.pdf (at 6).

29. SEC News Digest of July 1, 1999, *available at* https://www.sec.gov/news/digest/1999/dig070199.pdf.

Further, after *O'Hagan*, the SEC was able to employ both Classic and Misappropriation theories to a sole defendant, and to intertwine authority therefor. Witness the aggressive assertion in 2007 that a spouse could be either a misappropriator or a temporary insider per *Dirks*, even though only professionals such as accountants and lawyers were noted in that famed footnote 14:

> ... the phrase "solely for corporate purposes" should be construed broadly. It is true that the Supreme Court, when it first articulated the temporary insider principle, stated that temporary insider status exists where a person "[h]as entered into a special confidential relationship in the conduct of the business of the enterprise and [is] given access to information solely for corporate purposes. *Dirks*, 463 U.S. at 646 n.14) However, *O'Hagan* did not use the phrase "solely for corporate purposes," but stated that temporary insiders are those who temporarily become fiduciaries of a corporation. 521 U.S. at 652. [The Defendant], in view of her prior practice of maintaining in confidence information her husband told her about [the issuer], and of the corporate purpose such disclosures served, did temporarily become a fiduciary of the company.[30]

Clearly, for market traders and investors alike, a new, frightening world order had been established, and the closest thing to the unfettered SEC discretion of the Parity of Information period had been re-attained. Of course, more insider trading defendants mean more fines to be levied, a bonus for the SEC and the United States Treasury alike.

Thus, regardless of any inconsistencies along the way, after the *O'Hagan* decisions, *everyone* was now subject to the Prohibition. The conclusion appears a bit odd given that the Acts were initially pointed towards the professional demons of the Depression; still, perhaps such a vastly broad measure was necessary to ensure the paramount goal of market fairness. With the means no longer in question, the Commission could focus on remedies. O'Hagan received jail time but no criminal fine.[31] Subsequent criminal defendants would not be so lucky.

---

30. SEC Appellate Brief, *SEC v. Rocklage*, No. 06-1571 (1st Cir. 2006), *available at* https://www.sec.gov/litigation/briefs/2006/rocklagebrief0609.pdf. The *Rocklage* Brief is far from a maverick view of a Commission attorney, as it was signed by the SEC Solicitor at the time.

31. The DOJ's cases against O'Hagan resulted in imprisonment, while the SEC's subsequent summary judgment upon the DOJ case levied a bounty of $7.6 million (reflecting disgorgement of $4.3 million and penalty of over $3 million) against him.

Selected Bibliography

Kimberly D. Krawiec et al., *Don't Ask, Just Tell: Insider Trading After United States v. O'Hagan*, 84 Va. L. Rev. 153 (1998), *available at* http://scholarship.law.duke.edu/faculty_scholarship/2047/.

Summary Judgment and Order Requiring Payment of $7.6 Million Ordered Against Insider Trader, James O'Hagan, SEC News Digest Issue 95–158 (August 16, 1995), *available at* https://www.sec.gov/news/digest/1995/dig081695.pdf.

Eben Shapiro, *A Leading Lawyer's Fall is a Jolt to Minneapolis,* N.Y. Times (January 20, 1990), *available at* http://www.nytimes.com/1990/01/20/business/a-leading-lawyer-s-fall-is-a-jolt-to-minneapolis.html.

Hon. Ruth Bader Ginsburg, with Others, My Own Words (2016).

United States v. O'Hagan, 92 F.3d 612 (1996).

United States v. O'Hagan, 521 U.S. 642 (1997).

United States v. O'Hagan, 139 F.3d 641, *on remand,* (8th Cir. 1998).

United States v. Chestman, 947 F.2d 551 (2d Cir. 1991) (en banc), *cert. denied,* 503 U.S. 1004 (1992).

J. Scott Colesanti, *Taking Stock of the S.T.O.C.K. Act,* NY Bus. L.J. (2013).

Donna M. Nagy, *Reframing the Misappropriation Theory of Insider Trading Liability: A Post-O'Hagan Suggestion* (1998), *available at* http://www.repository.law.indiana.edu/facpub/615.

Carpenter v. United States, 484 U.S. 19 (1987).

SEC 1998 Annual Report.

SEC 1999 Annual Report.

Jeff Overley, *100 Oral Arguments: How a DOJ Attorney Made High Court History,* LAW360 (May 9, 2016), *available at* https://www.law360.com/articles/789864/100-oral-arguments-how-a-doj-atty-made-high-court-history.

United States v. Halper, 490 U.S. 435 (1989) (finding a $130,000 civil penalty to be "sufficiently disproportionate" so as to violate Double Jeopardy).

Chapter VIII (*Checkpoint #2*)

2001: The Full Arsenal Arrives with the Millennium

Within five years of the O'Hagan case, all of the present parts of the Prohibition had been set. It is tempting to sum up the prosecutorial weapons against insider trading in Rule 10b-5, but, in actuality, a number of other provisions play a role in the disciplining of violative activity. These provisions have been added to the arsenal at different times and for varying reasons, and often they are based upon a definition extracted from 10b-5 cases. Still, each is worthy of attention.[1]

A. Statutory Sections

Although varied provisions reference the crime, insider trading is not defined in any statute. In referencing the Acts, the SEC itself has acknowledged the subtle connection between the Prohibition and written law by stating, "Congress, by enacting two separate laws providing enhanced penalties for insider trading, has expressed its strong support for our insider trading enforcement program."[2] But the SEC could never have crafted the Prohibition without some form of legislative nexus, the main points of which are reiterated below.

1. Section10(b)

Section 10(b) is in effect the most vital weapon within the Prohibition. Simply put, the Section authorizes and justifies Rule 10b-5; more than one

---

1. Full copies of the provisions listed below are reprinted in the Appendix of this Book.
2. SEC Release No. 33-7881 (August 2000), at 16.

securities litigator has been chided for not stating the statutory provision and its subsequent enabling Rule in unison.

In recent years, the statutory section had been slightly modified. This enhancement was in response to the credit crisis in 2008, and it was effectuated by the Dodd-Frank law described later in the Book. But such modification worked chiefly to bring additional instruments within the reach of the '34 Act's anti-fraud provision. For continuing questions about scope of defendant (e.g., insider vs. outsider) and definitions of the elements (i.e., materiality, scienter, deception, securities connection), federal case law remains the best guidance. Most importantly, the core standard in these matters has changed very little since the *O'Hagan* decision of 1997.

2. Section 16(b)

Recall that Section 16(b) was the only legislative response within the Acts to the yet unlabeled violation of insider trading (and the birthplace of the term "fairness"). The octogeneric provision continues to be vital, somewhat difficult to adhere to, and dynamic. Questions over the statutory 2-year statute of limitations have risen all the way to the Supreme Court, while technical questions over the breadth of the subject securities and defendants have largely been resolved by SEC rulemaking.

3. Section 17(a)

The Section that inspired Rule 10b-5 has joined it as a basis for insider trading charges, as both the SEC and the DOJ have come to add the charge to their Complaints.

As an independent basis for private recovery, Section 17(a)(1) remains a conundrum—there is still a Circuit split regarding the issue of whether it implies a cause of action. That split has been largely mooted by the addition by Congress of a separate insider trading claim in 1988 (discussed later in Chapter X).

The Acts serve mainly as brief starting points for academic discussions, while SEC Rules most often form the substance of contemporary debate on the Prohibition. The relevant Rules are discussed below.

B. Rules/Regulations

1. Rule 10b-5

As the new Millennium arrived, the Commission had four full theories with which to utilize Rule 10b-5 to combat insider trading. These theories have been blessed by the Supreme Court; further, they are taught in law schools and translated for traders by compliance departments. The chart below details the specifics of each.

Theory	Duty	Victim	Case Authority
"Classic"	To shareholders*	Same shareholders	*Cady, Roberts; Texas Gulf Sulphur; O'Hagan*
"Misappropriation"	To source of information	Counterparties within the market	*O'Hagan*
"Temporary Insider"	To shareholders	Same shareholders	*Dirks; O'Hagan*
"Tipper/Tippee"	Either the source of the information, or the shareholders	Either the counterparties or the shareholders	*Dirks; O'Hagan*

* Whether "shareholders" connotes existing stock owners or new ones is subject to debate, as was discussed in Chapter VII.

However, an SEC Rule that has been interpreted countless times by the courts is not always the best fit for an investigation. Further, "duty theory" has, at times, been taken to its questionable (yet logical) extreme. For example, in *SEC v. Yun*,[3] the Commission premised a misappropriation upon the "theft" of inside information by a spouse from her husband and a subsequent tip to a fellow country club member. A jury found the two club members jointly and severally liable for $270,000 in disgorgement and fines based upon a conversation at a cocktail party.

On appeal, the Eleventh Circuit acknowledged the theft of the information by a spouse as a predicate for application of the Misappropriation Theory,[4] but

---

3. 327 F.3d 1263 (11th Cir. 2003).

4. The spousal relationship was codified as a predicate for a Misappropriation case through the SEC's promulgation of Rule 10b5-2 in 2000, as is described below. The Rule was likely not considered by the *Yun* court because the underlying facts dated from 1997.

disputed the tippee's liability for lack of a benefit (step #2 of the *Dirks* test). The jury verdict was reversed, and the seeming extension of Rule 10b-5 liability was thwarted. Decisions such as *Yun* thus occasionally prompt the Commission to apply a more pointed provision, such as the measure described below.

2. Regulation FD ("Full Disclosure")

In 2000, in an instance of omnibus rulemaking, the Commission addressed several lingering problems besetting the Prohibition. One included measure was aimed at issuers and was titled "Regulation FD" (i.e., "Full Disclosure").[5] The Regulation specifically covered stock issuing companies, their chief officers, and, in turn, their agents. It was designed to curtail the evil of "selective disclosure" by companies to their favorite analysts, investment professionals, or institutional investors.

The pejorative term "selective disclosure" had been used in the *Dirks* decision, although the SEC cited other sources in adopting FD, which reads in relevant part below:

§ 243.100.

Whenever an issuer, or any person acting on its behalf, discloses any material nonpublic information regarding that issuer or its securities to any person described in paragraph (b)(1) of this section, the issuer shall make public disclosure of that information as provided in § 243.101(e):

(1) Simultaneously, in the case of an intentional disclosure; and

(2) Promptly, in the case of a non-intentional disclosure.

The Regulation defines "promptly" as soon as is "practicable" but in no case more than 24 hours; "simultaneously" is left undefined (and, by implication, presumed to be more immediate than "promptly"). "Intentional" is explained as being satisfied by either knowledge or recklessness. "Material" comports with the definition stated in the Supreme Court case of *Basic Inc.* (i.e., infor-

---

5. In the vernacular of the SEC, a "regulation" is a set of rules. For example, Regulation A (which covers one form of exempted capital formation) is comprised of SEC Rules 251 through 263. Regulation FD (short for "Full Disclosure") is comprised of Rules 100 through 103. *See* 17 C.F.R. §§ 243.100–103 (2016).

Additionally, a Rule enabling a '33 Act provision is labeled with 3 digits (e.g., "Rule 405"), while a Rule enabling a '34 Act provision contains a letter and a hyphen (e.g., "Rule 10b-5").

mation that a reasonable investor would consider that altered the total mix of available data).[6]

The language of the adopting release[7] for Regulation FD also borrowed heavily from existing case law. For example, tippees of an issuer were said to have gained unique access to privileged information from selective disclosure "rather than from skill, acumen, or diligence" (the phrase used by Chief Justice Burger in his *Chiarella* dissent). Nonetheless, the cited sources for the lengthy release drew equally from popular press, case law, academic commentary and submissions to the Commission while the Regulation was opened for public comment (December 1999 through early 2000). As an example, in response to industry comments,[8] Regulation FD clarifies that a violation cannot form the basis for a private lawsuit.

The overarching rationale for the measure was said to be two threats to market integrity: 1) The similarity between selective disclosure and tipping as addressed by case law, and 2) The undesirable tendency of issuer management to treat non-public information as a "commodity" to be bestowed upon favored parties. Also, it was pointed out that "technological advancements" enabled management to now disseminate news more broadly.

The interesting aspect of Regulation FD is its non-obligatory nature: The regulation does not require a mandatory disclosure unless the issuer itself has selectively released material information.

Reg FD Applications

The Regulation was the subject of consent decrees with (or informal action against) four unrelated companies in November 2002. The disciplinary actions put various of the Commission's relevant weapons on display—one subject company consented to an injunction, another to an injunction and fine, and a third was simply admonished via a Section 21A report.[9]

---

6. *Basic Inc. v. Levinson*, 485 U.S. 224, 231–32 (1988).

7. SEC Release No. 33-7881, Final Rule: Selective Disclosure and Insider Trading (August 2000), *available at* https://www.sec.gov/rules/final/33-7881.htm.

8. The SEC stated that the "vast majority" of the 6,000 Comment Letters it received urged adoption of Regulation FD.

9. SEC Press Release 2002-169. A "Section 21A" report culminates an investigation without bringing formal Enforcement action against the investigative target.

Subsequently, in September 2003, the SEC settled with a public company and its CEO for a violation of Regulation FD in conjunction with Section 13(a) of the '34 Act.[10] The allegations in that matter, chiefly tied to data, read as follows:

> From October 1 through October 3, 2002, Schering's stock price fell by more than 17 percent, from $21.32 to $17.64 per share, with volume each day averaging more than four times the stock's typical daily volume (*i.e.*, over 20 million shares per day compared to an average of less than 5 million). Schering knew of this volume increase and price decline. This market reaction was substantially the result of heavy sales of Schering stock by the institutions whose analysts and portfolio managers met with [the CEO] that week in Boston. In particular, [two large funds] each sold more than 10 million Schering shares during that three-day period, accounting for more than 30 percent of the overall volume for the period.[11]

However, in 2005, a contested matter against a company tied more to management's words resulted in a court dismissal. The SEC had charged a CFO and a Senior Vice President with aiding and abetting an FD violation by making statements to institutional investors, among others, that company sales were "good" and "better" when contrasting public statements had been issued in the prior month. The court dismissed the Complaint, holding that the Regulation, while not defining either "material" or "nonpublic," nonetheless "was never intended to be utilized in the manner attempted by the SEC under these circumstances."[12]

Additional applications after 2005 are few and far between. Regulation FD nonetheless serves a vital purpose in defining *nonpublic* by providing information on what adequate remedial disclosure entails. Specifically, the broad dissemination standard could be deemed met by use of a company web site, the filing of a Form 8K, the issuance of a press release, and/or the holding of a press conference. More recently, the Commission has liberalized these means

---

10. SEC Litigation Release 18330 (September 9, 2003). Section 13(a) of the '34 Act requires companies registered with a national stock exchange to preserve records of, among other things, all documents required to be filed with a registration statement or any other document so required by the SEC "to ensure **fair** dealing in the security."

11. Complaint: *SEC v. Schering-Plough Corporation* (D.C. Cir. September 2003) (settled by imposition of a cease-and-desist order, a $1 million fine on the company, and a $50,000 fine upon its CEO).

12. *SEC v. Siebel Systems, Inc.*, 384 F. Supp. 2d 694 (S.D.N.Y. 2005) (citing, in footnote 8, SEC language near the time of Regulation's FD's adoption promising that "reasonable [disclosure] judgments made in good faith" would not be second guessed by the Commission).

to include, under certain circumstances, a widespread social media platform such as Facebook.[13]

3. Rule 10b5-1

The adopting Release behind Regulation FD bluntly stated the laudatory reasons that Rule 10b5-1 and Rule 10b5-2 (discussed separately below) were being simultaneously promulgated:

> ... the prohibitions against insider trading in our securities laws play an essential role in maintaining the **fairness**, health, and integrity of our markets. We have long recognized that the fundamental **unfairness** of insider trading harms not only individual investors.[14]

Rule 10b5-1 was designed to end the debate over whether a defendant could be found liable for merely being in *possession* of material, nonpublic information at the time of the subject trade, or, alternatively, must be proven to have *used* the subject information in deciding to trade. The debate was resolved by addition of a third term, "aware of." Alas, the easier pleading requirement did not catch on in all Commission Regional Offices. In a high-profile criminal case against Enron's executive officers, the distinction between "use" and "possession" was deemed mooted by other of the government's allegations.[15]

Further, the debate has been sidestepped in recent Rule 10b-5 cases by common employment of the allegation that the defendant "knew or was reckless in not knowing" that information was material and nonpublic and in Rule 14e-3 cases by clinging to the "possession" standard.[16]

The more lasting contribution of 10b5-1 may have come from its inclusion of a defense for trading pursuant to a written "plan" that predates the alleged receipt of inside information. That defense is stated at subsection (c)(1)(i)

---

13. SEC Release No. 69279, Report of Investigation Pursuant to Section 21(a) of the Securities Exchange Act of 1934: Netflix, Inc., and Reed Hastings (April 2, 2013), *available at* https://www.sec.gov/litigation/investreport/34-69279.pdf. The Report subtly acknowledged the use of "corporate social media sites"—if accompanied with notice and in compliance with the SEC's prior, formal guidance on the use of company web sites [SEC Release No. 34-58288 (Aug. 7, 2008)]—as a means of disseminating material, nonpublic information.

14. Release No. 33-7881, at 16.

15. United States v. Causey, Skilling, and Lay, Cr. No. H-04-025-SS (S.D. Tx. 2005).

16. *See, e.g.*, Complaint, SEC v. Rivas, et al., No. 17-cu-6192 (S.D.N.Y. August 16, 2017) (including both standards at paragraphs 125 and 129, respectively).

and, in the main, requires that the plan be in writing and not allow for any trading discretion by the subject employee. The "plan" defense found its basis in Comment Letters to the SEC that had noted the problems occasioned by legitimate reinvestments by corporate employees in retirement and stock option arrangements. Not surprisingly, subscription to such "10b5-1 plans" has been attempted in high profile cases as a defense to otherwise untenable trading.

4. Rule 10b5-2 ("Duties of Trust or Confidence in Misappropriation Insider Trading Cases")

The final addition of the August 2000 Release was a specific response to the pleading and proof requirements of the Misappropriation Theory, to wit, the predicate duty. In response to the defeat in *Chestman* in 1991, in which fiduciary relationships and their "functional equivalents" were examined by the Second Circuit, the SEC used its broad rulemaking authority to adopt a Rule containing a series of three provisions setting forth fiduciary duties which could establish duties underlying the breach required for a misappropriation.

The first duty covers persons making agreements to maintain information in confidence.

The second duty covers persons who "have a history, pattern or practice of sharing confidences."

And the third duty covers persons characterized as spouse, parent, child, or sibling (with the understanding that the presumption can be rebutted by a showing that no duty of confidence existed regarding the subject information).

The provisions in toto came under attack 2009 in the Fifth Circuit by defendant Mark Cuban. The District Court had dismissed the SEC's insider trading Complaint against Cuban, finding Rule 10b5-2 to "exceed the SEC's § 10(b) authority to proscribe conduct that is deceptive."[17] On appeal, the Fifth Circuit reinstated the Complaint for very narrow reasons, without addressing the Commission's rulemaking authority. The SEC followed through on the civil suit, and Cuban was found not liable by a jury in October 2013.

Nonetheless, Rule 10b5-2 remains a key tool for the Commission in Misappropriation Theory cases involving immediate family members or close acquaintances. The provision has been expressly cited in criminal cases in recent years (as is discussed in Chapter XI).

---

17. *SEC v. Cuban*, 634 F. Supp. 2d 713 (N.D. Tex. 2009).

5. Rule 14e-3

It is often forgotten that the Rule, at least in regard to tender offers, actually continues the Parity of Information theory—indeed, it was adopted by the Commission in direct response to the *Chiarella* loss of 1980. However, the measure has been dubbed "The Other Guy's Takeover Rule" because its trading ban does not apply to employees of the acquiring company or their agents. Often the key consideration is the satisfying of the requirement that the "offeror" (i.e., acquirer) had taken "substantial steps" to effectuate the tender offer at the time of the violation.

In practice, Rule14e-3 tends to serve as the basis for an add-on charge (e.g., the *O'Hagan* case). Further, its eventuality requirement works to make the measure most applicable when actual trading has resulted; stated otherwise, it is the not the tool to fight *dissemination* of tender offer information the SEC or others had hoped for.

C. Chief Cases

The Prohibition chiefly hailing from common law, a short list of cases often serves as primary authority for parts thereof.

1. *United States v. O'Hagan*

It bears noting that, although primarily recounted for formally approving the Misappropriation Theory, the famed written decision of Justice Ginsburg equally approved SEC rulemaking discretion. Specifically, by the Court's upholding Rule 14e-3, the Commission overcame yet another challenge to its implementation of anti-fraud provisions within the Acts.

Regardless, *O'Hagan* stands as the weapon of choice for cases aimed at outsiders. As noted previously in discussions of, among others, the *Chestman* case, the Theory can be combined with other weapons to reach informational chains involving both insiders and outsiders.

Finally, as the most recent Supreme Court case addressing the extent of the Prohibition, *O'Hagan* serves as precedent for all of the Prohibition's underlying theories.

2. *Dirks v. SEC*

The landmark case from 1983 continues as the primary authority for "tipper/tippee" cases. Such cases have grown to both constitute a major focus of the Prohibition and its main cause of setback: SEC losses at trial almost uniformly concern the question of whether information passed to non-securities professionals violated the law.[18]

The continued utility of the *Dirks* test was seriously questioned in 2015 by the Second Circuit in its *Newman/Chiasson* decision.[19] The two defendants—both fourth generation tippees—had been convicted in a hedge fund case. The investigation traced inside information through layers of both fund personnel and non-industry tippees. The ensuing trial found a duty of the tipper inherited by the downstream defendants; there also being a loose benefit to the tipper, there was a conviction.

Undoubtedly, the District Court had been justified in its charge to the *Newman* jury—numerous cases from the Second Circuit had interpreted "benefit" to include intangibles, and even an enhancement to reputation.[20] But the Second Circuit, which reversed, may simply have determined that the expansion of tippee liability had gone far enough. In adding a fifth requirement to the *Dirks* test, namely, the tippee's knowledge of the tipper's benefit, the Panel could not avoid reiterating the distance between the source of the inside information and the defendants, as well as the recent frequency of criminal insider trading charges:

> While we have not yet been presented with the question of whether the tippee's knowledge of a tipper's breach requires knowledge of the tipper's benefit, the answer follows naturally from *Dirks*. *Dirks* counsels us that the exchange of confidential information for personal benefit is not separate from an insider's fiduciary breach ... The Government's overreliance on our prior dicta merely highlights the doc-

---

18. *See, e.g.,* Kara Scannell & Luc Cohen, *Rajaratnam's brother acquitted by jury,* FINANCIAL TIMES (July 8, 2014) (describing *United States v. (Rengan) Rajaratnam* (S.D.N.Y. 2014) (finding defendant not guilty of conspiracy to commit insider trading and noting that it was the first loss for the sitting United States Attorney in 80 cases).

19. *United States v. Newman,* 773 F.3d 438 (2d Cir. 2014). The case—unrelated to the 1981 *Newman* case that first upheld the Misappropriation Theory—is discussed in detail in Chapter XI.

20. *See, e.g., United States v. McDermott,* SEC Press release 99-174 (December 21, 1999) (citing the tipper/tippee "close relationship" where a CEO tipped his paramour).

trinal novelty of its recent insider trading convictions, which are increasingly targeted at remote tippees many levels removed from corporate insiders ... We note that the Government has not cited, nor have we found, a single case in which tippees as remote as Newman and Chiasson have been held criminally liable for insider trading.[21]

The *Newman* decision served to halt or outright reverse a number of DOJ insider trading prosecutions. Further, the turnaround sparked public disparagement from the sitting U.S. Attorney for the Southern District, whose impressive string of insider trading convictions was halted by the *Newman* reversal:

As we think about what kind of cases we can and cannot prosecute— if you have a CEO who has access to material nonpublic information about earnings or anything else of a very sensitive nature and he decides that he wants to give it to a relative or a buddy or a crony knowing that person is going to trade on it to the tune of millions of dollars ... we would have to think long and hard, given *Newman*, whether to prosecute a person like that.[22]

The Supreme Court did not grant certiorari to *Newman*, presumably because the petition questioned only the *Dirks* interpretation while the Second Circuit decision rested on an additional basis (i.e., lack of scienter). However, in 2016, the Supreme Court did agree to hear a related case, *United States v. Salman*.

Salman concerned tips between brothers-in-law. The Ninth Circuit expressly avoided depending upon *Newman* and found the tippee guilty based upon language regarding gifts of tips from *Dirks* and sufficient trial evidence that he knew that the source of the information had made a gift of this information to his immediate tipper. Further, Salman's argument that a tangible benefit must be received by the original tipper (e.g., a check) in order to satisfy the *Dirks* test was rejected.

On appeal, the Supreme Court upheld the conviction based on a narrow analysis presuming a *Dirks* benefit when inside information is gifted between family members.[23]

---

21. 773 F.3d at 451.

22. Mark Hamblett, *High Court Declines to Hear "Newman"; Circuit Ruling Stands,*" NEW YORK LAW JOURNAL (October 6, 2015) (comments of Assistant U.S. Attorney Preet Bharara). Bharara and his unprecedented prosecution of insider trading cases between 2012 and 2016 are a subject of Chapter XII.

23. *Salman v. United States*, 137 S. Ct. 420 (2016), is also discussed at length in Chapter XI.

Subsequently, a Second Circuit panel heard the appeal of Matthew Martoma, who had been convicted by a jury of insider trading in September 2014. Later in the year, the Second Circuit issued its *Newman* decision restricting tippee liability; in December 2016, the Supreme Court appeared to strike the balance back in favor of the government in *Salman*. Martoma thus argued to the Second Circuit in 2017 that *Salman* did not affect the thrust of the *Newman* decision (i.e., that the tippee must have a "meaningfully close personal relationship" with his tipper).

The Second Circuit disagreed, upholding Martoma's conviction, 2–1. The majority opinion held that a tipper is liable whenever information is disclosed with the "expectation" that a tippee will trade. The dissent noted that "securities law is a field in which legal and ethical obligations are not coterminous."

Accordingly, the most palatable reconciliation of *Dirks, Newman, Salman,* and *Martoma* would seem to posit the following:

1. The *Dirks* test is still the foremost authority applicable to tipper/tippee situations;

2. In the Second Circuit, to establish liability, the government must show only an expectation that his tippee shall trade to prove the tipper's "benefit" (although the short-lived *Newman* requirement still has some suport on the Bench); and

3. In all Circuits, a family relationship eases the government's burden of proving benefit, which shall be presumed even in the absence of tangible profit or gain.

3. *Chiarella v. United States*

While *Chiarella* was mooted by two key developments in the quest to reach outsiders (the adoption of SEC Rule 14e-3, and the Supreme Court decision in *O'Hagan*), the decision still stands as the foremost authority for the defense of charges against a defendant arguably possessing neither a duty to shareholders nor a source of information. In that regard, the holding is timeless, as is evidenced by over 3,000 civil and administrative case citations to date.

D. Tangential Reforms after 2001

1. The Dodd-Frank Wall Street Reform and Consumer Protection Act of 2010[24]

In the fall of 2008, as the Dow Jones Industrial Average commenced what would ultimately crest as a 39% swoon, over 30 Bills were introduced in Congress to reform regulations of players, practices, and products. In the spring of 2010, these had largely coalesced into a Bill sponsored by the White House and personally endorsed by the President in public in April 2010.

The resulting Dodd-Frank Act, mammoth in scope, created new oversight panels and imposed over 300 studies of or revisions to the regulation of Wall Street. But its only true effect upon insider trading/the Prohibition was limited to changes in SEC administrative penalties and the addition of the Commodity Futures Trade Commission[25] as an enforcer. Accordingly, the statute is discussed (in part) in the next Chapter.

2. The S.T.O.C.K. Act of 2012

In his February 2012 State of the Union address, President Obama had to confront a Congressional approval rating hovering around 15%. As one of his responses, he called upon the federal legislature to quickly produce a law that would quell the rumors that had circulated for years that Congress was privy to inside information on the stock market.

By early April, Congress had almost unanimously passed the "Stop Trading on Congressional Knowledge (STOCK) Act." A largely symbolic measure, the STOCK Act amended the '34 Act to (technically) impose an express duty upon "members and employees of Congress" that runs to "the Congress, the United States Government, and the citizens of the United States."

Scholars were quick to note that such government employees (who often sign confidentiality agreements) could likely be reached as outsiders misappropriating information from a source. Interestingly, back in 1980, the specter

---

24. Pub. L. 111-203, H.R. 4171 (enacted July 21, 2010) (hereinafter "Dodd Frank" or "Dodd Frank Act").

25. Established in 1974, the CFTC is an independent agency charged with enforcing the Commodity Exchange Act. As a general rule, its jurisdiction centers on sophisticated products and institutional investors.

of a judge benefitting by purchasing a stock prior to writing a decision with stock price consequences was expressly posed by Justice Burger during the *Chiarella* oral argument.[26] At its subsection "h," the Act extends the duty forced upon Congress to "each executive branch employee, each judicial officer, and each judicial employee" as well.

In practice, the all-reaching duty imposed by the Act has never been applied, although relevant SEC subpoenas have triggered debates over the immunity imposed upon Congressional deliberations by the Constitution's Speech and Debate Clause[27] (a conflict not addressed by the Act). Interestingly, the STOCK Act also targeted those firms working with government officials, coined "political intelligence firms." At least one government action to date has sought to discipline a member of such a firm.[28]

Conclusion

The full range of Prohibition weapons implies a complementary protocol joining administrative, civil, and criminal regulators in a solitary fight. More accurately, the outline of the Prohibition continues to receive updates addressing scope and/or sanction as implemented by varied parties in interest. What should not be blurred by these tangential dictates is that their benefactor is most often the Securities and Exchange Commission, a civil plaintiff uniquely empowered for litigation, and thus the subject of the next Chapter.

Selected Bibliography

Michael G. Capeci, Note, *SEC RuleB5-2: A Call for Revitalizing the Commission's Efforts in its War on Insider Trading*, 37 HOFSTRA L. REV. 805 (2009), *avail-*

---

26. The full question posed to Chiarella's counsel read as follows:
"Suppose a judge trying a case in the trial court knows that economic consequences are going to have a great impact on the market. Assume he has some stock in the company and the impact is going to be to push the market down, so he sells and then alternatively assume it is going to go up as a result of his holding and he goes out to the bank and borrows some money and buys a lot of the stock, just the way this fellow [Chiarella] did here."

27. U.S. Const., Art. I, Section 6, clause 1 provides in relevant part that Senators and Representative, "in going to and returning from [their respective Houses] and for any Speech and Debate in either House shall not be questioned in any other place."

28. E.g., Securities and Exchange Commission v. David Blaszczak, et al., www.sec.gov/litigation/litreleases/2017/lr23899.htm (August 8, 2017).

able at http://law.hofstra.edu/pdf/academics/journals/lawreview/lrv_issues_v37n03_dd1_capeci_final.pdf.

J. Scott Colesanti, *Bouncing the Tightrope: The S.E.C. Attacks Selective Disclosure, But Provides Little Stability for Analysts*, 25 So. ILL. U. L.J. 1 (Fall 2000).

SEC Release, Selective Disclosure and Insider Trading, Exchange Act Release No. 33-7787, 64 Fed. Reg. 72,590 (proposed rules, Dec. 28, 1999).

SEC Press Release, SEC Brings First Regulation FD Enforcement Actions (November 25, 2002), *available at* http://www.sec.gov/news/press/2002-169.htm.

Massimo Calabresi & Bill Saporito, *The Street Fighter/U.S. Attorney Preet Bharara Is Taking Down Wall Street*, TIME MAGAZINE (February 13, 2012), *available at* http://content.time.com/time/magazine/article/0,9171,210 5971,00.html.

SEC Document, *Fair Disclosure, Regulation FD, available at* https://www.sec.gov/fast-answers/answers-regfdhtm.html.

SEC Release, Selective Disclosure and Insider Trading, 65 Fed. Reg. 51,789 (final rules, August 15, 2000).

SEC Release 2002-169, SEC Brings First Regulation FD Enforcement Actions (November 25, 2002).

Karen Schoen, *Insider Trading: The "Possession Versus Use" Debate*, 148 U. PA. L.REV. 239 (1999).

Raytheon's CFO steps down, USA TODAY, p. 8B (December 12, 2002).

Donna M. Nagy & Richard W. Painter, *Selective Disclosure by Federal Officials and the Case for an FGD (Fairer Government Disclosure) Regime*, 6 WISC. L. REV. 1285 (2012).

Securities Enforcement Alert, Kramer Levin Client Letter (August 2009), *available at* http://www.kramerlevin.com/files/Publication/41a82d72-06f8-4ad4-8701-00f6ace2047b/Presentation/PublicationAttachment/4467a25d-32af-402c-bea2-02136e094ecd/Alert_Cuban_SecEnf_v2.pdf.

Insider Trading: United States vs. Newman and Chiasson, INSIGHT (published by the ABA Business Law Section Corporate Governance Committee) (January 2015), *available at* https://www.americanbar.org/content/dam/aba/administrative/business_law/corpgov_article_2.authcheckdam.pdf.

Melissa C. Brown, *First Regulation FD Decision Finds SEC's 'Excessive Scrutiny' Chills Disclosure*, 37 SECURITIES REGULATION LAW REPORT 49 (December 19, 2005).

DavisPolk Client Memorandum, *Summary of the Dodd-Frank Wall Street Reform and Consumer Protection Act* (July 21, 2010).

Mark Hamblett, *SEC, House Clash over immunity in insider trading investigation*, NEW YORK LAW JOURNAL (June 13, 2016).

SEC Release 2015-266, SEC Charges Political Intelligence Firm (November 24, 2015).

Anne Marie Squeo, *Raytheon Is said to Be in talks To Settle SEC Disclosure Charges*, WALL STREET JOURNAL, p. B10 (July 17, 2002).

Part Three

The Players, and Their Tallies

Chapter IX

The Securities and Exchange Commission: The Unparalleled Plaintiff

The SEC serves a multitude of functions, foremost among which is the education investors, the enforcement of the "securities laws," and the issuance of guidance on capital formation. The tail truly wags the dog, as an agency of less than 3,500 employees spread over 12 offices (located in nearly as many Circuits) must oversee a market that is peopled by over 11,000 public companies and in excess of 15,000 intermediaries. Oddly, it must nonetheless "sing for its supper" (i.e., obtain an operating budget) each year from Congress.

The Commission's role in formulating expansive insider trading law may be overstated—while it started the ball rolling, the Prohibition wins and loses (even in settled cases) according to federal judicial approval. Accordingly, the SEC's greatest effect may be in defining the requisite duty, for the theories by which the breaches of those duties constitute securities fraud have more often than not emanated from judges. Whether Commission diligence in pursuing court approval adds up to persistence or creativity is in the eyes of the beholder.

A. The People Who Inspired, Grew, and Contained the Prohibition

Louis Bachelier was a 20th century French mathematician who combined the study of finance with that of probability. He taught at the Sorbonne and authored a celebrated book on games and chance. He also contributed the "efficient market hypothesis," which asserts that stock exchange prices are the best indicator of an issue's value because the market has absorbed all available information. Such precept may seem unremarkable, but one has to remember that while the first stock exchange is traced to 1602, stock sales still pale when compared with sales of insurance and debt in terms of volume.

The Efficient Market Hypothesis comes in three variations: weak, semi-strong, and strong. The strong theorem maintains that stock exchange prices communicate all information on an individual security. The semi-strong theorem ("Hypothesis") posits that the stock exchange price contemplates all available *public* information. It is this theory by which insider trading can be prosecuted, for if the market price already contemplates nonpublic information, then no one has an advantage. The Hypothesis occasionally draws express attention in a court ruling (normally one focused on whether or not the insider information was material). However, the Hypothesis is always at work in any insider trading case, for if there is no undeterminable amount of inside information driving prices, then there can be no defendants.

William O. Douglas, commonly known as a Supreme Court Justice for over 35 years, was the second Chair of the SEC. Truly, he had small shoes to fill: His predecessor, Joseph Kennedy, was openly known to have been appointed because of his familiarity with "bear raids" by which he had profited (and which were later outlawed by Section 16(c) of the '34 Act). Douglas, a former professor at the law schools of Columbia and Yale, brought a more cerebral approach to the Commission.

As Chair, Douglas pushed successfully for follow-up legislation to the Acts. Laws remedying particular Depression-era ills in public finance came about in the 1930s, while statutes governing investment advisers (distinguishable from stockbrokers by their form of compensation) and investment companies (fractionalized grouped holdings distinguishable from individual stocks) came to fruition in 1940. By that time, no less than six laws were enforced by the SEC,[1]

---

1. Namely, the '33 Act, the '34 Act, the Public Company Holding Act of 1935, the Trust Indenture Act of 1939, the Investment Advisers Act of 1940, and the Investment Company Act of 1940. In 1975, Congress added the Securities Investor Protection Act. Specific legislation was adopted by Congress in response to scandals/crises in 2002 (the Sarbanes-Oxley Act) and 2010 (the Dodd-Frank Act). In 2005, Congress repealed the Public Company Holding Act; the remaining eight statutes are collectively referred to as "the securities laws".

granting the young agency considerable power over varied aspects of the finance and investment business.

Further, Douglas tripled SEC staff and, via Congress, quadrupled its budget. Perhaps more importantly, the intellectual leader bestowed a reputation of efficacy upon Wall Street's overseer that lasts until today. Douglas, who was brought to the Commission by Kennedy (and left only because the modest $10,000 a year salary was placing him in debt), might have stayed forever if he could have. And the feeling was mutual—for years, the SEC web site opened with his patriotic quote about the Commission being "the investor's advocate." What is appreciated by all is the future Supreme Court Justice's commitment to expanding the reach of the SEC into meaningful corporate governance. If investors could not truly appreciate data and financials, the Commission would be forced to look out for them. If not born, a paternalistic agency had been crafted.

———————

Mary Jo White, a former United States Attorney for the Southern District of New York, is the most recent example of what all parties appreciate as the revolving door between private and public service. In late 2012, the esteemed former prosecutor left an enviable position as a partner at a high profile law firm to head the SEC for four years. Under her stewardship, the Division of Enforcement adhered to a "broken window policy" first espoused by police departments in troubled neighborhoods: wherever a violation occurred (i.e., a window was broken), there would be concerted response. Consequentially, the SEC under White set a record for cases brought.[2] As detailed in the press release announcing her departure:

> During Chair White's tenure, the Commission brought more than 2,850 enforcement actions, more than any other three-year period in the Commission's history, and obtained judgments and orders totaling more than $13.4 billion in monetary sanctions. The Commission charged over 3,300 companies and over 2,700 individuals, including CEOs, CFOs, and other senior corporate officers ... Other major cases involved insider and abusive trading, violations of anti-corruption rules and misconduct in accounting and financial reporting. In the last year alone, the Commission brought a record 868 enforcement actions.[3]

———————

2. As a civil agency, the SEC as a plaintiff cannot itself seek incarceration. Correspondingly, its defendants are optimally declared "liable" (instead of guilty), although its initial pleading in a case routinely includes "Charges," a criminal law term.

3. SEC Press Release 2016-238 (November 14, 2016).

The $13.4 billion figure perhaps deserves special attention, for it politely reminded elected officials, who had been calling for devastating change to the SEC, of its money-earning potential. Upon her return to private practice in late 2016,[4] Chair White had overseen the greatest tally of SEC enforcement statistics ever assembled, during a period of limited budgetary increase. The SEC Division of Enforcement, which, at 45 years old, is younger than the majority of judges who hear its cases, had become arguably the most feared batch of investigators and litigators in government. Even more impressive still is that the legion of attorneys proceeds under rules internally crafted with little statutory guidance.

Honorable Jed Rakoff is a difficult but compelling thorn in the Commission's side. His experience is both varied and deep: After graduating Harvard Law School, he spent seven years as a federal prosecutor (during which time he headed the securities fraud unit). Afterwards, he spent decades in white collar defense practice. He may be the only jurist to have both argued against the Misappropriation Theory and later found defendants guilty thereunder.

To wit, as a defense attorney in 1987, he had argued for Carpenter in the eponymous case; his efforts succeeded in stalling High Court approval of the Misappropriation Theory for almost a decade. As a federal judge in the Southern District of New York, he presently strives to depart from the harshness of the Federal Sentencing Guidelines. Beginning in 2009, he shocked conscience by twice questioning the right of the Commission to settle matters with corporate defendants without simultaneously naming the individuals responsible for the illegality. The learned judge was rebuked by the appellate court, but he had made his point that settlements need to be rational, and that all the deal-making had obscured the cause of the financial crisis of 2008.

---

4. White herself highlighted the SEC money bonanza in a speech at New York University School of Law two months before her departure from the Commission:

> By every measure, the SEC's enforcement program has been a resounding success … While numbers are a small part of the story, in the last three fiscal years, we have brought record numbers of enforcement actions, obtained unprecedented monetary remedies in the billions of dollars, and returned hundreds of millions of dollars to harmed investors.

NYU LAW MAGAZINE, Volume XXVII (2017), at 71. The difference between the referenced "billions" and "hundreds of millions" is, of course, comprised by fines; such monies largely go to the United States Treasury, while on occassion coming to rest at the SEC (as is discussed below).

Regarding the Prohibition, Judge Rakoff, a prolific writer and spokesman for change, has integrated the need for judicial resolution within the encumbrance of legal uncertainty, as the opening words to a 2015 opinion demonstrate:

> As a general matter, there is nothing esoteric about insider trading. It is a form of cheating, of using purloined or embezzled information to gain an **unfair** trading advantage. The United States securities markets—the comparative honesty of which is one of our nation's great business assets—cannot tolerate such cheating if those markets are to retain the confidence of investors and the public alike.
>
> But if unlawful insider trading is to be properly deterred, it must be adequately defined. The appropriate body to do so, one would think, is Congress; but in the absence of Congressional action, such definition has been largely left to the courts. This creates difficulties, because courts must proceed on a case-by-case basis ...[5]

However, even a common sense maverick like Jed Rakoff acts strongly to punish insider trading when facts are compelling and fairness dictates action. For example, while sitting in a different Circuit, he found insider trading liability in a tipping case, admittedly ignoring Second Circuit precedent.[6] And he imposed sizeable penalty in Second Circuit cases where the wrongdoing appeared evident.

Thus, the experienced senior judge finds himself repeatedly at the heart of disputes over government overreach, statutory limitations, and criminal sanctions. Outspoken and well-versed, Judge Rakoff serves at once as the foremost example that fairness as a standard can work and that the Prohibition, an extra-statutory creation, is in serious need of repair.

B. Support for SEC Authority, and Its Collection Efforts

The Constitution tersely states that Congress shall have the right to regulate commerce "among the several States";[7] such allocation is the starting point for all federal securities regulation.

---

5. *SEC v. Payton*, 97 F. Supp. 3d 558 (S.D.N.Y. 2015).

6. Namely, the *Salman* case, described in Chapter VIII.

7. U.S. Constitution, Art. I, Section 8, clause 3. Traditionally, it was difficult to find a healthy Constitutional debate about the federal securities laws. As of late, the Commission has come under fire for its internal hearings, which are presently alleged to violate the Appointments Clause of Article II. *See, e.g.*, Jonathan H. Adler, "En banc D.C. Circuit splits

Section 4 of the '34 Act, which created the Commission,[8] was scarce on guidance. Essentially, the statutory provision followed the model for independent regulatory agencies spawned by the New Deal in authorizing five Commissioners with staggered, 5-year terms, with no more than three pledging allegiance to the same political party.[9] Elsewhere, Section 4 focused on the remuneration for the Commissioners; the details of the agency's structure and standard operating rules were left to the SEC. Two statutory creations in the last 15 years have further delineated the Commission's roles while reminding that its monetary intake is always considerable. These creations are discussed below.

1. "Fair Funds"

Traditionally, monies collected by the Commission—no matter how labeled—were paid directly to the United States Treasury.[10] Retrieved monies designated as "disgorgement" were occasionally and unsystematically dispersed to investors identified as having been harmed by the wrongdoing. Settlements with defendants were, at times, creatively structured so as to maximize monies that could be returned to clearly victimized investors.

In 2002, as part of the Sarbanes-Oxley Act of 2002, the disgorgement and restitution process was formalized and legitimized. Section 308 of the Act created "Fair Funds," dedicated accounts identified by the name of the defendant from which monies would be returned to qualifying investor-victims. A Fair Fund can join disgorgement and fines received from a sole defendant into a dedicated holding for injured investors. The Funds are but discretionary in nature, as clarified by internal SEC regulations:

> *Payment to the United States Treasury under certain circumstances.*
> When, in the opinion of the Commission or the hearing officer, the cost of administering a plan of disgorgement relative to the value of the available disgorgement funds and the number of potential claimants would not justify distribution of the disgorgement funds to

---

over constitutionality of SEC administrative law judges," THE WASHINGTON POST, June 27, 2017 (discussing *Raymond J. Lucia Cos. v. SEC*).

8. It is a little known fact that, since it was created by the '34 Act, there was no SEC in existence to enforce the '33 Act. Federal securities regulation was thus left up to the Federal Trade Commission for the period of May 1933 to May 1934.

9. 15 U.S.C. § 78d (2016).

10. *See, e.g.*, Securities Act of 1933 Release No. 7891, *SEC v. LeBed*, Part III (September 20, 2000) ("It is further ordered that Respondent shall, within seven days of the entry of this Order, pay disgorgement of $272,826 and prejudgment interest of $12,174 for a total amount of $285,000 to the United States Treasury.").

injured investors, the plan may provide that the disgorgement funds and any civil penalty shall be paid directly to the general fund of the United States Treasury.[11]

The Fair Fund has become an impressive display of agency closure to investigated harm, as the Commission is wont to remind all observers—the SEC web site routinely updates payout figures since 2002, which were tallied as exceeding $14 billion as of 2014.

2. The "Reserve Fund"

Further, the Commission, which is not self-funding, was permitted a "reserve fund" by the Dodd-Frank Act of 2010. That provision amended Section 4 to read as follows:

(1) RESERVE FUND ESTABLISHED.

There is established in the Treasury of the United States a separate fund, to be known as the "Securities and Exchange Commission Reserve Fund" (referred to in this subsection as the "Reserve Fund").

(2) RESERVE FUND AMOUNTS.—

(A) IN GENERAL.—Except as provided in subparagraph (B), any registration fees collected by the Commission … shall be deposited into the Reserve Fund.

(B) LIMITATIONS.—For any 1 fiscal year—

(i) the amount deposited in the Fund may not exceed $50,000,000; and

(ii) the balance in the Fund may not exceed $100,000,000.

(C) EXCESS FEES.—Any amounts in excess of the limitations … that the Commission collects from registration fees … shall be deposited in the General Fund of the Treasury of the United States and shall not be available for obligation by the Commission.

(3) USE OF AMOUNTS IN RESERVE FUND.—The Commission may obligate amounts in the Reserve Fund, not to exceed a total of $100,000,000 in any 1 fiscal year, as the Commission determines is necessary to carry out the functions of the Commission. Any amounts in the reserve fund shall remain available until expended … Not later than 10 days after the date on which the Commission obligates

---

11. SEC Rule 1102(b).

amounts under this paragraph, the Commission shall notify Congress
of the date, amount, and purpose of the obligation.

It is evident that the SEC's permitted draw from the Reserve Fund is limited,
and that all other monies reside with the government. Despite '34 Act Section
4's efforts to keep its management bipartisan, and allowances made for its retention of monies, the Commission is forever focused on its budget. And that
budget is immediately susceptible to changes in the White House. Witness the
2008 plea of then Chairman Cox, a Republican, to members of a Democrat-
controlled Congressional subcommittee:

> As you know, until this year the Congress had not increased the SEC's
> budget for three years. If the President's budget request for another
> year is approved, then after years of flat budgets, the SEC will have
> received a roughly four percent increase over two years. After taking
> inflation and pay increases into account, this budget for F[iscal] Y[ear]
> 2009 would permit the SEC to keep staffing on par with levels in FY
> 2007—at about 3,470 full-time equivalents.[12]

Further complicating any attempts to read political tea leaves was the Obama
administration's simultaneous commitment to tighter regulation and
flattening of the Commission budget: The SEC's 2011 budget was not
increased from its 2010 level. To caption the obvious, perennial funding questions prod the Commission to play to headlines. However, apart from yearly
money troubles, the SEC enjoys unique autonomy. Other than the Congressional grip on its purse strings, checks on Commission operations are subtle
(*e.g.*, reports issued by the Government Accountability Office). Thus, the
agency passionately focused on enforcing the securities laws and its accompanying Rules does so with considerable discretion.

---

12. Chairman Christopher Cox, U.S. Securities and Exchange Commission, *Fiscal Year
2009 Appropriation Request* (May 7, 2008), *available at* www.sec.gov/news/testimony/2008/
ts050708cc.htm. The same Request noted as its greatest achievement in the prior year its
bringing of "one of the most significant insider trading cases in 20 years" (presumably the
UBS case, which named 15 defendants and was announced in March 2007), as well as "more
than $500 million in financial penalties" paid by defendants in SEC actions.

C. Procedural and Substantive Advantages

The Commission enjoys nearly unilateral determination of its priorities, enforcement strategies, accounting methodology, and hearing procedures.[13] Some of the more daunting SEC powers are highlighted below.

1. Subject only to "civil" rules

As a civil (i.e., non-criminal) agency, the SEC need not concern itself with a number of criminal law safeguards. Teenagers may be charged, trial losses are not foreclosed by double jeopardy, and cases are subject to a "preponderance of evidence" standard of proof.

2. Singular voice in Commission practice

The SEC unilaterally determines its operating rules. For example, the Commission determines its own quorum for purposes of Commissioner action. Accordingly, a Commission operated with 3 sitting Commissioners for months after the election of 2016.[14]

Separately, the SEC exercises the self-declared right to bar certain accountants and lawyers from practice before the agency. Staffing decisions are normally not examined (although a continuing question of the Constitutionality of the process by which its administrative law judges are appointed lingers in the courts).

3. Unfettered rulemaking authority

Politics occasionally leads this admirable agency down some regrettable paths: In one of the more embarrassing political gestures by the Commission, a Republican Chair in 2007 publicly opened for debate the idea of diverting investor lawsuits against public companies to arbitration.[15] That short-lived specter was immediately forsaken when the Credit Crisis of 2008 intervened.

However, SEC rulemaking authority is consistently replete. As cases such as *O'Hagan* and *Chestman* made clear, challenges to SEC legislations are truly speculative litigations. When the agency engages in Administrative Procedure

---

13. The complete "Rules of Practice" governing SEC procedure and penalties are available at https://www.ecfr.gov/cgi-bin/text-idx?SID=09ef3e57558d4099ffe43a56f1a32775&mc=true&node=pt17.3.201&rgn=div5.

14. https://www.sec.gov/Article/about-commissioners.html.

15. Either in response to or despite such transient Commission sentiments, the incoming President (Barack Obama) supported the provision in the 2010 Dodd-Frank Act that required the SEC to study mandatory securities arbitration for its effectiveness.

Act Section 553 rulemaking—an art at which it is superb—courts are extremely loath to unsettle the resulting regulation.

4. Widespread jurisdiction

The Acts expressly reference the Commission's ability to operate in extra-territorial fashion (see generally, *infra*, Chapter X, n.18), and the SEC is very rarely ordered to scale back its global reach. A humorous tale from 2000 describes the successful hauling into court of a foreign national re-establishing the ancient kingdom of Enenkio upon a temporary atoll island in the Pacific Ocean (and selling related bonds to American investors). On more mundane levels, the Commission routinely leaps over the "means of interstate commerce" hurdle in sundry ways.[16]

5. The distinct honor of going second

Indeed, the Commission often finds itself of being in an enviable triage position: If the DOJ succeeds in a parallel proceeding against the same defendant, a summary judgment motion by the SEC based upon the verdict follows.[17] When parallel criminal charges are filed, custom and realities demand that the SEC's civil suit get stayed pending resolution of the DOJ's matter. If the DOJ fails at trial, the SEC has literally viewed a trial run. For example, after the *Newman* setback to tippee liability in 2014 (described in detail in Chapter XI), the SEC brought the same type of case, successfully arguing an applicable reckless standard for non-criminal proceedings.[18]

The SEC Division of Enforcement, employing over 200 attorneys, is litigation-driven. Statistics bear out the fact that the Commission each year is involved in as many appeals as it is involved with new cases. Even a former

---

16. *See, e.g., Consolidated Development Corp.*, 40 S.E.C. 294 (1966) (use of stock exchange for transactions); *Carpenter v. United States*, 484 U.S. 19 (1987) (defendant's knowledge that his employer newspaper utilized the mails and wires in distribution); and *In the Matter of Arthur Lee Kunes*, Securities Act Rel. No. 8120 (August 9, 2002) ("Kunes offered securities through the Internet, a means of interstate commerce ...").

17. *SEC v. Hansen*, 13-CV-1403 (S.D.N.Y. April 12, 2017). In granting summary judgment in favor of the Commission, Judge Vernon Broderick held that the defendant was "collaterally estopped from denying the claims against him by virtue of his criminal convictions and the administrative decision rendered against him" (citing *United States v. Podell*, 572 F.3d 31, 35 (2d Cir. 1978)).

18. *SEC v. Payton*, 97 F. Supp. 3d 558 (S.D.N.Y. 2015). Judge Rakoff issued the decision distinguishing between criminal and civil standards for finding scienter, thus proving once again that he can be, at times, a Prohibition supporter.

SEC Commissioner has acknowledged that "it is not a good day at the Commission unless somebody gets sued."[19]

6. The deliberate lack of clarity in the Prohibition

It is axiomatic that the Commission, a lawyer-driven agency, alone determines the point of no return for its applications of regulation. For example, a 1991 case stretched the notion of "benefit" under the *Dirks* test to include a potentially increased reputation.[20]

More significantly, the concept of *duty*—vital to all of the theories underlying the Prohibition—has been pleaded, re-pleaded, or urged as an entirely non-factor. Relief on this last point came in one of the first "hacker cases," *SEC v. Dorozhko*. The District Court found for the defendant, ruling that a hacker of material, non-public information owed no duty to anyone and thus could not be brought within the Prohibition (i.e., he had engaged in simple theft).[21] "To eliminate the fiduciary requirement now would be to undo decades of Supreme Court precedent, and rewrite the law as it has developed. It is beyond the purview of this Court to do so," wrote the District Court. The opinion noted that academics had publicly pondered the question of how to charge hackers for years (i.e., the SEC had been on notice of the loophole but not acted to close it).

But the Second Circuit Court of Appeals reversed. Noting that the Commission's appellate case did not rest upon either the Classic or Misappropriation theories, the court rested its analysis on the affirmative misrepresentations attending "hacking":

> In our view, none of the Supreme Court opinions relied upon by the District Court—much less the sum of all three opinions—establishes a fiduciary-duty requirement as an element of every violation of Section 10(b). In *Chiarella*, *O'Hagan*, and *Zandford*, the theory of fraud was silence or nondisclosure, not an affirmative misrepresentation.[22]

In essence, the Second Circuit—viewing the difficulties in bringing Dorozhko, the insider trader within the Prohibition—simply recast him as a Rule 10b-5

---

19. *See* J. Scott Colesanti, *SEC Chiefs Past and Present at Fordham*, Bus. L. Prof. Blog (Sept. 28, 2010), *available at* http://lawprofessors.typead.com/business_law/2010/09/sec-cheifs-past-and-present-at-fordham.html.

20. *SEC v. Phillip J. Stevens*, 48 S.E.C. Docket 739 (S.D.N.Y. 1991).

21. 606 F. Supp. 2d 321 (S.D.N.Y. 2008).

22. *SEC v. Dorozhko*, 574 F.3d 42, 48 (2d Cir. 2009).

defendant. In turn, ~~silence in the presence of a duty was equated with silence in the absence of a duty.~~ The drawback to the Prohibition (i.e., charging computer hackers) was therefore nullified.[23]

The abrogation of the fiduciary duty in hacker cases contravenes at least two precepts of insider trading law. First, in finding the universal "affirmative obligation in commercial dealings not to mislead," the Second Circuit ignored the warning of *Chiarella* to avoid a "general duty between all participants in market transactions."

Second, in finding the fraud consummated at the point of misleading the victim, the *Dorozhko* court fulfilled the fear of the *O'Hagan* Dissenters that simple theft violated Rule 10b-5 (i.e., the defendant's crime was deemed consummated not at the time of trading, but at the time of deception). Overall, having identified indefensible activity (i.e., hacking), the duty analysis simply assumed a lesser role. As the reputable Second Circuit eloquently opined, "[W]hat is sufficient is not always what is necessary."

Regarding the District Court's observation that Dorozhko's hacking activities could be the subject of a number of criminal statutes,[24] the Second Circuit took no position. Likewise, the appellate court did stop short of directly contravening *Chiarella* by remanding the case to District Court for a determination of whether hacking in this particular case was deceptive. On remand, the District Court granted the Commission's unopposed motion for summary judgment and imposed disgorgement and an unspecified civil penalty.[25] Fairness had been obtained, although, as is true with the use of so many SEC advantages, certainty, definition and consistency were sacrificed.

Indeed, malleability of the Prohibition can thus be said to be what the Commission craves and protects at every juncture. As a reminder, the SEC withheld support from proposed legislative definitions of insider trading twice in the

---

23. In late 2016, the SEC charged hackers again, this time as parties who "used stolen nonpublic material information" in violation of, among other things, all three subdivisions of Rule 10b-5. *SEC v. Hong, et al.* (S.D.N.Y. December 2016), *available at* https://www.sec.gov/litigation/complaints/2016/comp-pr2016-280.pdf.

Between *Dorozhko* and *Hong*, the DOJ charged six traders who had stolen internal Merrill Lynch prognostications (daily "squawk box" audio transmissions) under the theft of services statute; those convictions were eventually overturned on grounds of prosecutor misconduct.

24. *Dorozhko*, 606 F. Supp. 2d 321 at n. 6.

25. U.S. Securities and Exchange Commission Release No. 21465 (March 29, 2010), *available at* https://www.sec.gov/litigation/litreleases/2010/lr21465.htm.

1980s. Via *Dorozhko*, the SEC was able to add hackers to the list of villains reached by Rule 10b-5; such elasticity would be hindered by a statutory definition of the Prohibition, and thus the Commission with the budget and the history and the cause retreated from endorsing formal change to the offense by Congress in 1984 and 1988 (as discussed in Chapter VI).

7. Congressional blank checks

Whenever asked, Congress has increased fines and the means by which the Commission can seek them. The chart below details the majority of SEC means of punishment, with statutory sources and contributing causes noted at the far right:

Topic	'33 Act Section	'34 Act Section	Chief Attributes	Crisis & Statute
Investigative Authority	Section 20, 22	Section 21	Nationwide service of process; venue where the transaction took place/ "wherever the defendant is found"	Depression & the Acts
SEC Hearings	Section 21	Various (e.g., Section 21B)	Appealable to D.C. Circuit	Depression & the Acts
District Court Trials	Section 22	Section 27	Proceed as other federal litigation	Depression & the Acts
Insider Trading Penalties	N/A	Section 21A	3X profit gained/loss avoided	Added by ITSA in 1984
Cease and Desist Authority	Section 8A	Section 21C	Penny Stock Reform Act of 1990 added; Section 929p of the Dodd-Frank Act of 2010 added civil penalties under the Acts (e.g., 21B(a))	Credit crisis of 2008
Criminal Penalties	Section 24	Section 32	"Knowledge" defense not applicable to fines	Scandals of 2001 & Credit Crisis

The means of discipline being numerous, and the resulting numbers approaching infinity, the pinnacle achievement of the Commission may be in accounting for all of the collected funds. Adding to the myriad agency duties attending a broad spectrum of remedies and sanctions are the provisions related to the Prohibition—at least in substance, if not in name.

D. Prohibition Substitutes

New ways have been repeatedly tried and successfully tested by the Commission to maximize the means of charging and collecting from insider trading. Seven of them are detailed below.

1. Section 13d/Beneficial Ownership Rules[26]

In 1990, the headlines roared with unprecedented SEC fines. One such case involved a "junk bond" expert named Michael Milken. Milken was accused of 98 counts of racketeering, insider trading, and mail fraud. He settled with the DOJ on six charges, the penalties for which included jail time, a lifetime bar from the securities industry, and payment of a fine of $600 million. Milken's name became synonymous with the insider trading scandals of the 1980s. However, the charges of which he was convicted via his plea deal predominantly related to beneficial ownership rules promulgated under Section 13 of the '34 Act.

More recently, a group of company insiders paid fines totaling $2.6 million in September 2014 for Section 16(a) and Section 13d reporting violations,[27] proving that the reporting requirement is still a moneymaker.

2. Parallel Provisions, within and outside of the '34 Act

The courts have often obliged the Commission by interpreting key elements within parallel provisions of the '34 Act in similar fashion.[28] Further, others of the securities laws also prohibit fraud in a manner that translates to application of Prohibition principles.[29]

---

26. Such SEC or stock exchange proscriptions ensnare members of insider trading rings by capturing defendants who hide true ownership of positions to keep trading plans private or otherwise evade government reporting obligations.

27. SEC Press Release No. 2014-190, *available at* https://www.sec.gov/news/press-release/2014-190.

28. *See, e.g., Brody v. Transitional Hospitals Corp.*, 280 F.3d 997 (9th Cir. 2002) (finding that the contemporaneous trading requirement of Rule 10b-5 also applies to Rule 14e-3).

29. *See, e.g.,* SEC Rule 204A-1, 17 C.F.R. §275.204A-1 (requiring investment advisers to file beneficial ownership reports).

3. Order Ticket/Record Keeping/Filing Rules

A fallback to charging insider trading is to charge violations of SEC books and records rules, violations of which can be extremely costly. Order ticket rules generally serve as a productive backup to theories of wrongful trading. For example, one case alone in 2007 yielded over $2 million in fines.[30]

Of course, the Ivan Boesky settlement of 1986, which detailed false filings with the Commission, yielded a record-setting $100 million fine against the arbitrageur. Boesky had been accused of high stakes insider trading (in 1987 he was separately sentenced to three years in prison).

4. Identification of Relief Defendants

Parties from whom the Commission seeks monetary recovery without an admission of guilt are known as "relief defendants." The practice is not particularly new, as the Commission was openly publicizing relief defendant cases as far back as 2005[31] (and even further, in the 1968 *Texas Gulf Sulphur* case). Nor is the naming of those believed to have received ill-gotten gains peculiar to the SEC, as the IRS uses the mechanism as well.

Regarding insider trading, the practice is downright lucrative. In 2017, the sports and financial pages enjoyed a crossover as a star professional golfer returned $1 million to the SEC for a transaction based on a wrongful tip; commentators were quick to note that the SEC's unified Complaint against the relief defendant and the primary defendant disclosed similar fact patterns.[32]

5. Charging of "Late Trading"[33]

The violation essentially lies in a trader promising an outdated or premature price to an investor, who commits to the trade out of trust for its unfairness.

---

30. https://www.sec.gov/news/press/2007/2007-41.htm.

31. *Securities and Exchange Commission v. Samuel D. Waksal and Jack Waksal, Defendants, and Patti Waksal, Relief Defendant*, SEC Litigation Release No. 19039 (January 19, 2005). Samuel Waksal, alleged to have tipped celebrity Martha Stewart, among others, settled by disgorging over $800,000 in profits and—along with his father—paying a penalty of over $3 million.

32. See www.sec.gov/litigation/complaints/2016/comp-pr2016-92.pdf, at 14 ("Walters Tips Mickelson, Who Trades in Dean Foods").

33. The SEC defines "Late Trading" as "the practice of placing orders to buy or redeem mutual fund shares after the time as of which a mutual fund has calculated its asset value."

In one 2004 case alone, the SEC obtained $125 million in penalties.[34] While the violation was chiefly brought to light by the efforts of New York Attorney General Eliot Spitzer, the offense boils down to insiders arranging trades for favored parties at favorable prices—those prices only have meaning in light of inside information, and such offense mirrors perfectly the horrors disclosed by the Pecora Investigation of the 1930s.

6. Charging of "Frontrunning"

Stock exchange investigators are familiar with the breed of insider trading peculiar to the floor of a trading center. The practice is called "frontrunning" (so-called because of the historical practice of one exchange Floor runner carrying a trade being physically outpaced by a rival who knew the terms of his order). In a more generic sense, frontrunning, which can be reached by Rule 10b-5, occurs whenever an industry professional acts on market information not accessible by others.

The offense is real and continuing and punishable under Section 17(a) or Rule 10b-5, as was evidenced in January 2017 when a trading center paid $22 million to the SEC to settle a complaint alleging "internalization" of customer orders.

When engaged in by Specialists (on stock exchange floors) or Market Makers (for all other trading venues), the violation is termed "interpositioning." In one disciplinary action in 2004, the SEC fined all of the NYSE Specialists a total exceeding $240 million based upon widespread evidence of the pernicious practice.

7. The Whistleblower Phenomenon

Prior to the Dodd-Frank reinvention of Commission whistleblower authority, the SEC distributed less than $160,000 to cooperating parties, always in cases involving insider trading. In the seven years since, the Commission has distributed over $158 million (in a variety of cases) to less than 50 whistleblowers. Truly, the monies redistributed to whistleblowers has become the most alluring topic in the debate of fund re-allocation, as is amply demonstrated by the growing tally's feature on the SEC web site.

The SEC describes its statutory whistleblower authority as such:

---

34. www.sec.gov/news/press/2004-22.htm. The case involved both Late Trading and Market Timing, the latter focusing on intra-day trading in mutual funds priced once a day.

Whistleblowers who provide the SEC with unique and useful information that contributes to a successful enforcement action are eligible for awards that can range from 10 percent to 30 percent of the money collected when financial sanctions exceed $1 million. By law, the SEC protects the confidentiality of whistleblowers and does not disclose information that might directly or indirectly reveal a whistleblower's identity.[35]

While but a fraction of these anonymous whistleblower awards reveal a specific insider trading case, such evidence does exist. Significantly, while Congress refashioned the Commission's whistleblower authority to go beyond insider trading cases, the SEC has in turn reinvented "whistleblowing" to include assistance from parties who have participated in the violation (and thus receive a correspondingly reduced payout). Similarly, there is payout to those giving tips that lead to the opening of an investigation, and even parties who simply aid an ongoing investigation (i.e., tantamount to paying the bounty hunter before the villain is caught).

Rule 10b-5 and the Prohibition are thus aided at the front end by numerous supplements (both direct and indirect). At the back end, these monies are bifurcated into buckets hiding subtleties. These two buckets are termed *disgorgements* and *fines*.

E. Disgorgement and Fines

As described earlier in the Chapter, traditionally, the SEC relayed all fines collected to its "parent"—the United States Treasury. This practice was mimicked by the stock exchanges, whose disciplined members settled penalties via checks made payable to the stock exchange itself. As both the size of fines and number of parties collecting them grew, it was inevitable that monies classified as fines would need to be formally distributed to victims of fraud (*i.e.*, via fair funds), or at least munificent third parties.[36]

---

35. SEC 2015-150, *SEC Pays More Than $3 Million to Whistleblower* (July 17, 2015).

36. For example, New York State Attorney General Eliot Spitzer donated monies collected by a 2002 settlement with Wall Street to, among other places, law schools establishing securities arbitration clinics representing investors and employees without the benefit of counsel.

Section 109 of the Sarbanes Oxley Act of 2002[37] also expressly allocated some fine monies for laudable programs, such as scholarships.[38] And as noted above, the Commission enjoys a reserve fund from which to draw, up to a point.

However, notwithstanding the Fair Fund program and the scholarship-type programs, the overwhelming majority of fines/penalties remain payable to the U.S. Treasury. Not surprisingly, in 2013, one publication openly commented that SEC fines in a period of less than 12 months theoretically covered the entire Commission budget for the year.[39] Some other noteworthy characteristics of disgorgement and fine allocations are noted below.

1. Disgorgements

The period of 2000–2001 saw a number of public companies looted by their management officials, as well as restated financials submitted to the SEC by legendary corporate giants. Congress, even under a conservative new President, was compelled to respond. The resulting Sarbanes-Oxley Act was primarily aimed at corporate greed aided by loose accounting practices. Passed in response to highly-publicized extravagance, the law succeeded in, among other things, forcing officials such as Chief Executive Officers and Chief Financial Officers to sign SEC filings and otherwise accept responsibility for accounting determinations. To indirectly target questionable withdrawals from company treasuries by insiders, the Act created a new self-regulatory organization called the Public Company Accounting Oversight Board.

As generally acknowledged by recent SEC financial reports, "Disgorged funds are normally distributed to those affected by the action, but in certain cases may be deposited in the General Fund of the Treasury."[40] Section 308 of SOX thus codified the requirement that fines find the defrauded, where possible. As the SEC acknowledges in its financials, approximately 80% of disgorgements in such funds reach harmed investors, who must make applications. Between 2002 and 2014, a total of 236 such dedicated funds returned over $14 billion to qualifying investors.

---

37. Pub. L. 107-204, 116 Stat. 745 (enacted July 30, 2002).

38. *See* 2017 United States Budget, p. 1070.

39. *SEC: Self-Funding vs. Congressional Appropriations*, FOX BUSINESS (May 17, 2013). The editorial noted that the $1.6 billion in fines obtained from just five defendants could carry the Commission for an entire year.

40. U.S. Securities and Exchange Commission Fiscal Year 2013 Agency Financial Report, at 147, *available at* https://www.sec.gov/about/secpar/secafr2013.pdf.

2. Fines

The SEC proudly discloses that awards (in the form of disgorgement or fine) are obtained in 92% of Enforcement cases; the same figures reveal that less than 50% of the accompanying dollar amounts are actually collected in the same fiscal year.[41]

Dodd-Frank did alter tradition a bit by allowing the Commission to pay up to $300 million annually from "sanctions" into the whistleblower award program described above.[42] Statistics show that, for the fiscal year 2015, while nearly $2 billion in fines was collected, less than 10% was reallocated to investors, leaving the U.S. Treasury, again, with the lion's shares of the SEC's awards.[43]

The point to be made is not that monies are being quietly diverted—by all evidence they are not, as the Dodd Frank Act and the Commission's practices are models of budgetary transparency in this regard. However, billions of dollars a year are nonetheless being generated for general government usage by the status quo, a sobering thought for those who wish change for the Prohibition and its implementation.

———

A review of SEC powers, their rationales and their revenues reveals some truisms:

Regarding the Prohibition

- The Prohibition has adhered to a pattern of SEC identification of an unfairness, court recognition of a related duty, and, in turn, SEC perfection of that duty.
- The working parts of the Prohibition actually emanate from defenses offered by the accused. Not all are addressed in meaningful fashion in each case.
- The Prohibition, although animated via Rule 10b-5, manifests itself in various agency rules and statutory frameworks.

———

41. U.S. Securities and Exchange Commission, Fiscal Year 2017 Congressional Budget Justification ("2017 Report"), at 41. The "Budget Justification" report used to be called the "Performance Appraisal Report," but a more blunt nomenclature has been adopted in recent years.

42. 2017 Budget of the United State Government at 1345. The budget summarizes the Whistleblower program as designed "to elicit high-quality tips by motivating persons with inside knowledge to assist the federal Government in identifying and prosecuting individuals who violate the Federal securities laws."

43. *Id.* at 40–41.

- Accordingly, *duty* is the lynchpin to the occasionally unpredictable science of prosecuting insider trading, and that fluctuating construct is most responsible for the eye-catching remedies. Further, the gamesmanship of the alternating theories comprising the Prohibition is not lost on the courts.[44]

Regarding the Monies

- The SEC's budgetary needs force the agency to crave headlines spurred by ever-ratcheting monetary rewards.
- Congress has acquiesced to SEC requests for greater type and depth of sanctions (normally following periods of highly publicized corporate scandal).
- Penalties have gravitated from a raison d'etre of general deterrence to one of specific deterrence, to one of almost inexplicable calculations.
- A sizeable portion of monies collected by the SEC—no matter how labeled—come to rest in the United States Treasury.

Still, with the seemingly unlimited bounty of court assistance, fairness compels regulators other than the unparalleled Commission to act, and the Acts expressly contemplated help from a variety of sources. Atop the money-makers is the reliable SEC, unique in litigation experience, as well as in collection of illicit gains. Such a favored status appears rational in light of the multitude of industry players and the sheer volume of securities trading. Such approach sometimes provides for an impressive regulatory recapture of cash; that recapture itself, at times, pales when compared to the rewards of private Rule 10b-5 litigation (the subject of the next Chapter).

Selected Bibliography

"What We Do," SEC web site, *available at* https://www.sec.gov/Article/whatwe do.html#org.
U.S. Securities and Exchange Commission, Office of the Inspector General Office of Audits/Assessment of the SEC's Bounty Program (March 29, 2010), *available at* www.sec.gov/oig/reportspubs/474.pdf.

---

44. *See, e.g., United States v. Kim*, 184 F. Supp. 2d 1006, 1013 n.3 (N.D. Cal. 2002) ("Presumably the government's reliance on the misappropriation theory reflects their conclusion that they cannot prove a mental state of the CEO of Meridian that would support liability when he revealed the merger information.").

SEC Press Release 2016-92, *SEC Announces Insider Trading Charges in Case Involving Sports Gambler and Board Member.*

THE COURT YEARS, 1939–1975/THE AUTOBIOGRAPHY OF WILLIAM O. DOUGLAS (1980).

Roberta S. Karmel, *Realizing the Dream of William O. Douglas: The Securities and Exchange Commission Takes Charge of Corporate Governance,* 30 DEL. J. CORP. LAW 79 (2005).

J. Scott Colesanti, *Not Dead Yet: How the* Finnerty *Decision Salvaged the Stock Exchange Specialist,* 23 ST. JOHN'S J. LEG. COMM. 1 (Spring 2008) (explaining "interpositioning" as a form of insider trading).

Gibson Dunn, Client Alert, *The Dodd-Frank Act Reinforces and Expands SEC Enforcement Powers* (July 21, 2010), *available at* http://www.gibsondunn.com/publications/Pages/Dodd-FrankActReinforcesAndExpandsSECEnforcementPowers.aspx.

June Rhee, *Public Compensation for Private Harm: SEC's Fair Fund Distribution* (April 30, 2014), *available at* https://corpgov.law.harvard.edu/2014/4/30.

William O. Douglas and the Growing Power of the SEC, available at http://www.sechistorical.org/museum/galleries/douglas/administeringLaw.php.

Securities Exchange Act of 1934 Release No. 43307 (Sept. 20, 2000), *In the Matter of Jonathan G. Lebed,* Order Instituting Cease-and-Desist Proceeding (finding violations of Section 17(a) and Rule 10b-5 by a 15-year-old respondent).

Rob Tricchinelli, *"Anything Goes" in SEC Courts, NBA's Cuban Argues,* BLOOMBERG BNA SECURITIES REGULATION & LAW REPORT, 47 SRLR 1796 (Sept. 15, 2015).

Steadman v. SEC, 450 U.S. 91 (1981) (finding the SEC responsible for proving its charges by a preponderance of the evidence).

Peter K. Vigeland, et al., *Should a Defendant Be Forced to Disgorge What He Never Possessed?,* NEW YORK LAW JOURNAL (April 25, 2014) (commenting on *SEC v. Contorinis,* 2014 WL593484 (2d Cir. Feb. 18, 2014), and defining disgorgement as an equitable remedy designed to force the defendant to give up the "amount by which he was unjustly enriched" that does not serve a punitive function).

Joel M. Cohen & Mary Kay Dunning, *Insider Trading: It's Not Just for Suits,* 18 BUSINESS CRIMES BULLETIN 4 (Law Journal Newsletters, December 2010) (reminding that, in view of an SEC case against railroad workers who had surmised a takeover of their employer, that "the prohibition against insider trading applies to everyone, not just to hedge-fund managers and financiers").

SEC Press Release, *Overseas Traders Paying Back All Profits Plus Penalties in Insider Trading Case* (March 24, 2017), *available at* www.sec.gov/news/press-release/2017-70-0.

Kokesh v. SEC, 137 S. Ct. 1635 (2017). The unanimous decision was most critical of the Commission's use of disgorgement, stating that "SEC disgorgement sometimes exceeds the profits gained as a result of the violation" and "Even though district courts may distribute the funds to the victims, they have not identified any statutory command that they do so."

Kurt Eichenwald, *Milken Set to Pay a $600 Million Fine in Wall St. Fraud*, N.Y. TIMES (April 21, 1990), *available at* http://www.nytimes.com/1990/04/21/business/milken-set-to-pay-a-600-million-fine-in-wall-st-fraud.html.

Cara Salvatore, *Labaton Sucharow Adds 3 to Sec Whistleblower Practice*, LAW360 (May 23, 2017), *available at* https://www.law360.com/articles/927247/labaton-sucharow-adds-3-to-sec-whistleblower-practice.

Shearman & Sterling LLP, Client Letter, *Securities Enforcement: 2016 Mid-Year Review*, (2016), *available at* http://www.shearman.com/~/media/Files/News Insights/Publications/2016/07/Securities-Enforcement-2016-Mid-Year-Review-NO-CITATIONS-LIT-071916.pdf ("The SEC's charging decision to name [golfer Phil] Mickelson as a relief defendant was likely motivated, at least in part, by (i) the lingering uncertainty of how *Newman* applies to civil SEC actions and (ii) the difficulty of proving that Mickelson had the requisite mental state—that is, at least recklessness—as a remote tippee.").

SEC Press Release 2007-156, *SEC Announces Distribution of $267 Million Fair Fund to Qwest Investors Injured by Accounting Fraud* (August 1, 2007), *available at* www.sec.gov/news/press/2007/2007-156.htm.

JENNIFER BOTHAMLEY, DICTIONARY OF THEORIES 168 (1993).

White Collar Crime 2013: Prosecutors and Regulators Speak, PLI Corporate Law Practice Course Handbook Series, *available at* https://www.akingump.com/images/content/2/4/v2/24956/White-Collar-Crime-2013-Prosecutors-and-Regulators-Speak.pdf.

John H. Sturc & Adam Chen, Gibson Dunn Client Letter, *Insider Trading: New Developments and How to Deal With Them* (November–December 2011), *available at* http://www.gibsondunn.com/publications/Documents/Sturc Chen-InsiderTrading-NewDevelopments-PracticalCompliance.pdf.

"About GAO," https://www.gao.gov/about/index.html, *last visited* July 4, 2017.

C. Ryan Barber, *The Unusual Condition the SEC Imposed on a Whistleblower's Award*, NATIONAL LAW JOURNAL (April 12, 2016) (noting that a review of the prior 19 final orders approving whistleblower awards and the present $275,000 award leads to the conclusion that a whistleblower "doesn't have to be squeaky clean").

Chapter X

Private Attorneys General

The Acts created a number of statutory causes of action to enlist private plaintiffs in the regulation of the market. Yet, the strongest means of deterring fraud was gradually reposed in the claims quietly found by the judiciary to be implied by the anti-fraud measures expressly delegated to the SEC.

In 1946, a federal judge in Pennsylvania held that Rule 10b-5 (a regulation) implied a private cause of action; several years later, after a nautical disaster in Texas, the class action was born. In 1964, the Supreme Court succinctly held that precedent in the area of securities law and elsewhere supported the equating of investor protection with investor lawsuits, lest victims be left to inadequate state remedies.[1]

*By 1995, **securities** class actions had ballooned to the point of threatening to overwhelm the entire genre. Congress responded drastically in the form of the Private Securities Litigation Reform Act ("PSLRA"), a limitation on claims so novel that President Clinton accused it of "closing the courthouse door" to legitimate investor claims and vetoed it. Congress overrode the veto, and private securities claimants have faced a tougher road to hoe ever since.*

But Congress taketh away, and Congress giveth. The ITSFEA Act of 1988 cemented both a private claim and a rationale that would routinely be utilized by the private Bar. On numerous occasions since, Congress has blessed the use of civilian counsel to further the securities laws. As a result, "private attorneys general" have remained a significant (at times, primal) money-earning force for deterrence.

---

1. *J.I. Case v. Borak*, 377 U.S. 426 (1964) (finding an implied, private cause of action in both derivative and direct forms under Section 14(a) of the '34 Act for those parties misled by management's proxy statement).

A. Class Actions, Origins and Targets

The **SS Grandcamp**, a French cargo ship that was to transport American fertilizer to war-torn nations, inexplicably exploded while docked in Texas City, Texas, on the morning of April 16, 1947. A fire ravaged the vessel and its moored neighbor for two days, causing a disaster the court would subsequently summarize as follows: "Both ships exploded, and much of the city was leveled, and many people killed."

Subsequently, 8,500 claimants filed lawsuits against the United States Government, alleging negligence in the preparation, storage, and/or handling of dangerous fertilizer. When their myriad claims were combined into a sole test case within the Fifth Circuit, America's first class action was born.

A bench trial on the claim of fatality Henry Dalehite, one such "test" plaintiff, revealed that the fertilizer was pressed into production by America's desire to help feed areas ravaged by World War Two, including Germany, Japan, and Korea. Army personnel were involved with appropriations, operation, and supervision of private entities contracted for the delivery of fertilizer, which was laden with combustible ammonium nitrate. The private ship Grandcamp was carrying at least three cargoes at the time of the disaster: The fertilizer, explosives, and sulfur. While the direct cause of the Grandcamp explosion could not be pinpointed, the government—via its U.S. Army agents—was blamed for "adopting the fertilizer program as a whole, in its control of various phases of manufacturing, packaging, labeling and shipping the product, in failing to give notice of its dangerous nature to persons handling it, and its failing to police its loading on shipboard."[2]

The trial judge ruled that the Federal Tort Claims Act ("FTCA") permitted the related lawsuits against the United States as sovereign and granted a $75,000 recovery for the family of Dalehite.

The Fifth Circuit unanimously reversed, finding that the negligence suit was not permitted by the FTCA. The Supreme Court, by a vote of four Justices to three, affirmed the Circuit Court. The decision focused on the "discretionary" functions exercised by the Army in both planning and executing the relief fertilizer program. Since all practices complained of by the plaintiffs involved discretionary (i.e., non-obligatory) acts, relevant decisions could not meet the jurisdictional basis required for a lawsuit against the government.

Dalehite's family and others thus lost out to a narrow reading of sovereign immunity in post-War years. But the procedural precedent was set. Large num-

---

2. *Dalehite v. United States*, 346 U.S. 15, 15 (1953).

bers of claims could be joined, and an astronomical array of undertakings could be simplified via a test case. The notion of mass tort plaintiffs (and deep pocket defendants) had taken hold.

———————

William Lerach was a California attorney. He specialized in securities class actions, and, in particular, Rule 10b-5 claims that highlighted "insider" transactions by corporate management prior to public announcements. Between roughly 1975 and 1995, his defendants spanned the spectrum of industry, including such financial titans as Enron, Goldman Sachs, Disney, and Apple Computer. At its peak, Lerach—whose firm at times commanded contingency fees up to 30% of a settlement—owned an estimated net worth of $700 million. So effective were Lerach's attorneys at expediently employing Rule 10b-5 that the official House Report on the PSLRA expressly referred to his public boasting of efforts on behalf of plaintiffs:

> Using professional plaintiffs, law firms often file complaints within days of a substantial movement in stock price ... Firms are able to do this by keeping a stable of professional plaintiffs who hold a few shares in a broad range of companies. As William Lerach, whose firm filed 229 different suits over forty-four months—one every 4.2 business days—told Forbes magazine: "I have the greatest practice of law in the world. I have no clients."[3]

Lerach was even heralded in San Diego, the city where he sued hometown corporations, as the foremost private enforcer of the Acts. Subsequently, as his name and successes grew, he came under government investigation. After years of examining his practice, the government convicted Lerach of obstruction of justice in 2007, and he lost his law license in 2009. Nonetheless, his contribution to securities law may last forever. It was Lerach's firm that, in a famed Ninth Circuit case, essentially frittered away the element of *reliance* in securities class actions so that the burden shifted to defendant corporations to disprove causality.

That case, *Blackie v. Barrack*,[4] concerned an appeal from an order of certification in favor of plaintiffs. The plaintiffs had alleged Rule 10b-5 violations based upon a corporation's belated disclosure of sizeable losses. The appellate court review focused on the commonality of class claims (and potential

———————

3. United States House of Representatives, Report No. 104-50 (Part 1) (February 24, 1995). For his part, Lerach (who refused to disclose his earnings to Congress) later wrote that the PSLRA did not significantly decrease class action filings, and that "the lion's share" of post-1995 filings became centered on continuing accounting irregularities and trading by corporate insiders.

4. *Blackie v. Barrack*, 524 F.2d 891, 906 (9th Cir. 1975).

conflicts among class members). In reviewing FRCP 23(a), the Ninth Circuit concluded that in what was essentially a misrepresentation case, individual questions of reliance were irrelevant:

> ... Moreover, proof of subjective reliance on particular misrepresentations is unnecessary to establish a 10b-5 claim for a deception inflating the price of stock traded in the open market. (cites omitted). Proof of reliance is adduced to demonstrate the causal connection between the defendant's wrongdoing and the plaintiff's loss. We think causation is adequately established in the impersonal stock exchange context by proof of purchase and of the materiality of misrepresentations, without direct proof of reliance. Materiality circumstantially establishes the reliance of some market traders and hence the inflation in the stock price—when the purchase is made the causational chain between defendant's conduct and plaintiff's loss is sufficiently established to make out a prima facie case.

Subsequently, the *Blackie v. Barrack* "fraud on the market" theory was codified by Congress in 1988 with the adoption of Section 20A of the '34 Act. Beyond its use as a class certification tool, *Blackie* was cited in Rule 10b-5 cases when beneficial to pleadings, and as a suitable definition of *materiality* for substantive purposes at trial.

The "fraud on the market" theory so took hold that Lerach became skilled at cross-examining defense experts so as to obtain a concession that his firm was preeminent in the field. When the Supreme Court eliminated aiding and abetting liability under Rule 10b-5 in the *Central Bank* decision of 1994, Lerach simply invented "scheme liability" (borrowing the term from subdivision "a" of the notorious Rule). By the time Lerach's fame grew so large as to invite Congressional scrutiny, his pleadings were the standard for class action litigation. However, with the attention came suspicion of Rule 10b-5 as well, for in stating the purpose for its bold PSLRA legislation, Congress wrote in 1995:

> Congress has never expressly provided for private rights of action when it enacted Section 10(b). Instead, courts have held that Congress impliedly authorized such actions. As a result, 10(b) litigation has evolved out of judicial decisionmaking (sic), not specific legislative action. The lack of congressional involvement has left judges free to develop conflicting legal standards thereby creating substantial uncertainties and opportunities for abuses of investors, issuers, professional firms and others.[5]

---

5. James Hamilton, *Private Securities Litigation Reform Act of 1995*, FEDERAL SECURITIES LAW REPORTS (January 10, 1996), at 73.

Those abuses were detailed by the 104th Congress as resulting in corporate America's rush to settle quickly filed class action lawsuits at a rate of 93% (at an average cost of $8.6 million per suit). In turn, the alarming costs to the American dream were expressly pinned to a coterie of lawyers operating profitable class action firms in the 1990s, labeling "professional plaintiffs" as a primary cause of the extravagant and costly litigation.

The sizeable successes of Lerach and his colleagues inspired the PSLRA to add some inventive restrictions on private class action litigation. Issuers were granted a safe harbor for their public prognostications if the information was accompanied by "meaningful cautionary statements." Securities plaintiffs had to verify complaints. Discovery was stayed pending a corporate defendant's motion to dismiss. And under FRCP 9(b), allegations of fraud were subject to a heightened pleading standard calling for a statement with "particularity" (which largely mirrored case law from the Second Circuit).

The new law ultimately added much to the class action plaintiff's work, but, ultimately, did not attain the goal of decreasing the number of class actions. Additionally, the Act did not diminish SEC authority, which was actually strengthened via codification of the agency's right to pursue aiding and abetting claims.[6] These developments thus placed firms like Lerach's in prime position to pounce when another corporate titan was accused of insider trading.

Martha Stewart was a radiant success story, starting with the rise of the former stockbroker to CEO and culminating with her addition to the Board of Directors of the New York Stock Exchange. All that stock market success ended in less than a year after she sold her shares of ImClone to avoid a loss of approximately $45,000 when the company's stock dropped 16% to $46 a share.

As background, ImClone was a public company hopefully awaiting word on FDA approval for Erbitux, a new cancer-fighting drug. On December 26, 2001, the CEO of the company learned confidentially from the federal agency that such approval would not be forthcoming; the world would not learn of this news for days. The CEO, Samuel Waksal, immediately began attempting to sell his shares of his own company before the public dissemination of the FDA decision could trigger a price plunge. Some Wall Street firms balked at Waksal's peculiar trade orders. Still, Waksal's relatives were permitted to sell their ImClone shares and avoid the loss. Waksal ultimately faced charges for

---

6. The PSLRA, voting upon which proceeded largely along party lines, effected changes to the Acts as of January 1, 1996. These changes are primarily contained within Sections 27 and 27A of the '33 Act, and Section 21E of the '34 Act.

insider trading based upon his successful tipping to his family and his unsuccessful attempts to personally exploit the confidential FDA notification.

Stewart, who in 1999 had enjoyed a highly profitable public offering of her own company ("Living Omnimedia"["LO"]), had not fared well in her private stock portfolio after the techno-stock downturn of 2000. On December 27, 2001, Stewart, who shared Waksal's broker at Merrill Lynch, learned indirectly from him that Waksal was attempting to sell and that ImClone's price was likely to fall. Stewart ordered the sale of all of her own ImClone shares, and avoided the loss. An SEC investigation into ImClone trading ensued, during which Stewart maintained that her sell order had been pursuant to a standing "stop loss" order at the brokerage. When word spread that Stewart's version of events differed from others, she resigned from the NYSE Board in October 2002. During this hectic time, Stewart repeated the (possibly false) defense of a standing instruction via her LO web site, seemingly to calm her shareholders about the outcome of the pending investigation.

The subsequent SEC Complaint against Stewart in June 2003 alleged that the celebrity had violated Section 17(a) and all three subdivisions of Rule 10b-5. The charging instrument accused Stewart of wrongdoing in acting upon information on Waksal's sales/attempted sales that she either knew or was reckless in not knowing the broker had leaked from Merrill Lynch. Curiously, when her SEC case was contemplated by the DOJ, the regional prosecutors decided against including an insider trading charge.[7] They did, however, fashion a more generalized claim of securities fraud premised upon Stewart's denials of wrongdoing on the LO web site; the district court trial judge dropped that claim before the case went to the jury.

Separately, Waksal pled to securities fraud in 2002 and was sentenced to seven years in prison. Stewart and the stockbroker were convicted in March 2004 after a 7-week criminal trial. The pair were each found guilty on four counts of obstruction of justice and misleading investigators. "This is a victory for the little guys. No one is above the law," announced one of the jurors. A few months later, Stewart was sentenced to five months in prison (a term she would complete under house arrest). Observers noted that a conviction of securities fraud could have increased her jail time tenfold.

On the courthouse steps after the verdict, the tearful 62-year-old protested the zeal with which the government had pursued its case against her. But the

---

7. See Naomi Aoki and Tatsha Robertson, "Stewart is Indicted, Steps Down," Boston Globe, June 5, 2003, at A1 ("Charges of insider trading were notably absent from the criminal case.").

harm was far from over. The SEC pressed forward with its stayed Complaint, in settlement of which Stewart agreed in 2006 to a 5-year ban from the industry and the payment of disgorgement and fine totaling approximately $195,000. Additionally, a 2002 class action by LO investors alleged a Rule 10b-5 violation premised upon Stewart's web site denials of guilt in the ImClone matter; the case was filed by Lerach's firm and settled in 2007 for $30 million.

B. "Fraud on the Market" and Section 20A on Class Actions

Some of the most famous American legal battles were commenced via the class action. *Brown v. Board of Education* and *Roe v. Wade* top that list. The class action process grew from maneuver to majesty in the late 1960s, thanks largely to quiet, technical changes promulgated by professors and lawyers, and adopted by the Supreme Court. To wit, the Federal Rules of Civil Procedure were amended in 1966 to re-balance Rule 23's required elements,[8] thereby updating the decades old Rules, which had made joinder not realistically feasible, and essentially changed putative class action claims from an "opt in" to "opt out" procedure.

In the 1970s and 1980s, securities cases occasionally clarified the breadth of the new Rule 23. *Coopers & Lybrand* held that the denial of class certification did not amount to a final decision, and thus was not appealable as of right.[9] The same year, the Supreme Court held in the *Oppenheimer* case that, as a general rule, plaintiffs bear all notification costs during the certification process.[10] A 1974 Court ruling required that individual class members be notified by the plaintiff in almost all cases, seemingly contravening the spirit of the broadened notice provision.[11] The costs of such notices thus weighed heavily in subsequent triage decisions.

---

8. After the change, putative class actions would have to prove 1) numerosity (i.e., joinder of all class members is "impracticable"), 2) common questions of law or fact, 3) representative claims/defenses typical of all class members, and 4) that the representative parties would "fairly and adequately protect the interests of the class." Fed. R. Civ. P. 23(a).

9. *Coopers & Lybrand v. Livesay*, 437 U.S. 463 (1978).

10. *Oppenheimer Fund, Inc. v. Sanders*, 437 U.S. 340 (1978).

11. *Eisen v. Carlisle & Jacquelin*, 417 U.S. 156, 179 (1974). The plaintiffs, obligated to notify class members at a cost of approximately $225,000, sought to shift this burden to the defendants. The Court ruled as follows: "In the absence of any support under Rule 23, petitioner's effort to impose the cost of notice on respondents must fail. The usual rule is that a plaintiff must initially bear the cost of notice to the class. The exceptions cited by the District Court related to situations where a fiduciary duty preexisted between the plaintiff and defendant, as in a shareholder derivative suit. Where, as here, the relationship between

However, securities class action lawyers had already solved the costs/problems of mass notice. And such firms succeeded in proving their utility on many occasions.

Advances in Securities Class Actions

In addition to a class action procedural victory in *Blackie v. Barrack* (which, in 1975, reduced individual investor reliance to proof of "fraud on the market"), securities class actions have strikingly pushed the envelope on insider trading cases on numerous occasions, some of which are charted below:

Class Actions That Pushed the Envelope

Case and Year	Allegation(s)	Takeaway
Affiliated Ute Citizens of Utah v. the United States[a]	Government agents misled tribal representatives on the value of their stock.	Damages set at what they would have received had there been no fraud, or, alternatively, true loss.
Diamond v. Oreamuno	Insider trading by Directors was a breach of fiduciary duty under state common law.	The corporation has an action against insider traders.
Shapiro v. Merrill Lynch	Investment banking house brokers shared inside information on mergers.	By countering *Moss v. Morgan Stanley*, *Shapiro* recognized "misappropriation," over a decade before *O'Hagan*.
Enron[b]	Public company officials faulted for selling stock pre-bankruptcy filing.	Awareness of impending bankruptcy deemed inside information.
Rosen v. Stewart[c]	CEO benefitted from misleading public statements to shareholders re her innocence.	Whereas the claim of manipulation was dismissed at criminal trial, the same claim was rewarded in class action.
Valeant Pharmaceutical[d]	Hedge fund knew of lucrative ultimate plans to reorganize the subject company.	Hedge fund benefitting from sale of company stock to 3rd party liable to company shareholders who sold.

[a] 406 U.S. 128 (1972).

[b] *Mark Newby, et al. v. Enron Corporation*, #01-CV-3624 (S.D. Tex. Oct. 2001).

[c] *Howard Rosen, et al. v. Martha Stewart, et al.* (S.D.N.Y. 2002), complaint *available at* http://securities.stanford.edu/filings-documents/1025/MSO02-01/20020820_f01c_Rosen.pdf.

[d] *Anthony Basile v. Valeant Pharmaceutical*, #14-CV-02004 (C.D. Cal. December 2014).

---

the parties is truly adversary, the plaintiff must pay for the cost of notice as part of the ordinary burden of financing his own suit."

Yet, despite such advances and the largesse of amended Rule 23, by 1988 *The New York Times* had declared the class action moribund — until Congress codified the "fraud on the market" in that year.

"Fraud on The Market" and Section 20A

The New York case of *Diamond v. Oreamuno* (discussed in Chapter III) found a derivative action premised upon insider trading in 1969. Four years later, a federal court created an additional venue for such class actions in *Shapiro v. Merrill Lynch*. But the watershed year for insider trading class actions arrived in 1988, when Congress — although again refusing to define the crime — meticulously outlined a new private claim possessing multiple but definitive parts.

First, the 20A cause of action[12] could be brought against "any person" for a violation of any '34 Act provision or any SEC Rule. Such nondescript violation when combined with a defendant's purchase/sale "while in possession of material, nonpublic information" created liability in favor of all investors who "contemporaneously"[13] purchased/sold.

Second, the limitation on such liability could not exceed the profit gained or loss avoided "in the transaction or transactions that [were] the subject of the violation."

Third, recovery was to be limited by disgorgements pursuant to court order sought by the Commission.

Separate subdivisions of Section 20A precluded respondeat superior liability for employers and created a five-year statute of limitations. Curiously, in establishing joint and several liability for all defendants, the Section seems to outlaw the mere communication of material, non-public information. However, such a reading may be overly optimistic, as the defendant still must violate another "provision of this title" (e.g., Section 10(b) of the '34 Act) or the rules and regulations thereunder (e.g., Rule 10b-5).

Finally, Section 20A expressly did not limit recovery under other insider trading causes of action, statutory or otherwise. Likewise, the DOJ and SEC were not limited in any attempts to secure penalties.[14]

In practice, the Section 20A claim is pleaded much like its predecessor, the Rule 10b-5 claim, as is evidenced by the 2013 example below:

---

12. Section 20A is reprinted in its entirety in the Appendices to the Book.

13. "Contemporaneously" under Section 20A is indefinite but generally limited to transactions (e.g., a buy and a sell) within a few days of each other.

14. 15 U.S.C. § 78t-1 (2016).

119. By virtue of the foregoing, Defendants, in connection with the purchase or sale of securities, by the use of the means or instrumentalities of interstate commerce, or of the mails, or a facility of a national securities exchange, directly or indirectly: (a) employed devices, schemes, or artifices to defraud; (b) made untrue statements of material fact or omitted to state material facts necessary in order to make the statements made in the light of the circumstances under which they were made, not misleading; or (c) engaged in acts, practices or courses of business which operated or would have operated as a fraud or deceit upon persons.

120. Defendants thereby violated Section 10(b) of the Exchange Act and SEC Rule 10b-5.

121. Plaintiffs contemporaneously purchased and/or sold securities of the same class as those sold and/or purchased by the Defendants.

122. By virtue of the foregoing. Defendants are jointly and severally liable to Plaintiff and the Class for the SAC Insider Sales pursuant to Section 20A of the Exchange Act (*all statutory and Rule cites omitted*).[15]

The PSLRA of 1995 targeted law firms lodging securities class actions, but the 20A claim had a seven-year head start. The law firms that survived the PSLRA attack had become specialized at the practice (as well as the Rule 10b-5 claim), and the number of class actions filed under the Acts never really faced fear of demise. Nearly 30 years of data on the Section 20A insider trading claim has revealed some worthy settlements. The debate on the utility of such awards (and the awards of securities class actions in general) continues to thrive.

Notably, like the majority of securities class actions, over 90% of insider trading class actions settle before trial. Such resolution furthers deterrence hinders transparency: Onlookers know not who specifically was to blame, or exactly what went wrong. Unlike the general class actions, the Section 20A claim appears to primarily be used as an "add on" claim (i.e., a safety claim to back up the Rule 10b-5 cause of action). This role is opportuned by the provision expressly authorizing joint and several liability among defendants.

Opponents of the mechanisms note that, for both types of class actions (i.e., Rule 10b-5 suits and Section 20A suits), existing shareholders indirectly bear the cost of settlement. While such cost is sometimes borne by insurance, its

---

15. Complaint, *Birmingham Retirement Relief System v. S.A.C. Capital Advisors LLC* (S.D.N.Y. April 2013), *available at* http://securities.stanford.edu/filings-documents/1049/ELN00_02/2013412_o01c_13CV02459.pdf.

threat is significant enough to have inspired several SEC Commissioners in recent years to warn against court approval of sizeable awards.

Payouts

As is the case with securities class actions in general, the monies returned to investors is depleted by legal fees. An organization providing yearly statistics on securities class actions tracks settlement value as a percentage of alleged losses between 1 and 20%. Further, this consultant organization lists attorney fees as between 10% and 30% recovery, although the trend has been decreasing over time.[16]

Countering questions of class member payout is the data showing that piggyback actions do succeed in scaring off insider trading by insiders. Stated otherwise, pointed class actions such as those authorized by Section 20A do seem to weigh in the mind of management. A 2016 study conducted by business/accounting professors concluded that, based upon a 13-year sample, insider trading class litigation has a discernible deterrent effect upon "opportunistic insider selling." The study, which focused on Rule 10b-5 as the vehicle for the class actions, elaborated that the empirical data suggested that the determined deterrent effect on opportunistic management buying/selling lasted for five years.[17]

The deterrent effect is made obvious by the sheer enormity of the recoveries. Oracle paid $100 million in 2005 to settle private claims of insider trading; SAC Capital Advisers similarly handed over $135 million in 2016. Apart from Rule 10b-5 awards, Section 20A recaptures are real and noteworthy. Some other more noticeable awards are detailed below:

- In *Kaplan v. S.A.C. Capital Advisors*, a second settlement of over $95 million was reached, 2 years after that firm's landmark settlement of $1.8 billion with the government.

- In *Hayes v. MagnaChip Semiconductor Corp.* (N.D. Cal. December 2016), a settlement of over $23 million was reached.

---

16. NERA Economic Consulting, *Recent Trends in Securities Class Action Litigation*, yearly reports *available at* http://www.nera.com/content/dam/nera/publications/2016/2015_Securities_Trends_Report_NERA.pdf *and* http://www.nera.com/content/dam/nera/publications/2017/PUB_2016_Securities_Year-End_Trends_Report_0117.pdf.

17. C.S. Agnes Cheng, Henry He Huang & Yinghua Li, *Does Shareholder Litigation Deter Insider Trading?*, 1 JOURNAL OF LAW, FINANCE, AND ACCOUNTING 275, 282, 303 (2016) ("After litigation, insiders are likely to revise their beliefs in the costs and benefits of their trading, thus changing their post-litigation trading behavior.").

- And in *In re Pfizer, Inc.* (S.D.N.Y. April 2016), the judge approved a $468 million settlement.

Further, in *In re Longtop Financial Technologies* (S.D.N.Y 2012), a jury trial premised on Section 20A found the company's CFO liable for damages; he later settled for $2.3 million. Additionally, the court entered a default judgment against the company and its CEO for over $880,000.

Thus, irrespective of whether it is used as a primary cause of action or as a frill appendaged thereto, the Section 20A claim is alive and kicking. And adding billions to the Prohibition's tally.

C. Other Forces, Great and Small: States, "SROs," Foreign Lawsuits

Other plaintiffs in interest, if not setting records for awards, are continually on the beat as regulatory police for the Prohibition. Some of the more noteworthy enforcers are described below.

- States have developed an interest in regulating insider trading. A California statute embodied in Section 25401 of the state Corporation Code mimics Rule 10b-5. In New York, State common law weighing breaches of fiduciary duty or misrepresentations can be interpreted broadly so as to permit a quasi-inside information claim.[18]

- Foreign plaintiffs have availed themselves of America's Rule 10b-5 under the "impact test," which upholds application of the securities laws when domestic investors could be harmed by foreign issues. Such lawsuits are sometimes inspired by the unquestioned jurisdiction of the SEC pursuant to the '34 Act's Section 30.[19] The rise of "foreign cubed" fraud suits (i.e., involving a foreign plaintiff,

---

18. *See, e.g., Wey v. New York Stock Exchange, Inc.*, 15 Misc. 3d 1127A (N.Y. Sup. Ct. April 10, 2007) (upholding certain claims by NYSE seat holder against former Exchange official alleged to have (falsely) denied the entity's plans to go public).

19. *See, e.g., Schoenbaum v. Firstbrook*, 405 F.2d 200 (2d Cir. 1968). That oft-cited decision for matters of extra-territorial application codified the "impact test" when it stated: We hold that the district court has subject matter jurisdiction over violations of the Securities Exchange Act although the transactions which are alleged to violate the Act take place outside the United States, at least when the transactions involve stock registered and listed on a national securities exchange, and are detrimental to the interests of American investors ...

a foreign defendant, and a foreign stock) led to the Supreme Court's express roadblock in 2010 when such claims attempt to rely upon Rule 10b-5.[20] Nonetheless, the seemingly bizarre usage of American law and courts by foreign nationals buying foreign stocks continues.

- Stock exchanges and FINRA (termed "Self-Regulatory Organizations," or "SROs" under the '34 Act) continue to investigate and punish insider trading, an offense for which financial intermediaries must be able to evidence dedicated detection procedures. The resulting fines for flawed systems are appreciable.[21]

However, the largest recoveries (and greatest fear of corporate America) remain securities class actions, which, ironically, are still often defined by what they are not. Stock exchange arbitrations simply preclude them. The 2005 Class Action Fairness Act[22] defines class actions as lawsuits with 100 or more plaintiffs; the 1998 Securities Litigation Uniform Standards Act[23] places the threshold for "covered class actions" at 50 plaintiffs. The SEC, although favoring cluster cases such as *Texas Gulf Sulphur* (13 defendants), often finds many parties settling and thus normally oversees relatively small litigations. The DOJ faces defendants with explicit criminal rights who can motion for severed trials.

The relevant facts are undeniable. Securities class actions are omnipresent and enduring. While an American Bar Association web site first lists ease for the defendant as the reason for the existence of class actions in general,[24] for securities defendants, the ease may not be so evident. A review of filings from the last two decades reveals an average of over 200 filings a year, peaking after periods of appreciable market decline, and with a great many integrating a Rule 10b-5 claim.[25]

---

20. *Morrison v. National Australia Bank Ltd.*, 561 U.S. 247 (2010).

21. *Disciplinary and Other FINRA Actions*, FINRA (June 2015), at 7 (noting a $200,000 fine for a firm's failure to adequately supervise procedures with the potential "to mask beneficial ownership and to be used as vehicles to engage in illegal activity, such as money laundering, insider trading and market manipulation"), *available at.* https://www.finra.org/sites/default/files/Disciplinary_Actions_June_2015.pdf.

22. 28 U.S.C. §§ 1332(d), 1453, and 1711–1715 (2016).

23. "SLUSA," Pub. L. 1050353, passed to further the goals of the PSLRA of 1995, was designed to close the "state loophole" when plaintiff firms rushed to file securities class actions in state courts.

24. Julie Cantor, *Class Actions 101: What Are These Lawsuits All About, Anyway?*, *available at* https://apps.americanbar.org/litigation/litigationnews/practice_areas/class-actions-law suits.html (*last visited* August 10, 2017).

25. *See* The Stanford Securities Class Action Clearinghouse, www.securities.stanford. edu/list-made.html, last visited March 14, 2017.

Overall, there has been an estimated $89 billion in securities class action settlements from cases filed in the Southern District of New York in the last 20 years.

The newest regulator of note is the Commodity Futures Trading Commission. Empowered by the Dodd Frank Act and reinforced each year thereafter by a budgetary increase that far surpassed that of the SEC on a percentage basis, the CFTC enhanced its own insider trading prohibition and used it in disciplining two parties in 2015.

In terms of purely advancing regulation, perhaps more impressive than any case noted in the above chart is a class action pending in the Second Circuit. In that 2014 filing, a leading class action firm targeted controversial "high frequency trading" by accusing the 14 largest broker dealers and certain securities exchanges with violating Rule 10b-5 and Section 20A and consequentially "diverting billions of dollars annually from buyers and sellers of securities to themselves."[26] In 2015, the SEC fined one of the exchanges for inaccurate order portrayal. In November 2016, upon court request, the SEC filed an Amicus Brief in support of the notions that the federal District Court has jurisdiction over such a lawsuit, and that absolute immunity does not extend to registered securities exchanges when such entities act beyond the interests of members.[27] Clearly, in this action, private litigation has beaten the SEC to the punch.

Some Takeaways

- Aided by Congressional wish for a mosaic, private securities litigation has flourished. Occasional efforts by Congress to rein in that power have succeeded foremost in prodding a form of super-Bar capable of both applying the extant law and expanding it.

- While Section 20A decreases liability by the amount of SEC award, there is no authority stating that DOJ recoveries in criminal trials similarly cap Section 20A liability; conversely, there is direct support within the statutory cause of actions allowing for dual government penalties (although some jousting could focus on whether *disgorge-*

---

26. Complaint, *City of Providence, Rhode Island v. BATS Global Markets, Inc., et al.* (April 18, 2014), *available at* https://www.rgrdlaw.com/media/cases/279_complaint.pdf at ¶ 2.

27. https://www.sec.gov/litigation/briefs/2016/providence-bats-global-markets-1116.pdf. The lawsuit was dismissed by the District Court and then reinstated by the Second Circuit in December 2017.

ments are limited to one plaintiff). Thus, a blossoming in DOJ cases also signifies a blossoming in class actions—and vice versa.

- The data proves that private class action litigation can sometimes precede SEC investigation, damnation, or Prohibition advancement. And the argument that securities class action litigation takes too long (e.g., up to four years between filing and settlement for 40% of all cases) had been diminished by the government's elongation of investigations and their resolution.

- An appreciable contribution has also been made by the States and the stock exchanges, which are not encumbered by pleading requirements set by the federal causes of action.

- A similar contribution may, again, come from invested judges. It was Supreme Court Justice Clark who both maximized recovery under Section 16(b) (in *Smolowe v. Delendo*) and affirmed the notion that provisions in the Acts imply private claims (*J.I. Case v. Borak*). Moreover, today's jurists routinely uphold the huge settlements touted by the press.

There is no simple answer as to why class action litigation thrives, or what measures best cabin it when the practice runs amok. More often than not, it has been Congress spurring the notion that private monetary recovery enhances deterrence, and the enormous settlements that result readily justify attempts by law firms at the art form. The careful reader will note that on the two occasions on which Congress created insider trading private actions (i.e., 1934 and 1988), the SEC was left out of the picture. Regardless of favored enforcer, the effect is clear: Insider trading class actions routinely produce awards numbering in the tens of millions. In a regulatory system that calls for cash penalties to terrorize tortfeasors, such mechanism continues to both generate tacit support and produce tangible returns.

Selected Bibliography

Lampf v. Gilbertson, 501 U.S. 350 (1991).

Douglas Martin, *The Rise and Fall of the Class-Action Lawsuit*, N.Y. TIMES (January 8, 1988) ("But some experts further suggest an area of possible growth is securities class actions, which have been running fairly steady for the last decade at about 100 cases a year.").

Benjamin Kaplan, *Continuing Work of the Civil Committee: 1966 Amendments of the Federal Rules of Civil Procedure*, 81 HARV. L. REV. 357 (1967).

DavisPolk Client Memorandum, *Supreme Court Declines to Apply Class Action Tolling and Upholds Dismissal of Individual Securities Cases Filed After Expiration of Statutes of Repose* (June 27, 2017).

Schoenbaum v. Firstbrook, 405 F.2d 200 (1968).

William Lerach & Al Meyerhoff, *Why Insiders Get Rich, and the Little Guy Loses*, L.A. TIMES (January 20, 2002), *available at* http://articles.latimes.com/2002/jan/20/opinion/op-meyerhofflerach (discussing insider sales at Cisco Systems, Sunbeam Corp., and Oracle Corp.).

Cornerstone Research, *Securities Class Action Filings/2017 Midyear Assessment*, *available at* https://www.cornerstone.com/Publications/Reports/Securities-Class-Action-Filings-2017-Midyear-Assessment.

Sherman L. Cohn, *The New Federal Rules of Civil Procedure*, 54 GEO. L.J. 1204 (1966).

Stewart found guilty, CNN.com (March 10, 2004), *available at* http://money.cnn.com/2004/03/05/news/companies/martha_verdict/.

C.S. Agnes Cheng et al., *Does Shareholder Litigation Deter Insider Trading?*, 1 JOURNAL OF LAW, FINANCE, AND ACCOUNTING 275 (2016).

Paul Vizcarrondo, Jr., Wachtel, Lipton, Rosen & Katz, *Liabilities Under the Federal Securities Laws*, (August 2013), *available at* http://www.wlrk.com/docs/OutlineofSecuritiesLawLiabilities2013.pdf.

Robert J. Anello & Richard F. Albert, *Revisiting Criminal Insider Trading Liability*, NEW YORK LAW JOURNAL (June 3, 2014).

Terzah Ewing, *Queen for Day: Martha Stewart Earns Initial Public Offering Crown*, WALL STREET JOURNAL (October 20, 1999), *available at* https://www.wsj.com/articles/SB940365459655529718. The article notes that Stewart's Living Omnimedia, Inc. came to market at almost twice the expected selling price.

PATRICK DILLON & CARL M. CANNON, CIRCLE OF GREED/THE SPECTACULAR RISE AND FALL OF THE LAWYER WHO BROUGHT CORPORATE AMERICA TO ITS KNEES (2010). The book details the victories and defeat of California trial attorney William Lerach.

J. Scott Colesanti, *The Private Securities Litigation Reform Act of 1995*, 26 SECURITIES REGULATION L.J. 139 (Summer 1998).

William S. Lerach, *The Private Securities Litigation Reform Act of 1995 — 27 Months Later: Securities Class Action Litigation Under the Private Securities Litigation Reform Act's Brave New World*, 76 WASH. UNIV. L. REV. 597 (January 1998), *available at* http://openscholarship.wustl.edu/cgi/viewcontent.cgi?article=1528&context=law_lawreview.

Chapter XI

The DOJ: Zealous (But Pointed) Crusader

Much has been written about the active criminalization of Wall Street practices in the 1980s. Takeover activity increased over 500% from the prior decade. Public suspicion of those illegally benefitting from "merger mania" peaked. The responsive, joint SEC/DOJ crusade into insider trading netted hundreds of millions of dollars in fines. When the hoopla subsided, some bold indictments were tossed, and the number of criminal Prohibition cases trended towards a more traditional tally.

Much has also been written about the outrage against Wall Street occasioned by the most recent financial crisis. The conventional wisdom pins dramatic upturns in criminal cases to the public's desire for accountability for the harrowing times of 2008. But, in fact, Congress had urged increased criminal regulation of insider trading as far back as 2006, while concurrently suggesting hedge funds as the focus.

Specifically, a series of hearings in the Fall of 2006 commenced after accusations by a discharged SEC employee that his requests for testimony of a hedge fund official were internally suppressed. The hearings commenced with one noted law professor testifying to both a surge in insider trading and a corresponding link to increased hedge fund activity. The link was emphasized by the professor's declaration that hedge funds were "the principal destabilizing force in corporate governance" at the time.[1]

---

1. Testimony of John C. Coffee, Jr., Hearing Before the Committee on the Judiciary United States Senate (Second Session), September 26, 2006, at 61–66. Interestingly, Professor Coffee also declared that not just investors but "all" people are victimized by insider trading, as the crime reduces economic growth (at 61).

The ensuing financial crisis triggered the pointed declaration from the Obama administration that Wall Street should pay. Armed with the backing of Congress and the White House, a United States Attorney in New York set out on an unprecedented crusade against alleged hedge fund insider traders. After seemingly countless convictions, fairness may have found an ally in two of the defendants caught in the maelstrom.

A. The People and Guidance behind the Acceleration

Gary Aquirre was an SEC investigator. He claimed that in 2005 he requested the testimony of a hedge fund official at Pequot, then the largest such fund in the world. Aquirre alleged that when he persisted for the deposition, he was fired for political reasons.[2] A subsequent Judiciary Committee hearing explored Aquirre's claims. As part of this inquiry, the SEC Director of the Division of Enforcement testified. Facing the specter of dereliction of duty, the Director advised the Committee that insider trading investigations into hedge funds are hindered by the large volume of trades, the corresponding multiple numbers of "prime" (i.e., trade executing) brokerages, and the regulatory tradition of organizing investigations by subject stock (as opposed to by individual trader). The Director also emphasized the Commission's long track record of working with the Department of Justice and state regulatory authorities.[3]

The SEC and DOJ escaped harsh rebuke, but the link was cemented, as noted in the statements of two Senators at the outset of a Committee hearing in December 2006:

> SENATOR SPECTER: ... We are dealing with communications between individuals where there appears to be inside information on a pending merger and some $11 million is gained by transactions related to that. And the matter is referred to the SEC, and nothing is done for 2 years ... where you have hedge funds with as dominant a role as they are playing in the economy, ... these are very, very important matters ...

---

2. Aquirre sued the SEC in 2007 for wrongful termination. The SEC ultimately settled Aquirre's wrongful termination claim for $750,000.

3. Testimony of Linda Chatman Thompson, Director Division of Enforcement U.S. Securities and Exchange Commission, Hearing Before the Committee on the Judiciary United States Senate (Second Session), December 5, 2006, at 1276–78.

SENATOR GRASSLEY: ... Now, today's hearing is the second by this Committee relating to penalties for criminal enforcement of illegal insider trading, and the third that has discussed the evolving role involving hedge funds ... I share Chairman Specter's concerns about the extent of insider trading and its impact on public confidence in the **fairness** and integrity of the stock market ...

Aquirre's suspicions were ultimately rewarded: Pequot and its CEO settled SEC insider trading allegations in 2010, agreeing to pay $18 million in disgorgement and an additional $10 million in penalties. The cause of hedge fund illegality had been located. If four decades of targeting insider trading had not eradicated the pernicious practice, at least its latest conduit had been identified.

Barack Obama, the nation's 44th President, had reserved a soft spot for the little guy in stock market disputes long before he ascended to the White House in January 2009.

A little known fact is that Obama, as a young attorney, argued to preserve a victory as plaintiff's counsel in a securities arbitration against a brokerage house.[4] He also served as a law professor for 12 years, a tenure described as follows: "[A]t a school where economic analysis was all the rage, he taught rights, race and gender."[5] As the junior Senator from Illinois, he garnered attention for his outspoken desire to give shareholders a greater voice in company affairs. His novel "say on pay" initiative urged public companies to allow minority shareholders to vote for a non-binding resolution. The resolution would encourage limits on CEO compensation packages.

In 2004, Obama delivered the keynote address at the Democratic National Convention. That stirring performance highlighted his own rise from working to ruling class, while downplaying the view among his fellow citizens of America as a success because of the "power of our military, or the size of our economy."

---

4. *Baravati v. Josephthal, Lyon & Ross*, 28 F.3d 704 (7th Cir. 1994). In that case, attorney Obama (along with co-counsel) successfully represented a stockbroker who claimed he had been defamed by his employer's required "U-5" termination notice to regulators. The stockbroker's arbitral award for damages was upheld by the federal appellate court on appeal.

5. http://www.nytimes.com/2008/07/30/us/politics/30law.html. The picture accompanying the article shows Professor Obama writing on a chalkboard that displays "CORPORATIONS" AND "BANKS" along with "RELATIONSHIPS BUILT ON SELF-INTEREST" (all caps in original).

As President, Obama traveled to New York City in April 2010 to support passage of the Dodd-Frank Act. During that speech, he literally wagged his finger at Wall Street chiefs in attendance who were thought to have over-speculated before the credit crisis of 2008.

Separately, within his first year as President, Barack Obama signed Executive Order 13519, titled "Establishment of the Financial Fraud Task Force."[6] That impressive committee was staffed by representatives from over 20 agencies, including the SEC, the FBI and the IRS. The Task Force's aim was to provide information to the Attorney General concerning criminal prosecution of financial crimes and violations including securities fraud, mail fraud and wire fraud. But Order 13519 was, in many ways, merely a formality—a champion Prosecutor was already in the making, and his targets had come ready made.

───────────

Preet Bharara immigrated to the United States from India as a child. A naturalized citizen, he rose to graduate Harvard University and Columbia Law School, and to later serve as chief legal counsel for the United States Senate Judiciary Committee. After years as a federal prosecutor, he became the United State Attorney for the Southern District of New York in August 2009.

When Bharara became U.S. Attorney, the target had already been set. Hedge fund defendants were easy prey: They were rich, arrogant, and, as subsequent trials showed, did quite often flout the letter of the law. Bharara thus commenced an impressive spree of criminal cases against them. At its peak, Bharara's Department of Justice web page detailed $500 million in settlements via the Civil Frauds Unit. The page also modestly disclosed convictions of "scores of insider trading defendants"—in fact, over 100 insider trading cases (many with sizeable criminal fines) were successfully prosecuted during his tenure (i.e., 2009–2016; hereinafter "the Period"). Defendants from across the country joined Second Circuit citizens in being sentenced by a small roster of New York judges. The focus of these cases was hedge funds and their employees, either as defendants or as consumers of inside information. All of the cases utilized Rule 10b-5. The most noteworthy convictions are detailed below:

───────────

6. *Available at* http://www.presidency.ucsb.edu/ws/?pid=86893.

Case	Background	Penalties
S.A.C. Capital Investors	$14 billion hedge fund accused of a "culture" of insider trading in 2012.	Settlement of $1.8 billion fine/disgorgement; closing of Fund; limitation on CEO's trading activities.
Raj Rajaratnam	Head of Galleon Group, a $7 billion hedge fund.	Convicted, sentenced to 11 years in prison; $155 million disgorgement and fine.
Winifred Jiau	Member of "expert network."	Convicted, sentenced to 4 years in prison (prosecutors asked for 10 years).
Zvi Goffer	Trader at Galleon hedge fund.	Convicted, sentenced to 10 years in prison.
Raj Gupta	Member of Goldman Sachs Board found guilty of tipping Rajaratnam.	Convicted, sentenced to 2 years in prison.
Todd Newman and Anthony Chiasson	Hedge fund analysts at S.A.C. found guilty as fourth generation tippees of inside information.	Sentenced to 6½ and 4½ years in prison in 2012; convictions overturned in 2014.
Arthur Cutillo	Former member of white collar law firm; accused of sharing information on mergers with Goffer of Galleon.	Convicted, sentenced to 30 months in prison (separately disbarred).

Sparing few, Bharara's office prosecuted lawyers, traders, CEOs, and analysts, as well as fellow Indian immigrants Gupta and Rajaratnam (the latter leading to the then longest criminal sentence for insider trading in American history[7]), and Rajaratnam's younger brother (acquitted in 2014). One defendant was brought back from overseas; another proceeded pro se. Attendant criminal fines for insider trading—regardless of separate SEC fines for the same offense—grew to be palpable and universal.[8]

Moreover, while the Southern District of New York routinely leads such statistics in insider trading cases, Bharara exponentially grew both the focus on and ramifications of the crime. Beyond the success of this famed U.S. Attorney, insider trading itself had become institutionalized—as a violation, as a cause

---

7. The record was surpassed in July 2013 with the Third Circuit's sentencing of lawyer Matthew Kluger, who was given a 12-year sentence for illegal insider trading activity spanning 17 years.

8. For example, Sam Waksal, Martha Stewart's "tipper," had received a fine of only $3 million in 2003.

of action, and as a moral wrong. On top of the focus on fairness, the notion of massive criminal fines as a form of general deterrence slowly but indelibly crept into both the Prohibition and the judicial psyche. Additionally, the monies traced to the insider trader's actions were part of the equation within the Federal Sentencing Guidelines, a standard that Bharara himself helped to make more harsh on Rule 10b-5 defendants.

Alas, the champion Prosecutor did not last to reap the benefit: He, along with 46 other United States Attorneys, were fired by the new President in March 2017. However, Bharara's record may never be surpassed. His Southern District of New York office won over 90 insider trading convictions between 2009 and 2016; by comparison, the *entire Department of Justice* (which oversees 93 U.S. Attorneys in 94 districts) obtained a total 88 convictions in insider trading cases between the fiscal years 2001 and 2006.[9]

B. Changes to the Law, Direct and Indirect

The DOJ actually was rarely within the thoughts of the 1933 and 1934 Congresses. The inclusion of criminal fines within an insider trading provision was rejected. Section 32 of the '34 Act—a short passage, the numbers of which get raised periodically—says simply that incarceration is possible; the length of that imprisonment was increased to 20 years in 2010. Internationally, European mimicry of the American criminalization of insider trading has varied: France first outlawed the crime in 1970, the European Union did not compel its members to outlaw the offense until 1989, and the United Kingdom imposed its first criminal sentence in 2009.

Nonetheless, Rule 10b-5 had been used successfully in criminal trials against fraudsters under the Acts for decades. With all those Period cases being brought in the Second Circuit, changes to the Rule's application were likely inevitable. In three distinct areas, criminal application of the Prohibition was altered dramatically between 2010 and 2017. These areas are discussed in proposed degree of increasing significance below.

---

9. "Illegal Insider Trading: How Widespread is the Problem and Is There Adequate Criminal Enforcement?", Hearing Before the Committee on the Judiciary United States Senate (second Session), September 26, 2006, at 11. For further comparison, Rudolph Giuliani—another active S.D.N.Y. U.S. Attorney—has been credited with bringing 48 insider trading cases between 1984 and 1986. CNN: "The Eighties" (Episode II) (2016) (last aired on November 24, 2017).

1. The Sentencing Guidelines:
At Worst Ignored, at Best, Disparate

The United States Sentencing Commission ("USSC") was created by Congress' Sentencing Reform Act of 1984. The law had been a response to glaringly disparate sentences for federal crimes such as tax evasion, as well as the need for appellate review thereof. The original USSC was staffed by three judges and four others. With little support and unpredictable acceptance, the agency met a deadline of crafting Federal Sentencing Guidelines within 18 months between 1985 and 1987. Along the way, over 10,000 cases from the period of 1984–1985 were reviewed and 13 public hearings (bringing forth over 200 witnesses) were held.

Those initial Guidelines went effective in 1988. Since then, over 1.7 million criminal defendants have been sentenced pursuant thereto; 100 thousand related appeals have been lodged. The Guidelines have also been amended by the continuing USSC (sometimes, at the direction of Congress). With over 800 amendments, the Guidelines are now over 600 pages long.[10]

In the main, the Guidelines wrest discretion from federal District Court judges by providing a range of sentences premised upon "Offense Levels" and the defendant's criminal history. At present, over 700 federal crimes and 43 offense levels are contemplated. Critics, perhaps predictably, include judges and defense counsel. Supporters include prosecutors and other judges. What is incontrovertible is that convicted insider traders have never fared well under the Guidelines: The calculation of profits group all monies reaped by various parties related to the subject information in order to meet a very modest threshold of $6,500, and a separate Guideline provision may be added where the defendant exhibited an "abuse of trust" (e.g., a bank manager or an attorney).

In 2005, the Supreme Court ruled that the Guidelines were only advisory, and not mandatory.[11] However, jurists continued to use them as a starting point for all sentencing determinations, and, with their detailed structure for analyzing the crime of insider trading, few manuals proved more useful.

In November 2012, the Guidelines were amended to provide a floor of 15 months incarceration for those convicted of insider trading by participating

---

10. Symposium, "30 Years Later: A Look Back at the Original Sentencing Guidelines," Hofstra University Maurice A. Deane School of Law (October 23, 2017)(remarks of Brent Newton, Deputy Staff Director, USSC).

11. *United States v. Booker*, 543 U.S. 220 (2005). The Booker Court held that, by using the guidelines to enhance sentences, judges were violating the defendant's Sixth Amendment right to have a jury determine all relevant facts. Accordingly, the Guidelines were demoted in status from mandatory to advisory.

in an "organized scheme." This notion of *conspiratorial* insider trading added eight discretionary factors to aid judges in determining whether a group effort was manifested.[12] The factors range from the vague (e.g., "the duration of the offense") to the self-explanatory ("the dollar value of the transactions"). Ironically, the factor weighing "number of scheme participants" adds the instruction that "such a scheme may exist even in the absence of more than one participant." If such an organized scheme is established, the offense level is automatically raised to 14. The change in level, as described within the Guidelines as required by the Dodd-Frank Act, was designed to distinguish calculated or systemic efforts at the crime from "fortuitous or opportunistic instances of insider trading."[13]

A note within the Commentary to the relevant provision explained the nearly limitless damage calculation:

> Background: This guideline applies to certain violations of Rule 10b-5 that are commonly referred to as "insider trading." Insider trading is treated essentially as sophisticated fraud. Because the victims and their losses are difficult if not impossible to identify, the gain, i.e., the total increase in value realized through trading in securities by the defendant and persons acting in concert with the defendant or to whom the defendant provided inside information, is employed instead of the victims' losses.[14]

A study of insider trading sentences for the period of 2008 through 2013 (even disregarding cases overturned on appeal) disclosed an average sentence of 17 months, almost 32% higher than in the prior five-year period.[15] Anecdotally, practitioners note that Ivan Boesky, the "king of insider trading" from a prior generation, received a three-year prison sentence in 1987.

---

12. The specific list of factors is as follows: 1) number of transactions, 2) their dollar value, 3) number of securities involved, 4) duration of the offense, 5) number of scheme participants, 6) efforts to obtain material, nonpublic information, 7) number of times such information was obtained, and 8) efforts at concealing the offense. United States Sentencing Commission Guidelines Manual §2B1.4—Commentary 1.

13. United States Sentencing Commission Guidelines Manual 2016, Supplement to Appendix C, at 1–3 (discussing Amendment 761, which modified §2B1.4).

14. 2015 Federal Sentencing Guidelines Manual, Commentary to §2B1.14. Interestingly, Section 3571 of the U.S. Code ("Sentence of fine") generically limits fines for felonies to either $250,000; twice the defendant's cash; or twice the victim's loss. 18 U.S.C. §3571 b, d.

15. Nate Raymond, *Insider traders in U.S. face longer prison terms*, REUTERS (September 2, 2014), *available at* www.reuters.com/article/us-insidertrading-prison-insight-idUSKBN0 GX0A820140902.

During the Period, lengthy incarceration became its own mission, a development Judge Rakoff publicly called "irrational."[16] At a March 2013 conference of prosecutors and white collar defense attorneys, Judge Rakoff stated, "My modest proposal is that [the Guidelines] be scrapped in their entirety and replaced with a non-arithmetic multi-factor test."[17] As the senior judge has also publicly commented, "[T]he arithmetic behind the sentencing calculations is all hocus-pocus—it's nonsensical, and I mean that sincerely. It gives the illusion of something meaningful with no real value underneath."[18] Consequently, Judge Rakoff has been quoted on several occasions outright imposing sentences under those called for by the Guidelines.

Such temperance has proven to be the exception, and not the norm. And the government numbers on underlying trades and profits offered by the Prosecution have arguably been adopted without serious question by the Bench.

2. Varying "Scienter" for Purposes of Sections 10(b) and 32

During Bharara's string of victories, Rule 10b-5 was cited in all three of its subdivisions (i.e., device/scheme, misleading statements, and fraud/deceit). Any distinction between this trio of applications was relegated to historical footnote. Additionally, '33 Act Section 17(a) was often quietly added to indictments.

Scienter and knowledge, when distinguishable in court rulings, were generally intertwined and lowered. Section 32 permits a defense to incarceration where the defendant has "no knowledge" of an SEC Rule or Regulation. Traditionally, Section 32 knowledge was interpreted as the doing of a

---

16. *Id.* The same article noted that fellow SDNY District Judge Richard Sullivan, who sentenced several of the defendants prosecuted by Bharara, had stated, "I think anyone who engages in this kind of conduct for the amounts of money that are involved here has to be on notice that they're going to be looking at a lengthy jail term."

In an earlier Period case, Judge Sullivan had been much more pointed. In sentencing Zvi Goffer, a convicted "ringleader" of professionals trading on tips of pending takeovers, the S.D.N.Y. judge stated "Insider trading is very, very hard to detect and because of that has to be dealt with harshly." Judge Sullivan also denied Goffer's plea for leniency by noting that Goffer had chosen to go to trial, stating to the defendant, "You gambled and you lost." Goffer received a 10-year sentence and was ordered to pay $10 million in forfeiture. Basil Katz, "Goffer sentenced to 10 years for insider trading," Reuters (September 21, 2011).

17. Peter Lattman, *For White-Collar Defense Bar, It's Happening in Vegas,* N.Y. TIMES (March 7, 2013).

18. Leah McGrath Goodman, *Nonsensical Sentences for White Collar Criminals,* NEWSWEEK (June 26, 2014).

wrongful act,[19] or the intention to commit the act prohibited.[20] The Second Circuit later ruled that the intent to deceive is sufficient.[21] More recently, the *O'Hagan* case referenced a generic "evil mind."[22] The government, while arguing the 2016 *Salman* case before the Supreme Court, repeatedly stated that recklessness and conscious avoidance did not qualify as scienter in criminal applications of Rule 10b-5.

The cases from the Period have dignified coded language, boasts, and other trappings of audio recordings somehow hinting at nefarious behavior. For example, a defendant in the Galleon case alleged to have extracted inside information from a source was heard on tape saying, "I played him like a finely tuned piano."[23] The same individual was said to have been coached to avoid SEC detection by the instruction "to play around a position." Accordingly, it would seem that the Prohibition, rather than demanding a particularized form of intent, is now satisfied by a displaying of the defendant's willingness to profit at the expense of the law.

Separately, cases from recent years have weighed heavily a defendant's computer searches for ways to escape SEC scrutiny, or recklessness in not appreciating the source of tipped information. Meanwhile, the prosecution in *Newman* (discussed in the next section) alleged that the two defendants "must have known" the source of the inside information. A September 2017 SEC Complaint alleged "deceptive intent" evidenced by trading in family-titled accounts.[23] Overall, the scienter standard—if possible to distinguish its purpose as satisfying Section 10(b) or Section 32—has been completely divorced from statutory requirements. The standard has proven to be open-ended, and appears to disfavor sophisticated or industry professional defendants.

3. Disrupted Precedent: The *Newman* Setback to the Prohibition

Todd Newman was a portfolio analyst at a hedge fund. Anthony Chiasson was a portfolio manager at a separate hedge fund. The defendants, who were

---

19. *United States v. Peltz*, 433 F.2d 48 (2d Cir. 1970).

20. *United States v. Schultz*, 464 F.2d 499 (2d Cir. 1972).

21. *United States v. Dixon*, 536 F.2d 1388 (2d Cir. 1976).

22. *O'Hagan*, 521 U.S. at 665–66.

23. The defendant, Danielle Chiesi, later consented to a plea imposing a 30-month sentence.

23. SEC v. Peter C. Chang (N.D. Calif. 2017), at ¶ 62.

alleged to have been part of a group of professionals sharing inside information, were said to have collectively earned over $72 million for their respective funds. The two men were named together in an indictment unsealed in January 2012 and prosecuted together as tippees as defined by *Dirks* for violations of Rules 10b-5 and 10b5-2; further, each was charged with conspiracy to commit securities fraud.

The case proceeded on a theory of illegality stemming from *Dirks*. However, the matter was much unlike the famed 1983 holding in that the tip flowed through several layers of players. The tipping chain most at issue—originating with an employee of a finance unit within a public company called NVIDIA—is diagramed below:

Chris Choi (insider; NVIDIA)

  → **Hyung Lim (outsider, unrelated company)**

     → **Danny Kuo (outside analyst)**

       → **Messrs. Tortora & Anoukakis (outside analysts)**

         → **Messrs. Newman & Chiasson (outside analyst/ port. manager)**

A similar tipping chain, commencing with Rob Ray, an employee within the investor relations department at Dell Computer, also ended with Newman and Chiasson, three steps from the source of the insider information.

At trial, the government proceeded on the theory that Newman and Chiasson, as sophisticated industry personnel, must have known the source was an insider subject to a duty. The defendants moved for a jury instruction that the defendants could only be convicted if there were a benefit to the tipper and the defendants knew of the benefit; the court, applying well-established Second Circuit law, found the instruction on knowledge of the benefit unnecessary. Newman and Chiasson were convicted, and the two defendants were sentenced to 4½ years and 6½ years, respectively. Further, fines and disgorgement totaling over $8.7 million were imposed.[24]

On appeal, the Second Circuit reversed, adding a new requirement to the *Dirks* test in the process. Specifically, the court agreed with the proposed trial jury instruction that the defendants needed to know of the tipper's benefit, stating

---

24. *United States v. Newman*, 773 F.3d 438, 444–45 (2d Cir. 2014).

that the requirement "follows naturally from *Dirks*." Further, the court found a lack of evidence establishing scienter where a tippee was shown only to be a friend or acquaintance, or where only a gift or reputational benefit could be shown. In these regards, the court—while continuing to dignify the *Dirks* test—held that the government needs to simultaneously prove "a meaningfully close personal relationship that generates an exchange that is objective, consequential, and represents at least a potential gain of a pecuniary or similarly valuable nature."[25]

Perhaps the appellate court was reacting to Bharara's concentration on insider trading. Maybe the court had recognized the irrational open-endedness of the Circuit's non-factor of "benefit" for over 30 years, a requirement so loose that it had been deemed satisfied (even in criminal cases) by a romantic relationship. Or perhaps the business Circuit was tacitly suggesting that the Prohibition recall its initial focus on *non-public* information—surely, as information travels through four generations of tippees, time passes and news becomes repeated by many. Regardless of the express motive, the *Newman* decision resounded throughout the Circuits and immediately rang as a citation in legal briefs. Some of the notable language from the decision is repeated below:

- "We have defined willfulness in this [Rule 10b-5 scienter] context 'as a realization on the defendant's part that he was doing a wrongful act under the securities laws.'"
- "Because the Government failed to demonstrate that Newman and Chiasson had the intent to commit insider trading, it cannot sustain the convictions on either the substantive insider trading counts or the conspiracy count."
- "Although the government might like the law to be different, nothing in the law requires a symmetry of information in the nation's securities markets."

The effect of the *Newman* reversal was immediate and real. In excess of a dozen criminal cases were overturned or at least re-thought.[26] As late as three years after the Second Circuit decision, a related case was reheard.[27] Further,

---

25. 773 F.3d at 452.

26. *See, e.g., United States v. Conradt*, 2017 U.S. App. LEXIS 16065 (2d Cir. August 23, 2017); *United States v. Martoma*, 2017 U.S. App. LEXIS 16084 (2d Cir. August 23, 2017). Martoma's case was subject to a re-hearing in 2017. His conviction was upheld. See below.

27. *Martoma*, 2017 U.S. App. LEXIS 16084. Martoma, a portfolio manager at S.A.C. Capital Advisors, had been convicted in 2014 and sentenced to nine years in prison. In August 2017, a Second Circuit Panel upheld his conviction and sentence in reversing the 2015 *Newman* decision issued by the same Circuit. The majority opinion cited the Supreme Court decision in *Salman*, holding:

in 2015, an SEC administrative law judge dismissed a Complaint brought by the SEC Division of Enforcement on the grounds that no benefit could be shown for the tipper. That decision was upheld by another level of the Commission in July 2017.[28]

The *Salman* Case

The DOJ had asked the Supreme Court for review of *Newman* on the ground that the *Dirks* benefit had been altered; the Court denied the DOJ's petition. However, two years after *Newman*, the Court granted cert to a Ninth Circuit case involving a conviction based upon tips between family members. In that case, *United States v. Salman,* the defendant obtained information from a brother-in-law that earned him over $1.5 million.[29]

The brother-in-law received the tips from his younger brother, who, as an employee in Citigroup's healthcare investment banking department, was well situated to advise on mergers and acquisitions involving the company's clients. Salman did not pay or otherwise recompense his brother-in-law for the inside information. A jury found Salman guilty of one count of conspiracy and four counts of insider trading under Rules 10b-5 and 10b5-2. Salman was sentenced to three years imprisonment and ordered to pay $730,000 in restitution.

On appeal, the Ninth Circuit affirmed Salman's convictions, holding that a tip to a "trading relative" serves as a benefit under the *Dirks* test.[30] The issue on appeal to the Supreme Court was thus framed as whether an intangible gift of inside information to a family member could support the conviction of a tippee.

Whether the recipient of the [tip] gift is an existing friend or a potential future friend whom a gift is intended to entice, the logic—that a tipper benefits by giving inside information in lieu of a cash gift—operates in a similar manner.

The dissenting judge wrote an impassioned opinion decrying the new ability in the Circuit for prosecutors to "seize on this vagueness and subjectivity" in punishing "the absentminded [defendant] in addition to persons with corrupt intentions." The dissent also took issue with a prior Circuit opinion being reversed without the benefit of an en banc hearing. See also Chapter VIII.

28. *SEC v. Ruggieri* (2017). *See S.E.C. Upholds Dismissal of Wells Fargo Insider Trading Case,* N.Y. Times (July 16, 2017). The two sitting Commissioners split on the decision, thereby affirming the prior dismissal by the SEC administrative law judge.

29. *Salman v. United States,* 137 S. Ct. 420, 424 (2016). *See supra* Chapter VIII for an introduction to the case.

30. Honorable Jed Rakoff of the Second Circuit sat by designation on the Ninth Circuit case and authored the unanimous panel opinion. *United States v. Salman,* 792 F.3d 1087 (9th Cir. 2015).

The Oral Argument

The *Salman* argument before the Supreme Court provided a benefit to all observers of Prohibition law. The debate summarized extant law, exhibited roads not taken, and reminded listeners of compelling policy arguments. In the end, the common law moved only infinitesimally, but the Prohibition was viewed as somehow getting stronger.

Counsel for Salman commenced by concentrating on the lack of a statutory definition of insider trading. The vagueness problem, it was urged, "should limit this crime to its core" (i.e., cover only the insider or the tipper who is benefitted). Justice Ginsburg interrupted to ask how the strict requirement of a tangible benefit would assist regulation, for the insider could simply avoid detection by making the trade himself and then gifting someone the resulting profit. Counsel responded that Salman's brother-in-law had neither traded nor received a benefit; still, the Bench seemed wedded to the idea that helping a family member was tantamount to a "benefit" to any defendant.

Counsel for Salman also argued that the gift language in *Dirks* was merely dictum, while mentioning that other countries have insider trading laws with definitions. When pressed for a concrete rule, counsel offered that the benefit need not be cash but it did need to be "tangible."

The government position was argued by Solicitor Dreeben, who had successfully argued the *O'Hagan* case nearly 20 years earlier. Dreeben asserted that a "pecuniary gain" rule similar to the one offered by Salman would soon result in insider trading through family and close friends. The government then offered a test that would find benefit in any tip not serving "a corporate purpose." Several members of the Bench queried whether such a rule could handle a hypothetical involving a gratuitous tip to a stranger; Dreeben responded that the closest the government had come to bringing such a case was in matters in which a benefit was surmised from the existence of a friendship of sorts.

The experienced oralist was clear on the other safeguards against government overreaching: Knowledge must be proven in all criminal cases, stating that "[c]onscious avoidance is not enough" and recklessness is not enough. Ultimately, the Bench inquired if, since "most of these cases involve relatives and friends," a rule could be fashioned to define a benefit between such parties. Dreeben responded, "I'm fine with that," thus preserving the government's victory.

The Written Decision in *Salman*

In an 8–0 decision, the High Court readily disposed of Salman's proffered bright line test argument that the status quo was unconstitutionally vague, and all other arguments. The Court ruled that *Dirks'* definition of benefit remained intact and "easily" disposed of the appeal. In a provocatively narrow decision, the Court confined its holding to issuing a reiteration of *Dirks* that a gift will serve as a presumed benefit when the tipper is a relative. The Second Circuit decision in *Newman* was declared wrong insofar as that decision interpreted the *Dirks* test to exclude gifts as benefits. However, the ongoing relationship language of the Second Circuit's decision was not addressed. Consequentially, the holding (and import) of *Salman* for the time being was simply that a gift of inside information to a relative satisfies the *Dirks* benefit test.

Accordingly, as a direct result of the volume and reach of insider trading cases brought during the Period, the benefit portion of the *Dirks* test went from being a no-brainer to an obstacle for investigators and enforcement attorneys alike. No longer could the Commission presume that judges and juries would lump tipper with tippee; no longer could DOJ attorneys assume that an audio recording cryptically establishing a chain of information satisfied the law. Even when the 2017 *Martoma* case seemingly corrected *Newman*, one Circuit judge was compelled to reason the opposing view. The extensive reach of Preet Bharara had actually succeeded in raising the standard of proof faced by the SEC and DOJ. This higher bar in certain cases was but one ramification of the Period and its sweeping indictment of hedge fund personnel and their colleagues.

C. The Aftermath of Intense Criminalization

In late 1989, a federal judge attended a legal conference in lower Manhattan meant to examine and laud the government's victory in Princeton/Newport,[31] a securities fraud trial. The case had received much press because the United States Attorney for the Southern District had utilized the RICO statute to freeze the defendant's funds. The guest judge surprised the crowded room by looking at prosecutors and advising them to "cool their jets," as he had grown tired of secretaries and spouses and laymen sitting in his witness box each day to testify in insider trading cases. That period of criminal prosecution of the undefined crime was mild compared to the most

---

31. The Princeton/Newport trial of August 1989 centered on a business partnership that had worked with Drexel Bernham Lambert, a firm at the epicenter of the "junk bond" scandal of the 1980s. The sham transactions at issue took place in 1984 and 1985. A jury convicted six defendants of all but one of 64 counts.

recent crusade; correspondingly, the Period cases already exhibited some lasting effects. Four of them are discussed below.

1. Criminal Investigative Techniques/ Independent Investigation by DOJ

That same Princeton/Newport case referenced above had highlighted an audiotaped admission by one defendant, "Welcome to the world of sleaze." However, co-conspirators wearing wires came a distant second to the use of widespread authorized wiretaps since 2010, a tactic that has been said to have been employed by Bharara's offices to intercept over 2,000 phone calls to/from one target alone. The use of wiretaps, while ostensibly communicating a seriousness of purpose, invites a high degree of scrutiny of investigation. The tool, aimed most often at narcotics defendants, is approved upon request for authorization over 99% of the time. These arguably rubber-stamped applications are normally limited to a 30-day duration. The use of wiretaps has steadfastly increased; in turn, the targeted communication devices are now predominantly portable phones.[32] Perhaps most significantly, the expensive means of surveillance is always evaluated in terms of ultimate conviction (i.e., the decision to employ a wiretap concomitantly ratchets up the pressure to find a law was broken).

Bharara—who inherited some of the investigations he prosecuted, and thus was not responsible for all of their wiretaps—was characteristically unapologetic about his office's use of the investigative technology, as he told PBS in January 2014:

> It's important for a lot of reasons, not the least of which is that you can prove your case a little bit more easily depending on what you have on a wiretap. But also it sends an important deterrent message. It tells people that in an age when some people may have thought that they could be very casual about engaging in insider trading activity, that maybe the government is listening.[33]

Insider trading cases are notoriously plagued by their dependence upon circumstantial evidence, which is aided greatly by the indisputable, recorded concessions of egotistic characters. The press was quick to note the shift of insider

---

32. www.uscourts.gov/statistics-reports/analysis-reports/wiretap-reports.

33. Jason M. Breslow, *Preet Bharara: Insider Trading is "Rampant" on Wall Street*, Frontline (January 2014), *available at* http://www.pbs.org/wgbh/frontline/article/preet-bharara-insider-trading-is-rampant-on-wall-street/.

detection to criminal technique.[34] The cases against the Galleon Management hedge fund were particularly noteworthy. Interestingly, the SEC's first use of wiretap evidence—specifically approved by a judge—was in actuality a fluke: Hedge fund chief Raj Rajaratnam, defending parallel proceedings, had been provided transcripts in criminal discovery that his lawyers were obliged to turn over to SEC attorneys as part of civil discovery; the judge ruling on their admissibility noted that their content had already, in part, been made public by the U.S. Attorney's office.[35]

Apart from the use of wiretaps, criminal prosecutors "flipped" co-conspirators and adjusted sentencing recommendations for cooperating witnesses. Regardless of the propriety of the use of such criminal law tactics for a regulation entrusted to enforcement by an agency, the dependence upon oversight by prosecutors is unpredictable. Indeed, even more glaring than the tactics used by Preet Bharara and his 200 attorneys may be the DOJ's emergence as an independent securities regulator. Traditionally, the DOJ brought to trial cases developed by the SEC. As recently as the year 2000, "signal" cases were brought mutually.[36] In the Martha Stewart matter, the DOJ rejected the SEC's claim of insider trading and brought its own spate of charges (including obstruction of justice, of which Stewart was convicted). By 2012, the DOJ was largely investigating and prosecuting cases on its own: A web page from August of that year ("Insider Trading, Proactive Enforcement Paying Off") advertised fruitful FBI investigations of hedge fund personnel, an attorney, and a corporate executive.[37]

The internalizing of Prohibition policy by a prosecutorial office is a questionable undertaking at best. Simply put, the U.S. Attorney after Preet Bharara may not feel as strongly about committing resources to policing the stock market. Further, the criminalization of the Prohibition inevitably triggers new delays and scrutiny (both judicial and Congressional) normally attending Constitutional

34. *See, e.g., SEC v. Ginsburg*, 362 F.3d 1292, 1301 (11th Cir. 2004) (basing tips of inside information on phone records linking tipper to his brother and father, and to trades soon thereafter).

35. *SEC v. Galleon Management, LP*, 683 F. Supp. 2d 316, 317 (S.D.N.Y. 2010) (noting that the subject wiretaps had "already [been] partially disclosed publicly").

36. SEC Press Release 2000-33, *SEC and US Attorney Bring Charges Against 19 Individuals, Including Wall Street Professionals, for $8 Million Insider Trading Scheme* (March 14, 2000). The two cases were filed against the same defendants, and signaled the application of Rule 10b-5 to the communication of inside information via the Internet.

37. www.fbi.gov/news/stroies/august/insider-trading-enforcement-paying-off.html, last visited July 8, 2017.

skirmishes, battlegrounds that the SEC Division of Enforcement has happily avoided for so many years.[38]

2. Invitation to Congress

The *Newman* decision unpredictably heightened SEC pleading requirements (albeit temporarily) and thus was viewed by the press as weakening the Prohibition. Consequently, no less than three Bills were introduced in the 114th Congress to outlaw tipping without tangible benefit. These Bills, which were pending at the end of 2016, are summarized below:

- H.R. 1173 would impose liability upon anyone intentionally disclosing inside information in the absence of a "legitimate business purpose." Interestingly, the Bill specifically evaluated scienter in view of the defendant's job, assets under management, and financial sophistication.
- H.R. 1625 targeted, among others, those recklessly spreading material non-public information.
- And S.702 would prohibit both trading on material information known to be non-public and knowing/reckless dissemination of the same where subsequent trading is foreseeable.[39]

Moreover, Congressional revisitation of Prohibition subtleties appear unproductive in light of the duplication of efforts: Existing provisions within the '34 Act already serve to bar individuals from industry employment who have been convicted of felony fraud involving the "purchase or sale of any security" (i.e., barred from employment per the "statutory disqualification" rules found in Sections 3(a) and 15).

3. Penalties Unrelated to Wrongdoing

On a larger scale, both SEC and DOJ fines—generously tied to downstream profits—have become largely fictitious when viewed against the defendant's actual gain. During the Period, fines were levied by both the SEC and the DOJ

---

38. In March 2016, a judge refused to dismiss a civil lawsuit by hedge fund David Ganek against Preet Bharara and others alleging that a search warrant and accompanying publicity served to end a $4 billion fund called Level Global Investors LP. In March 2017, the Second Circuit heard arguments on the case, *Ganek v. Leibowitz et al.*, No. 161463 (2d Cir. 2017). In October 2017, the District Court decision was overturned, and the suit against Bharara and his aides was dismissed.

39. Michael V. Seitzinger, *Federal Securities Law: Insider Trading*, Congressional Research Service (March 1, 2016), at 13.

at a torrid pace. Sometimes, the same defendant paid twice or three times—
and no "foul" was ever called. For example, Raj Rajaratnam, who received the
longest insider trading criminal sentence ever in 2012, ultimately paid over
$155 million for wrongful trades amounting to a little over $31 million; the
'34 Act—while providing for treble damages and referrals to the DOJ for
parallel proceedings—does not cap cumulative awards (Rajaratnam's lawyers
unsuccessfully urged the courts to weigh double jeopardy concerns).

The *Chiarella* oral argument before the Supreme Court had exposed the
lack of a clear correlation between an insider trader's gain and subsequent
penalty. That gap was filled by the Insider Trading Sanctions Act, which added
to Section 21 of the '34 Act the formula of "profit gained or loss avoided" (while
allowing the SEC to seek a penalty of three times the same). Four years later,
the Insider Trading Securities Fraud Enforcement Act created an express cause
of action for those on the other side of a convicted insider trader; that recovery
was formulated as similarly tied to gain/loss avoided (to be discounted by the
monies paid as fines). Between the *Chiarella* case and ITSA the Supreme Court
heard the *Dirks* case, during the oral argument for which the Court rejected
the notion that a tipper was liable for all tippee profits.

Nonetheless, such formulas and considerations were subverted during the
Period, and the sheer amount of monies collected for insider trading between
2008 and 2014 was astronomical. While often these monies were admirably allocated to victims and programs (or returned upon appellate reversals), a percentage, by default, continued to be added to the United States budget. It is
safe to say that a lack of correlation between penalty and unjust enrichment
became the norm and not the exception. This disturbing consequence can be
traced to a case from early in the Criminal Period which helped to ensure that
the "profit gained or loss avoided" would be astronomical, thus justifying strict
criminal penalties and eye-catching fines.

In *United States v. Contorinis*, a director of an investment banking firm,
was found by a jury to have traded on inside information on several occasions.
The information (about a supermarket chain merger) emanated from a connection at UBS, a global financial company. Contorinis was subsequently ordered to forfeit $12.6 million, an amount reflecting profits gained of $7.3
million and losses avoided of $5.3 million by the banking firm's Paragon
Fund. On appeal, the Second Circuit adjusted the amount approximately
$427,000 because criminal forfeiture is normally tied to actual gain by the
defendant.[40]

---

40. *United States v. Contorinis*, 692 F.3d 136 (2d Cir. 2012).

In the related SEC action, the District Court cited the $7.3 million profit figure. On appeal (and over Contorinis' protest), the Second Circuit—contrary to the panel that had heard the criminal appeal—approved the high figure, reasoning that the defendant, as tipper, was responsible for all gains by his tippee (i.e., the Paragon Fund). The notion of limiting the defendant's harm to his personal gain was not seriously considered again during the Period.

Further, even when solely determining length of prison sentence, the Second Circuit has evaluated the defendant's gain in light of third party profit. As an example, a convicted insider trader named Winifred Jiau was found in 2011 to have been paid $200,000 for her role in an insider trading conspiracy. Her crime, however was linked to the mammoth $30 million overall gain of a hedge fund allegedly tipped by a network of Jiau and 10 other professionals, and Jiau thus received a hefty four-year prison sentence.[41]

Outside of the Second Circuit, other courts do not subscribe to the "fund" measure of damages. For example, in *SEC v. Blatt*, the Fifth Circuit reminded that that disgorgement is remedial in nature and limited disgorgement to the fee earned by each defendant for his part in the scheme.[42]

Further, the addition of a monetary escalation actually works against deterrence: The ill-founded rumor that small investors/gains are not prosecuted for insider trading. It bears noting that a high profile criminal case from the late 1990s centered on two defendants who, together, reaped approximately $170,000 from their insider tips.[43] Accordingly, one casualty from the Period may be the belief that government does not punish small investors running afoul of the Prohibition.

4. Intensified (Yet Selective) Criminalization

Bowing to criticism, the SEC in 2013 formally confirmed a procedural concession: Defendants would be compelled to admit wrongdoing in an SEC settlement if previously found guilty of parallel charges. But the Commission reiterated that the "no admit, no deny" policy would continue to apply to the majority of cases.[44]

---

41. *See United States v. Jiau*, 734 F.3d 147 (2d Cir. 2013). Jiau was,at times, a pro se defendant.

42. 583 F.2d 1325 (5th Cir. 1978).

43. *United States. v. McDermott*, 245 F.3d 133 (2d Cir. 2001).

44. See Speech, Chair Mary Jo White, "A New Model for SEC Enforcement Producing Bold and Unrelenting Results" (November 18, 2016).

Perhaps the plainest result of the Period cases manifested itself in the form of the DOJ's spot at the regulatory table. Formal referrals from the SEC per the Acts were believed to be obsolete, as many DOJ cases actually preceded Commission investigation. Further, the notion of the SEC and DOJ complementing each other—testified to by SEC officials before Congress—never materialized. Indeed, such a supplemental regime may have been mooted long before the Financial Crisis. For example, it had long been thought that "conspiracy to commit insider trading" was solely within the purview of criminal authorities. However, in 2005, the SEC obtained a consent judgment against CEO Samuel Waksal for, among other things, attempted insider trading in his company's stock upon receipt of confidential news that its lead drug would not receive FDA approval.[45] The charge of "attempted insider trading" sufficiently covers acts preceding the trade, expanding Rule 10b-5 and rendering the use of alternative criminal charges for foiled plots unnecessary. Thus, the need to use DOJ criminal authority to charge conspiracy was likely a myth even before the tumult of litigation following the Crisis.

Nonetheless, criminal cases have multiplied. In late 2016, the head of the Department of Justice Criminal Division acknowledged that—generally speaking—younger, inexperienced federal prosecutors were sometimes letting matters proceed too far and inappropriately filing cases. "There are districts where oversight is not what it should be," the Department chief stated.[46]

The DOJ's pointed crusade of 2009–2016 succeeded in swelling government statistics, coffers, and jails. The convictions during the Period dignified extravagant estimations of the damage done, which justified higher sentences (which, ironically, in turn added criminal fines to the mix). However, the crusade also touched but a handful of the 9,000 hedge funds in operation, clouded Prohibition law, heightened pressures on the SEC, and resulted in some sentencing calculation asymmetries of its own. Rule 10b-5 may still be (recklessly) applied to all types of parties, to inexplicable remedy, and to indeterminate fairness. Judge Rakoff may have lost the battle to reject SEC settlements that failed to name responsible individuals, but the DOJ fully executed a war plan against

---

45. Litigation Release No. 19039, *Securities and Exchange Commission v. Samuel D. Waksal and Jack Waksal, et al.* (Jan. 19, 2005), *available at* https://www.sec.gov/litigation/litreleases/lr19039.htm ("Waksal tried to sell a substantial amount of his own ImClone stock.").

46. C. Ryan Barber, *Some Federal Cases "Shouldn't Be Filed," Head of DOJ Criminal Division Says*, NEW YORK LAW JOURNAL (December 9, 2016) (quoting Assistant Attorney General Leslie Caldwell).

hedge fund defendants whose primary distinctions among Prohibition defendants appeared to be great wealth.

Selected Bibliography

Stephen Breyer, "The Federal Sentencing Guidelines and the Key Compromises Upon Which They Rest," 17 HOFSTRA L. REV. 1 (1988).

J. Scott Colesanti, *Wall Street as Yossarian: The Other Effects of the Rajaratnam Insider Trading Conviction*, 40 HOFSTRA L. REV. 411 (2011).

Jodi Kantor, *Teaching Law, Testing Ideas, Obama Stood Slightly Apart*, N.Y. TIMES, July 30, 2008).

United States Sentencing Guidelines, Section 2B1.4 (as amended, December 2016).

Donna M. Nagy, *Salman v. United States: Insider Trading's Tipping Point?*, 69 STAN. L. REV. ONLINE (October 2016).

Paul Monnin & Sam Puathasnanon, *SEC Is Misguided on Disgorgement from Portfolio Managers*, LAW360 (October 20, 2016).

Massimo Calabresi & Bill Saporito, *The Street Fighter*, TIME MAGAZINE (February 13, 2012). U.S. Attorney Bharara was featured on the cover of the same TIME issue, with the overlaying words, "THIS MAN IS BUSTING WALL ST."

Bethany McLean, *The Trader Seeking Revenge Against U.S. Attorney Preet Bharara*, FORTUNE (December 29, 2016). The article describes the 2015 lawsuit filed by a hedge fund chief who alleges that a wrongful FBI raid of his $4 billion firm in 2010 lead to its downfall.

Barack Obama, Keynote Address, 2004 Democratic National Convention, *available at* http://www.pbs.org/newshour/bb/politics-july-dec04-obama-keynote-dnc/.

Department of Justice Memorandum, *Individual Accountability for Corporate Wrongdoing* (Sept. 9, 2015), *available at* www.justice.gov/dag/file/769036/download.

Steve Fishman, *Get Richest Quickest. In the precarious hedge-fund bubble, it's either cleanup—or flame out*, NEW YORK MAGAZINE, p. 28 (November 22, 2004).

Christopher L. LaVigne & Brian Calandra, Client Letter of Shearman & Sterling LLP, *Insider Trading Laws and Enforcement* (May–June 2016), *available at* http://www.shearman.com/~/media/Files/NewsInsights/Publications/2016/06/PCRM_0316_LaVigneCalandra-(2).pdf (noting the upsetting of over a dozen insider trading convictions after the 2014 *Newman* decision by the Second Circuit).

Mark Hamblett, *High Court Declines to Hear "Newman"; Circuit Ruling Stands*, NEW YORK LAW JOURNAL (October 6, 2015).

B. Colby Hamilton, *Federal Judge Grants Sweeping Suppression Motion in Wey Fraud Case*, NEW YORK LAW JOURNAL (June 14, 2017).

Scott Flaherty, *SDNY Securities Fraud Chief Heads to Milbank*, NEW YORK LAW JOURNAL (December 15, 2016) (noting that the famed securities fraud unit boasted of "20 senior federal prosecutors").

Walter Pavlo, *Insider Trading: Civil or Criminal Crime?*, FORBES (October 24, 2013).

Stephen Labaton, *"Junk Bond" Leader Is Indicted by U.S. in Criminal Action*, N.Y. TIMES (March 30, 1989), *available at* http://www.nytimes.com/1989/03/30/business/junk-bond-leader-is-indicted-by-us-in-criminal-action.html?pagewanted=all.

Jonathan Stempel, *Lawyer's record 12-year prison term for insider trading is upheld*, REUTERS, *available at* http://www.reuters.com/article/us-insidertrading-kluger-idUSBRE96814J20130709.

David A. Vise & Stephen Coll, *SEC Accuses Drexel, Executive of Fraud*, WASHINGTON POST (September 8, 1988), *available at* https://www.washingtonpost.com/archive/politics/1988/09/08/sec-accuses-drexel-executive-of-fraud/ed5b006a-e95c-4aea-896a-06571d8644de/?utm_term=.8a0ebd06ffa9.

Gretchen Morgenson, *S.E.C. Settles With a Former Lawyer*, N.Y. TIMES (June 29, 2010).

Walter Pavlo, *Winifred Jiau Gets 4 Years in Prison, and What a Journey*, FORBES (September 21, 2011), *available at* https://www.forbes.com/sites/walterpavlo/2011/09/21/winifred-jiau-gets-4-years-in-prison-and-what-a-journey/#2bf032b622cc.

Gretchen Morgenson, *SEC Settles Suit with Employee It Fired for $755,000*, N.Y. TIMES (June 29, 2010), *available at* http://www.nytimes.com/2010/06/30/business/30sec.html.

Antoinette Gartrell, "Insider Trading Ruling Muddies Question of Tipster Benefits," SECURITIES REGULATION & LAW REPORT (September 4, 2017).

Jordan Maglich, "Once Reserved for Drug Crimes, Wiretapping Takes Center Stage in White Collar Prosecutions," FORBES (May 21, 2013).

Zachary Kouwe and Dan Slater, "2 Bear Stearns Fund Leaders Are Acquitted," N.Y. Times (June 10, 2009) (quoting the prosecutor of Enron officials, "These acquittals provide a cautionary tale for white-collar investigations premised on facially 'smoking gun' emails.").

Chapter XII (*Checkpoint #3*)

The Evolution of the Insider Trading Fine, and the Final Accounting

The prosecution of insider trading commenced in earnest in 1961. Since then, it has grown from the priority of some well-meaning scholars and officials to the gravy train for the well-meaning and self-serving alike. Both the relevant history and likely future support a re-evaluation of the mission of punishing insider trading, or at least an adjustment to the relevant authorities keeping us safe therefrom.

A. The Dynamic Concepts

The hallmarks of the Prohibition have changed repeatedly, often without warning, and sometimes without reason.

For example, the required mental state of the defendant grew from none (1968) to scienter (1980), to recklessness (2012).

A duty to all (1961) became a duty to some (1980) and back again (S.T.O.C.K. Act of 2012).

The victims included the market (1968), then those who bought or sold the information (1988), and then the source of the inside information (1997).

The mission begun as ensuring equality of information (1968) has morphed into Supreme Court confession that such is beyond reach (1997).

And, of course, the resulting sanctions traveled a path from suspension from the industry (1961), to rescission of profits (1968), to incarceration (1981), to unlimited monetary fines, detailed by the chart below:

Event and Year	Provision/Scope	Development
Adoption of "swing trading" measure (1934)	Officers, directors and 10% shareholders subject to strict liability under Section 16(b).	16(a) reporting penalties gradually grow from injunctions (1966) to fines.
Texas Gulf Sulphur decision (1968)	Rule 10b-5 is applied to insider trading; defendants include all corporate employees.	"Rescission" now recoverable.
Congressional revisions to '34 Act (1984 and 1988)	Section 21 of '34 Act	SEC can seek treble damages for insider trading; covers "profit gained and loss avoided."
Boesky and Milken plea deals (1986–1990)	Rule 10b-5; SEC Rule 13d	Wrongful enterprise standard utilized (e.g., Milken's $1.8 billion junk bond trading). Damages now unlimited.
Fair Fund adoption (2002)	Rule 10b-5 and others	Disgorgement to be more routinely shared with victims. Some monies still treated as fines.
Dodd-Frank Act (2010)	Section 8A cease and desist hearings; Rule 10b-5	Money damages added to admin. hearings (Penny Stock Reform Act of 1990 also affected damages).
Period (i.e., DOJ) cases (2009–2016)	Rules 10b-5 and 10b5-2; Section 17(a)	Sentencing Guidelines extended (directly/indirectly); double jeopardy argument weakened; defendant's gain irrelevant—a tipper liable for all subsequent gains by tippee entities or persons.

B. Evolution of the Prohibition Fine

With quick glance, it becomes evident that, since 1997, so much more concerted attention has been paid to penalty than to the contours of the crime itself. To wit, with the Supreme Court approval of the Misappropriation Theory in 1997, the SEC was freed to bring "cluster cases" involving industry professionals and laymen alike (see Chapter VII). A trio of theories enabled application of Rule 10b-5 equally to those within the subject corporation and those who would serve or benefit from knowing them. With the Prohibition's scope significantly broadened, increased penalties were the next conquests (see Chapter IX). The swift addition of the United States attorneys to the mix grew these goals exponentially, while also prompting a redefined definition of the crime within the Federal Sentencing Guidelines (see Chapter XI). Those Guidelines—designed to minimize disparate sentencing—by so mercilessly valuing the money amounts involved in the transactions actually showcased differing judicial beliefs, ranging from passionate faith in strict enforcement to ardent desire for Congress to legislate the crime.

Meanwhile, the statutory limits to fines were immaterial, as Congress has never accumulated civil penalties with criminal, nor capped total criminal fines in any one case.[1] And lower court jurists seeking guidance from Congressional acts have rejected claims of double jeopardy while (perceptively) noting that the nation's legislature has, since 1933, consistently sought only to enhance the deterrent effect of strict enforcement of the securities laws. Finally, as a watershed event, the *Contorinis* decision—an SEC action—ensured that the Circuit most likely to hear a Prohibition case was permitted in both civil and criminal actions to link all of a scheme's profits to one person (a position ridiculed by the Supreme Court in oral argument on the *Dirks* case in 1983; see Chapter V).

As a result, by 2016 the Prohibition was routinely generating monies termed fines, penalties, forfeitures and/or awards in nearly unfathomable amounts. Three Period criminal cases alone generated over $110 million in fines/forfeitures.[2] The SEC boasted of over insider trading actions during the same time frame, with accompanying disgorgement and fines conservatively estimated at $250 million (with disgorgement, like forfeiture, disbursement-oriented in theory but account-swelling in fact). And, of course, the class action settlement concurrently grew, punctuated by awards in the *S.A.C. Capital* case ($135 million) and the *Pfizer* case ($468 million). Even without incorporating related actions under different headings and whistleblower awards, there is a tremen-

---

1. Section 32 of the '34 Act, while textually limiting monetary fines per criminal charge, carries no total limit for cases involving multiple charges.

2. Criminal forfeitures are earmarked for victim compensation, while fines are paid directly into the U.S. Treasury. However, the final accounting gets more difficult when victims do not claim funds or otherwise cannot be identified; the most recent report lists all S.D.N.Y. forfeitures at $1.4 trillion for fiscal year 2016, with about 10% of that being returned to victims within a year of recovery. Regardless of transient or ultimate destination, the fact remains that hundreds of millions of dollars were recouped from insider trading during the Period, whereas, prior to the Period, the monies collected by criminal prosecutors from insider trading paled in comparison.

dous amount of money changing hands—particularly for a crime traced to an administrative Rule, repeatedly unscripted by Congress, and subject to strongly differing judicial support. Indeed, the adoption of Rule 10b-5 may have been the best investment the Commission ever made.

C. Points to Ponder

The Prohibition has proceeded on a path that is thoroughly unpredictable. Its chief targets can be set by meandering Congressional testimony or the priorities of unelected officials. The statute, effectuating provisions, and government applications can be so diverse as to inspire mirth, were not the ever ratcheting sanctions so dire.

The DOJ asks for periods of incarceration that inspire either inexplicable adherence or outright aversion from the federal bench. Its ever-increasing pool of insider trading fines flows into the United States Treasury.

The SEC acquiesces to greater enforcement efforts by others while utilizing massive recoveries as a cause for existence. When that cause becomes questionable, it somehow receives even broader authority to punish.

Both parties succeed in justifying the efforts by the monies recaptured, although the fines are most rationally explained by the defendants' ability to withstand them[3]—a very weak form of deterrence. Resultingly, "fine" has taken on several meanings, the most useful of which may be money recovered from the defendant in excess of his gain and coming to rest with the government.

Questions posed outright by the Supreme Court are answered belatedly (e.g., the addition of "loss avoided" as a basis for penalty) or, worse yet, directly countered (e.g., holding a tipper responsible for all subsequent chain profits).

As a result, Rule 10b-5—essentially the death penalty for securities misdealings—concurrently grows in use and vagary. While the investor expectations go up, the intellectual honesty actually depletes.

With insider trading devolving into a carousel spinner awarding fortunes to too many players, the urge grows to exhort government to do better. A fine starting point for reform starts with refining the Prohibition itself, the subject of the next and last Chapter of the Book.

---

3. For example, Winans (an unemployed reporter) was find $4,500. He was the sole source of the inside information. Rajaratnam (the benefactor of tips) was a hedge fund mogul, and was fined over $100 million.

Chapter XIII

Wishing Away the Oasis

Amidst the cashier's checks and their opposing editorials, three very simple truths emerge: In adopting Section 10(b) of the '34 Act, Congress created an anti-fraud measure with the vaguest of standards, the SEC consistently pushed this standard to extremes, and the judiciary repeatedly created the legal means for the expansion. Perhaps this design fulfills our nation's unique concept of interstitial rulemaking, but, then again, any protocol emanating from unelected officials which results in billions of dollars in remedy probably deserves a closer look.

A. The Historical Re-Cap

In 1933, a law professor (Felix Frankfurter) and his circle gave Congress a bill that essentially included a tort (Section 17(a)). In 1934, Congress answered the cries for an end to insider privilege with a remedy that went beyond the common law, Section 16(b). In 1942, some SEC officials tweaked these dual measures to cover an unforeseeable offense, creating Rule 10b-5.

Through litigation, the Rule was applied to new categories of defendants (non-officers/directors/large shareholders) and to new, consequential penalties (injunctions and fines). The federal judiciary agreed; one judge even concluded that a private cause of action sprang from the tort. Years later, the Supreme Court blessed the private cause of action via a footnote.

Legions of enforcement actions were brought by the SEC, throughout the land. All was more well than not until 1980, when the Supreme Court noted that a defendant (Chiarella) had not committed the tort. Still, a means of restating the tort was offered by the Chief Justice (the Misappropriation Theory). The restated tort enjoyed mixed success until 1997, when the Supreme Court approved it.

Since then, the Prohibition has enjoyed unlimited applications by a surprising array of plaintiffs in interest. Yet, the current status quo is arguably not serving *fairness* at all. To wit, if predictability and certainty should attend a Rule of Law, then the Prohibition has failed. Witness below the fact patterns that escape its reach.

B. Not So Rhetorical Hypotheticals

Note the commonality among the 10 hypotheticals listed below:

1. A trader on the national desk of a major broker-dealer notices that customer X appears to "guess" the market direction more often than not. He begins to mimic the purchases of the customer (a trading process coined "piggybacking"). The trader earns profits; the customer is arrested for insider trading. When later questioned by the SEC, the trader states that he knows not the nature of the customer's trading decisions—only that the trades are often profitable.

2. A neighbor hears a Wall Street trader mention that ABC Co. is about to make an offer for CDE Co. The neighbor had been contemplating selling her CDE Co. shares. Instead, she holds onto the shares, and profits handsomely when the confidential news of the offer hits the press.

3. A man confidentially learns from his job at a law firm that a 100-year-old printing company is about to declare bankruptcy. The man remembers that he has a certificate indicating ownership of 500 shares of the popular company in his attic. He sells his shares to a neighbor for $5,000 cash, delivering the certificate in person. The next week, the news is publically broadcast that the printing company is bankrupt, and all shares are declared worthless.

4. A man at a New Jersey bus stop is approached by an employee of XYZ, Inc. The employee blurts out, "I'm telling everyone—buy XYZ today. Merger news is coming tomorrow." The man at the bus stop complies and makes a profit when news of the merger is released the day after his purchase.

5. A printing shop employee deduces from masked documents that public companies ABC, Inc. and DEF Co. are about to merge. He buys stock in both companies prior to the news becoming public; he contemporaneously informs his supervisor at the printing shop, who says only, "Man's gotta make a buck somehow in this economy."

The employee makes $30,000 after selling his shares one day after the news breaks.

6. A patient hears his chiropractor tell his assistant the confidential news that ABC Co. is about to announce a dividend reduction. The doctor expressly tells the patient, "You can't trade on that information." The patient ignores the admonition and sells his ABC Co. stock before the news breaks, avoiding a $3,500 loss.

7. A burglar of a private home notes a folder reading "CONFIDENTIAL MERGER INFORMATION" on a desk in the study. He takes the folder, along with cash and jewelry. He later reads the contents of the folder and uses the material, non-public information to trade to a profit when news of the merger becomes public.

8. A manager of a branch office is privately assured by the company's research department that a planned Initial Public Offering is already over-subscribed. He requests his usual order of pre-IPO "syndicate placement" and is allocated 1,000 shares for his personal account. The IPO is highly successful, and the manager earns $40,000.

9. A non-industry person receives a tip to buy 100 shares of XYZ Co. from a deliveryman. The layman knows enough to ask his tipper how he knows of this great tip; the deliveryman says, "Don't worry, it's legit." In fact, the deliveryman learned the XYZ Co. inside information from a cousin working on a merger.

10. A hedge fund chief receives an e-mail from one of his portfolio managers alerting him that the manager had received "a second-hand read" (i.e., company code for confidential bad news) on the earnings estimates of a company held by the hedge fund. The chief sells shares before the company announces that it has underperformed earnings. He later advises regulators that he receives hundreds of e-mails (and effects hundreds of trades) each day, and he does not read every one of them. He is not charged.

None of these activities, although **unfair**, are readily reached by Rule 10b-5. Further, the last example was not a hypothetical, but a real, recent case.[1] The explanations appear below.

---

1. *See* Sheelah Kolharkar, *When the Feds Went After the Hedge-Fund Legend Steven A. Cohen*, THE NEW YORKER (January 16, 2017) (discussing the decision by the United States Attorney office not to charge S.A.C. Capital CEO Steven Cohen with insider trading).

1. The first example (piggybacking) deals with a practice decried but not outlawed. It would seem inequitable that a broker privy to trade orders not known to the public could base his trading decision on what a successful professional does. Note that the onus is on the employing broker-dealer to adopt a policy outlawing such copycat trading; in such instance, if the copycat still trades, he has possibly "stolen" the information from his employer, and could potentially be deemed a misappropriator. But a scienter problem still exists, for the professional's trades are no doubt sometimes unprofitable, and thus the copycat is trading on a *guess*, and not a *fact* (which was emphasized as the heart of insider information long ago by *List v. Fashion Park*[2]).

2. The second example (the insider "holder," as opposed to trader) has not committed fraud "in connection with" the purchase or sale of securities. This element has been averted in cases such as *Dabit* and *Madoff*, but the former was a class action particularly focused on the Congressional intent behind a 1998 law, and the latter was a consensual conviction.

3. The third example (the cash transaction) does not invoke the "means of interstate commerce," thus rendering Section 10(b) inapplicable. Indeed, the jurisdictional means has been liberally stretched by the courts,[3] but it is nonetheless a universal requirement to invoke a federal law.

4. The fourth example (the gratuitous tip) is not illegal outside of the Second Circuit. The Second Circuit *Martoma* correction of its prior holding in *Newman* in 2017 defined "benefit" within the tipper/tippee test as the tipper's expectation that the tippee will trade. But the Supreme Court has not held, and other Circuits — such as the Third. involved in the hypothetical — would require some form of benefit to the tipper.

5. The fifth example describes an exception to the Prohibition — per the Supreme Court decision in *O'Hagan* (i.e., full disclosure by an

---

2. 340 F.2d 457 (2d Cir. 1965).

3. *See, e.g.,* SEC Interpretation: Use of Web Sites to Offer Securities (March 23, 1998); Complaint: *SEC v. Andrews and Christensen* (Utah April 2017) (mailing of doctored account statements); *Chiarella*, 445 U.S. 222 (mailing of trading confirmations). Stock exchange transactions, of course, are the most common and most unquestioned form of jurisdictional means, as they are expressly listed in Section 10(b).

4. *O'Hagan*, 521 U.S. at 654.

outsider to the source of the information removes insider trading liability under Rule 10b-5).[4]

6. The sixth example (patient in chiropractor's office) would have to be prosecuted as a misappropriation, only it is doubtful that such a budding patient-client relationship would serve as the "functional equivalent" of a fiduciary relationship under state law.

7. The seventh example (burglar taking a confidential folder) presents another lack of relationship. The court would need to create an exception as was done in *Dorozhko* regarding theft by a hacker.

8. The eighth example (the IPO allocation) is not only omnipresent in the securities business but also the subject of SEC written guidance, which for years has confessed that the Commission does not regulate such matters.[5] More to the point, Rule 10b5-1 expressly exonerates trades "pursuant to a contract, instruction, or plan" predating the subject transaction (as routine IPO allocations to brokerage employees customarily are).

9. The ninth example (the "legit" tip) speaks to the degree of knowledge of a tippee. In the Second Circuit and elsewhere, the remote tippee must know that a duty has been breached, which does not seem to be the case here.

10. The last example (the e-mail glut) has been publicly disclosed and aptly chronicled. The U.S. Attorney convicted two individuals at a hedge fund called S.A.C. Capital Advisors, and obtained (along with the SEC) $1.8 billion from the firm. However, the company's chief was not charged, and his proffered defense of reading only 11% of his daily e-mails seemingly had teeth.

Thus, despite over 50 years of application, SEC and DOJ focus, and billions of dollars in reward, the Prohibition still proves impotent in very possible scenarios. The vagaries alone justify a consideration of changes to the Prohibition. Modifications of both the short term and long term nature are discussed below.

---

5. *See Initial Public Offerings: Eligibility to Get Shares at Broker-Dealers, available at* https://www.sec.gov/fast-answers/answersipoelightm.html ("Brokerage firms also may sell shares in the IPO only to selected clients. For example, some firms limit sales of shares in an IPO to those customers who have certain cash balances in their accounts, are active traders with the firm, or subscribe to one of their more expensive 'premium' services.").

C. Short Term Changes

To stave off court antagonism towards the Prohibition, there are quick fixes that would bolster what sometimes appears to be unfettered SEC discretion. Here are some suggestions:

1. Clarify the Rule 10b-5 Duty Via Rulemaking

When the *O'Hagan* decision held that the notorious lawyer owed a duty to either his employer or the employer's client, the vagary seemed almost quaint. Over two decades later, the indecision persists. For example, in charging a member of an investor relations firm in 2014 with wrongfully availing himself of inside information, the Commission summarily stated that the defendant's "self-centered misconduct betrayed both his own firm and his firm's clients whose confidential information he exploited for personal gain."[6]

The Misappropriation Theory has been around for too long to be saddled with such indecision. Either limit the injury to the immediate source of the information (e.g., a law firm), or declare the information to be the rightful property of the client (e.g., the company contemplating a tender offer). The distinction can be clarified in meaningful fashion through SEC rulemaking, which has proven to be beyond judicial reversal for reasons ranging from the *Chenery* cases of the 1940s to the doctrine of *Chevron* deference, born in 1984.

2. Follow the Statutory DOJ Referral Protocol

As far back as the 1990s, the defense Bar began noting that the statutory referral protocol was not being followed. That brief standard implies that matters under SEC investigation can escalate to criminal referral based upon recognition of evidence; today it has largely been forgotten,[7] notwithstanding the DOJ's own policies now calling for greater communication between its attorneys handling civil and criminal matters.[8]

---

6. SEC Press Release 2014-142, *SEC Charges Investor Relations Executive With Insider Trading While Preparing Clients' Press Releases* (July 22, 2014).

7. Former Chair Mary Jo White acknowledged in her March 2014 speech that the SEC "is certainly not the source of or involved in every securities fraud [criminal] prosecution..." www.sec.gov/news/speech/2014-spch033114mjw.

8. *See* the 2015 "Yates Memo," Individual Accountability for Corporate Wrongdoing (September 9, 2015).

Simply put, a more formal referral process ensures consistency of approach and avoidance of over-criminalization. The two government entities are intended by Congress to act in complementary fashion, as was last evidenced by the adoption of ITSA in 1984. At that time, the '34 Act was amended to provide for higher SEC fines, and the DOJ was relegated the role of enforcing that fine when not timely rendered.

3. Self-Impose Double Jeopardy

On a related note, more coordination between the DOJ and SEC on fines seems only reasonable.

A haunting example: In 2011, Raj Rajaratnam was convicted of insider trading and sentenced to 11 years in prison, at the time the longest prison sentence of any insider trading conviction ever. He was also compelled by the same federal court to pay over $63 million in fines and restitution based upon trading profits set by the SEC at approximately $33 million. The SEC immediately moved for summary judgment based upon the same transactions for which Rajaratnam was criminally convicted. Although the defendant protested double jeopardy, he was civilly fined another $92,805,705, bringing his payment total (and total of monies paid to the U.S. Treasury) to over $155 million. The 500% penalty far exceeds the treble damages called for by Section 21A of the '34 Act.[9]

If *Newman* shows that fairness has now grown to encompass the criminal defendant in insider trading cases, then perhaps some restraint needs to be shown by the government.

4. Eliminate Differences in Approach between Regional Offices

Mark Cuban, a Fifth Circuit defendant, was alleged in 2008 to have sold shares after receiving insider information of a forthcoming PIPE offering (i.e., private investment in public equity). He was charged with violations of all three subsections of Rule 10b-5 and alleged to have acted with scienter. Comparatively, Martha Stewart, a Second Circuit defendant, was alleged in to have sold shares after receiving a phone message. She was charged with violations

---

9. *See also SEC v. Palmisano*, 135 F.3d 860 (2d Cir. 1998) (imposing a $9.2 million disgorgement and a civil fine of $500,000 after a criminal case ordering unspecified restitution).

of Rule 10b-5 for trading while in *possession* of inside information and acting either with knowledge or recklessly. As previously discussed, since 2000, SEC Rule 10b5-1 enables the SEC to simply allege *awareness* in Complaints, a standard not cited in either the Cuban or Stewart cases.

Separately, a case called *Talbot* featured the battle over whether an outside director owes the classical duty to the Board in the absence of a written agreement (the Ninth Circuit held that, ultimately, he did[10]). A 2016 Sixth Circuit case attributed a lawyer's duty to a Board to a writing, a higher standard to meet.[11]

To be sure, the regional offices of the SEC follow different trial strategies and pleading protocols. However, SEC Rules adopted to provide certainty are being avoided, and cases hard fought to establish discernible law are being ignored. Such choices are unclear and again work to undermine confidence in the Prohibition.

D. Long Term/Doctrinal Modifications

If the Prohibition ultimately faces judicial modification, then change now is warranted. No rule of law over 80 years in the making is going to succumb overnight. Still, it is possible to improve the sometimes blunt instrument along a long timeline. Here are 10 substantive suggestions to ensure fairness over the long haul:

1. Confine Investigations to the Boardroom

In this regard, perhaps there is wisdom in the jury process. The strange distinction between the clear fiduciary duty for insider cases (i.e., Classical Theory) and the dubious, cobbled duty for outsider cases (i.e., Misappropriation Theory) has been aptly noted by scholars. It has likewise been sufficiently catalogued by the press that the SEC has problems at insider trading trials; upon inspection, that commentary could be refined to problems with *outsider* cases that proceed to trial. Maybe the jurors instinctively feel what the experts have noted: Insider trading charges should be reserved for the insiders. As was stated

---

10. *SEC v. Talbot*, 530 F.3d 1085 (9th Cir. 2008).

11. *SEC v. James C. Cope, Esq.* (M.D. Tenn. 2016), *available at* https://www.sec.gov/litigation/complaints/2016/comp23675.pdf (noting that "Board members, such as Cope, were required to sign certifications yearly, stating that the Director 'ha[d] read, underst[ood], and w[ould] comply' with the insider trading policy. In January 2015 and again in January 2016, Cope signed such certifications as part of completing his annual Director and Officer questionnaires ...").

previously, at least one juror in the Martha Stewart trial exalted at punishing someone she saw as a benefactor of corporate privilege (although the defendant was on trial for obstructing justice).

Moreover, a sole focus on fundamental corporate information was publicly urged by Milton Friedman—one of the creators of Rule 10b-5—in 1983.[12]

2. Seek a Statutory Definition of Insider Trading

From a high-profile former AUSA to a current federal judge, the calls for a statutory provision resound each decade. While drafting a one-size-fits-all provision may pose its own set of new problems, it at least aids the judiciary in commencing its analysis.

Additionally, a statutory definition would provide for uniformity in compliance efforts. Indeed, even well-meaning financial service providers are left to their own devices to craft meaningful training programs and safeguards. Witness the disparity among the two employee trading compliance procedures detailed below, both seemingly issued in good faith:

> You may not buy or sell securities issued by [employer] or any other public company if you are in possession of material nonpublic information relating to those companies. This restriction applies to transactions for you, members of your family, [employer] or any other person for whom you may buy or sell securities. In addition, you may not recommend to others that they buy or sell that security.[13]

> You must submit a pre-clearance request in [internal trading system], or in accordance with local procedures where [such system] is not available, and receive an approval before undertaking any personal investment transactions permitted under this policy, including purchases, sales, options exercises and gifts.[14]

The stylistic choices in the two compliance passages above alternatively place the burden on a trader and his compliance department. While each appears logical, each also represents the flip side of the coin regarding responsibility to prevent insider trading.

---

12. See supra Chapter V n. 29 and accompanying text.

13. https://www.sec.gov/Archives/edgar/data/701276/000119312504074901/dex9917ii.htm.

14. https://www.sec.gov/Archives/edgar/data/1100663/000119312514241353/d74574 1dex99p2.htm.

3. Learn from Foreign Regulatory Models

In the 1980s, the Prohibition stood far apart and above all foreign imitators. Britain once denied the SEC basic information on an insider trading suspect. The European Union had yet to act to inspire insider trading regulations. When the EU did act in 1989, Germany was very late in coming to the insider trading table, dragging its feet until adopting its Securities Trading Act in 1994.

But the belated regulation introduced a novel notion, namely, that wrongdoers could be separated into information disseminators and actual traders. Further, drawing upon the model of the Prohibition and its chief enforcer, the SEC, Germany established "BaFin," a federal regulatory agency committed to policing the market. Although BaFin was a start-up agency enjoying none of the SEC's benefits of a leviathan budget and state/criminal counterparts, the agency grew respectably. By 2010, BaFin was reporting over 50 cases a year to the public prosecutor (including 14 cases resolved by fines, 10 convictions, and an incarceration of 3 years). Clearly, the copycat agency has amply succeeded in investigating, referring, redressing, and distinguishing insider trading cases.

Germany's "administrative offense" for those who simple relay inside information seems a tad more reasonable than the all-or-nothing approach of the Prohibition (e.g., individuals linked by an informational chain and resulting trade all face possible incarceration and share joint and several monetary penalties). Even where "relief defendants" are separated from prosecutions, that is due solely to SEC discretion.[15] Distinctions traceable to the '34 Act or even SEC rules thereunder would presume much more credibility, among both jurists and the public.[16]

4. Reach More Cases without Rule 10b-5

The battle to have the Misappropriation Theory approved by the Supreme Court made eminently clear the fact that the subject behavior was often reach-

---

15. *See, e.g., SEC v. Walters, et al.* (Phil Mickelson as Relief Defendant), No. 16 CIV 3722 (S.D.N.Y. May 19, 2016). The professional golfer, although trading on a tip from someone subject to both SEC and DOJ charges for insider trading, was asked only to refund $1 million to the Commission.

16. *See* Stephen Gandel, *Why Phil Mickelson Got a Mulligan on His Insider Trading Scandal,* FORTUNE (May 21, 2016) ("Phil Mickelson should be heading to jail or at least under arrest and to trial, if insider trading laws were still working the way they should.").

able via other federal laws. For example, in the *Carpenter, Bryan,* and *O'Hagan* cases, the underlying trading activity was charged (successfully) under the mail fraud statute.[17]

5. Strive for SEC Continuity

The Commission has had 32 Chairs in 83 years; by comparison, the IRS has had 48 chiefs in nearly twice as long (155 years). Three of the last six SEC Chairs have held the position for less than two full years. The last five Directors of Enforcement at the SEC have held the position, on average, less than four years. Such abbreviated tenures are particularly glaring in that these officials left voluntarily (the Chair position, per the '34 Act, is a five-year appointment). This transience seems to have started around 2001, before which the Chair held office for seven years, and the Director of Enforcement for a decade.

The highest officials at the Commission are forever haunted by political pressures, and there shall always be the lure of astronomical Wall Street salaries. But the revolving door at the Commission has accelerated to warp speed. Truly, the top "independent regulatory agency" has become beholden to political and market forces alike.

The Commission enjoys great freedom to fashion its own standard operating procedure. For example, by its own quorum rules, the Commissioners enjoys the liberty to exercise authority even when staffed by less than the full contingent of five Commissioners called for by Section 4 of the '34 Act. An internal rule demanding five-year commitments from Enforcement Directors would provide for greater consistency on such crucial topics as deference to other regulators, coordination with the DOJ and, in general, triage strategy. It bears noting that the lack of coordination/communication between the SEC and other parts of government is universally cited for the difficulties in responding to the early days of the Credit Crisis of 2008.

As for the longevity of the Chairs, that remains up to the President who selects them. It is worth noting that Arthur Levitt, the Chair with the longest tenure (over seven years), has publicly stated that the lack of White House interference kept him committed to the Commission.[18] Additionally, in response

---

17. 18 U.S.C. § 1341 (2016). The statute punishes, among other things, "artifice to defraud" and fraudulent misrepresentations. On remand, the Eighth Circuit scaled back O'Hagan's convictions.

18. Speech at Adelphi University, Garden City, New York (November 12, 2007). The esteemed former SEC Chair took questions from the author and others on his record-setting tenure at the Commission.

to Credit Crisis, the Dodd-Frank Act of 2010 placed the SEC Chair as a permanent member on such inter-agency structures as the Financial Stability Oversight Board.

All of which favors the retention of upper management at the Commission, whether by internal rulemaking, higher salaries, and/or political will.

6. Educate Public Companies

FINRA, as the largest regulator of broker-dealers, routinely educates its constituency on insider trading rules in determined fashion. For example, a webinar titled "Monitoring for Insider Trading and Understanding FINRA's Regulatory Tip Process" explains the following:

- what triggers an insider-trading investigation;
- insider trading provision of FINRA's supervision rule (3110 (d));
- suggestions for responding to regulatory inquiries;
- "red flags" for identifying potential insider trading and other fraud; and
- an overview of the regulatory tip and intelligence gathering process.[19]

Likewise, a short video titled "Insider Trading 'Red Flags' and Filing a Tip With FINRA" alerts firms to spotting illegal trading practices, communicates the results of recent cases, and suggests the protocol for informing the regulator of wrongdoing.[20]

True, FINRA's broker-dealer constituency numbers only about a third of the total of public companies that file with the Commission. However, the SEC has an annual budget of over $1 billion. Perhaps some of the enforcement resources (or at least the investor education budget) could be re-allocated to more direct interaction with the public company community on this topic.

7. Deal with High Frequency Trading in Meaningful Fashion

High frequency trading involves purchases/sales tied to computer programs taking advantage of expensive, millisecond fast trading software. The trading

---

19. http://www.finra.org/industry/monitoring-insider-trading-and-understanding-finras-regulatory-tip-process.html.
20. http://www.finra.org/industry/insider-trading-red-flags-and-filing-tip-finra.

practice was publicized by a bestselling book in 2014, and it has caused debate every year since.[21] Surprisingly, the practice has been approved by the Commission. And the public—the respect of which has always been the aim of the Prohibition—does not know why.

The Commission has somewhat tuned to the new frequency but only in indirect fashion. A disciplinary action announced in early 2015 focused on transparency of order execution and netted over $14 million in fines.[22] Additionally, in 2017, the Commission approved the IEX Exchange, a stock exchange for institutional players expressly designed to slow trading (and thus provide a more fair market). However, overall, the promised regulation of the highly technological playing field remains a goal. The attainment of that goal would go a long way to re-assuring investors that the SEC is the dog wagging the tail of Wall Street. Simply put, a 20-minute trading advantage was seen as unfair in 1961, and, with today's quotes and trade executions occurring in fractions of a second, academics, practitioners and laymen alike are left wondering why a millisecond advantage is not seen as equally predatory.

8. Bring Back the *Materiality* Analysis

Judge Bonsal questioned whether a preliminary ore find was material. Since then, any information that can be linked to a stock rise/fall passes the test of materiality. SEC and DOJ charging instruments need only include a price increase after information dissemination to prove that information was material (when the dollar amount of that price increase is unremarkable, a percentage increase is offered).

Written standards for material events already exist in SEC Rule 405, Form 8K, and even the interpretive releases for Regulation FD. Confining material events to a definitive listing (e.g., news of preliminary negotiations; planned resignation of a high ranking corporate official) would increase certainty, further deterrence, and, overall, heighten fairness.

---

21. *See generally* MICHAEL LEWIS, FLASH BOYS/A WALL STREET REVOLT (2014). *See, e.g.*, Jake Zamansky, *High Frequency Insider Trading—and It's Completely Legal!*, FORBES (2013), *available at* https://www.forbes.com/sites/jakezamansky/2013/07/09/high-frequency-insider-trading-and-its-completely-legal/#5a8cae5f2bd2; Beverly Goodman, *SEC Still Mulling New Rules on High Frequency Trading*, BARRONS (2014), *available at* http://www.barrons.com/articles/SB50001424052748703754104577239231746043566; Usman W. Chohan, *The real problem with high frequency trading*, BUSINESS INSIDER.COM (2016), *available at* http://www.businessinsider.com/the-real-problem-with-high-frequency-trading-2016-1.

22. *See* SEC Press Release 2015-7 (regarding a subsidiary of UBS Securities).

9. Delegate More Duties to Compliance Personnel

The scandals occasioned by Carpenter, Levine, and Waksal were all detected and hindered by compliance departments. Thousands of people—many of them registered within the securities industry—work in the compliance departments of public companies.

Instead of inspiring a steady atmosphere of fear in these workplaces, greater incentives should be provided for companies that self-prevent, self-investigate, and self-report. While whistleblowing awards share this mission, such a monetary olive branch assumes the employee is willing to cut all ties with the employer. Use of provisions within the Acts exempting transactions from disciplinary action[23] could be effectively used by the SEC to absolve cooperating industry personnel seeking only to right a wrong.

10. Compel Congress to Let the SEC Self-Fund

To ask the SEC to decrease its insider trading efforts—whether trumpeted publically to the world or in more cloaked fashion to Congress—is tantamount to asking the desert traveler to wish away the oasis. An agency that each year must justify its continued existence to the legislative body that funds it is simply going to continue boasting of its noteworthy achievements in the prior 12 months; for all of the reasons discussed earlier herein, those achievements take the form of largely unquestioned astronomical monetary recoveries after SEC Complaints are issued and its theories salvaged by the judiciary.

Such questionable pattern is reason enough to let the SEC's funding track the FDIC or IRS models, both of which inspire agency confidence born of permanence by letting the hunters keep what they hunt in meaningful fashion.

Insider trading is morally wrong and clearly illegal. Yet, the Prohibition—if exercised well—results foremost in spectacular accolades for its practitioner. This achievement takes the form of headlines, higher governmental office, astronomical monetary recovery, and/or a new job on Wall Street. Meanwhile, the investing public, which is concerned foremost about the perception of a level playing field, as well as the regulated securities industry, which must un-

---

23. Specifically, Section 28 of the '33 Act ("General Exemptive Authority") and Section 36 of the '34 Act (same provision title).

derstand a regulation in order to be deterred by it, know little of the details of or the choices behind the unwritten law.

The one predictable characteristic of this recurring, unscripted government mission is a dynamic notion of *fairness*.

Fairness to the market, phrased as "integrity."

Fairness to investors, known as generating "investor confidence."

Fairness to victims of fraud, called "disgorgement."

Fairness, on all of these occasions, inextricably linked to maximum monetary penalty (even in criminal cases). And when such a notion reaches untenable excess, it translates into a new market abuse.

Like it or not, the powers that be have targeted the common law crime of insider trading as an evil to be quelled at all costs, and thus "fairness" has become its own corporate entity, with ever-ratcheting, eye-catching returns. Like every other money-making concern on Wall Street, *Fairness, Inc.* should be subject to clear rules and more transparent enforcement, rather than an ever-expanding protocol deputizing an agent on every corner.

Over 75 years ago a small band of agency officials worked quickly to halt a fraud. By all accounts, their hearts were in the right place. But their cure was born too elastic, grew unsupervised by Congress, and matured with only cash as its yardstick. As a result, today there are too many "regulators" taking too many swipes at the brass ring. Likewise, too little is being done to ensure that the market is "fair" by a universal standard.

The Commission can, of course, continue on its present path of ever-ratcheting fines and unfathomable money collection. However, the Prohibition is primarily judge-made law, and, as of January 2018, the Republican President is predicted to ultimately nominate at least 10% of the federal bench. The scaling back of interpretations antagonistic to business growth is inevitable. **Fairness** as a standard cuts both ways, and its application to defendants is inevitable in cases where the law is unwritten—indeed, the Second Cicuit judges deciding the *Newman* case believed fairness exonerated remote tippees, and even jurors will utilize fairness as a touchstone whether emphasized by a defendant or not.[24] Equally likely, the Supreme Court will at some point re-ex-

---

24. *See, e.g.,* Jason Grant & Mark Hamblett, *Jury Finds Ex-Banker Guilty of Insider Trading,* NEW YORK LAW JOURNAL (August 17, 2016) (quoting a male juror: "We gave [the defendant] as much **fairness** as anybody could possibly give him" after a guilty verdict in *United States v. Sean Stewart,* No. 15-cr-00287 (S.D.N.Y. 2016), a much-publicized case involving a Yale University graduate who tipped his father on tender offers).

amine its holding in *O'Hagan* with a keener eye towards intellectual risk and reward. To rein in the corporate-caliber bonuses and codify limits to prosecutorial excess would seem to be the fairest means of ensuring that the regulated American market as we know it continues in unparalleled fashion. Where law is unwritten, an agency's rationality is evaluated every day. On too many days, Fairness, Inc. appears to be in business for itself.

Selected Bibliography

Michael Lewis, Flash Boys/A Wall Street Revolt (2014).

Jeremy Schara, Note, *Knowledge is Salvation: Informing Investors by Regulating Disclosures to Safeguard Best Execution*, 43 Hofstra L. Rev. 1231 (2015), *available at* http://scholarlycommons.law.hofstra.edu/hlr/vol43/iss4/9.

SEC Press Release, *Overseas Traders Paying Back All Profits Plus Penalties in Insider Trading Case* (March 24, 2017), *available at* www.sec.gov/news/press-release/2017-70-0 (detailing an agreement to pay nearly $300,000 in disgorgement, penalties and interest, reached just 6 months after the filing of the Complaint. The Complaint had alleged violations of SEC Rules 10b-5 and 14e-3, as well as Section 17(a) of the 1933 Act.).

Mark Hamblett, *Longtime Prosecutor Tapped for EDNY Judgeship*, New York Law Journal (Sept. 15, 2016).

Homer Kripke, *The Myth of the Informed Layman*, 28 Bus. Law. 631 (1973) ("The way to do a real job of disclosure to the investing public is through the improvement of the information in the annual report to stockholders.").

SEC Release 2016-123, *SEC Approves IEX Proposal to Launch National Exchange, Issues Interpretation on Automated Securities Prices* (June 17, 2016) ("At the same time, the Commission issued an updated interpretation that will require trading centers to honor automated securities prices that are subject to a small delay of 'speed' bump when being accessed.").

Complaint, *Securities and Exchange Commission v. Mark Cuban*, No. 3-08C V2050-D (N.D. Tex. 2008).

After setbacks, NY prosecutors resume insider trading crackdown, Reuters (June 23, 2016), *available at* http://www.reuters.com/article/us-usa-insider trading-idUSKCN0Z915C.

Dunstan Prial, *SEC: Self-Funding vs. Congressional Appropriations*, FOX Business (May 17, 2013), *available at* http://www.foxbusiness.com/politics/2013/05/16/sec-self-funding-vs-congressional-appropriations.html.

Department of the Treasury, 2016 FSOC Annual Report, *available at* https://www.treasury.gov/initiatives/fsoc/studies-reports/Documents/FSOC%202016%20Annual%20Report.pdf.

Michael Bobelian, *As Preet Bharara Drops Seven Insider Trading Charges, Some Enforcement Might Move Out of New York,* FORBES (October 23, 2015), *available at* https://www.forbes.com/sites/michaelbobelian/2015/10/23/as-preet-bharara-drops-seven-insider-trading-charges-some-enforcement-might-move-out-of-new-york/#2cb8750a3680.

SEC Press Release, *Enforcement Director Andrew J. Ceresney to Leave SEC* (December 8, 2016), *available at* https://www.sec.gov/news/pressrelease/2016-259.html.

Note, "Cutting the Party Line: How the SEC Can Silence Persisting Phone Call Tips," 39 HOFSTRA L. REV. 447 (2010) (by Kristen A. Truver) (urging revision of Regulation FD in order to close an "unforeseen loophole" allowing for selective disclosure).

SEC Press Release, *SEC Chair Mary Jo White Announces Departure Plans* (November 14, 2016), *available at* https://www.sec.gov/news/pressrelease/2016-238.html.

E-mail from BaFin Investigator Rudolf Weber, April 20, 2010 (on file with author).

Jenny Anderson, *Wall St. Turns to the Time Out as Punishment,* N.Y. TIMES (December 8, 2004) (describing 5-day suspensions of employee registration embraced by the SEC and FINRA, the nation's largest broker-dealer regulator).

Jaffee v. Redmond, 518 U.S. 1 (1996) (recognizing a federal psychotherapist-patient privilege, based upon the common law of many states).

What is Physician-Patient Privilege and Why Is It Important?, *available at* https://www.hg.org/article.asp?id=31873.

John Cassidy, *What Good Is Wall Street?,* THE NEW YORKER, at 49 (November 29, 2010).

Peter Truell, *An Employee on Wall St. Is Arrested,* N.Y. TIMES (November 7, 1997), *available at* http://www.nytimes.com/1997/11/07/business/an-employee-on-wall-st-is-arrested.html ("[New York City] Prosecutors said yesterday that they had arrested a brokerage firm employee responsible for protecting market-sensitive information and charged her with using the information to profit from insider trading.").

Mark Schoeff Jr., *House panel seeks to freeze SEC budget,* INVESTMENTNEWS.COM (June 10, 2015).

Appendices

Full, Current Versions of Insider Trading Provisions

Appendix I:
Section 16(b) of the Securities Exchange Act of 1934 ("SEA")

Sec. 16. Directors, Officers, and Principal Stockholders

... (b) For the purpose of preventing the unfair use of information which may have been obtained by such beneficial owner, director, or officer by reason of his relationship to the issuer, any profit realized by him from any purchase and sale, or any sale and purchase, of any equity security of such issuer (other than an exempted security) or a security-based swap agreement involving any such equity security within any period of less than six months, unless such security or security-based swap agreement was acquired in good faith in connection with a debt previously contracted, shall inure to and be recoverable by the issuer, irrespective of any intention on the part of such beneficial owner, director, or officer in entering into such transaction of holding the security or security based swap agreement purchased or of not repurchasing the security or security-based swap agreement sold for a period exceeding six months.

Suit to recover such profit may be instituted at law or in equity in any court of competent jurisdiction by the issuer, or by the owner of any security of the issuer in the name and in behalf of the issuer if the issuer shall fail or refuse to bring such suit within sixty days after request or shall fail diligently to prosecute the same thereafter; but no such suit shall be brought more than two years after the date such profit was realized.

This subsection shall not be construed to cover any transaction where such beneficial owner was not such both at the time of the purchase and sale, or the sale and purchase, of the security or security-based swap agreement involved, or any transaction or transactions which the Commission by rules and regulations may exempt as not comprehended within the purpose of this subsection.

Appendix II:
S.E.C. Rule 10b-5

§ 240.10b-5 Employment of Manipulative and Deceptive Devices

It shall be unlawful for any person, directly or indirectly, by the use of any means or instrumentality of interstate commerce, or of the mails or of any facility of any national securities exchange,

(a) To employ any device, scheme, or artifice to defraud,

(b) To make any untrue statement of a material fact or to omit to state a material fact necessary in order to make the statements made, in the light of the circumstances under which they were made, not misleading, or

(c) To engage in any act, practice, or course of business which operates or would operate as a fraud or deceit upon any person,

in connection with the purchase or sale of any security.

[Dec. 22, 1948, as amended Aug. 11, 1951]

Appendix III:
S.E.C. Rule 14e-3

§ 240.14e-3 Transactions in Securities on the Basis of Material, Nonpublic Information in the Context of Tender Offers

(a) If any person has taken a substantial step or steps to commence, or has commenced, a tender offer (the "offering person"), it shall constitute a fraudulent, deceptive or manipulative act or practice within the meaning of section 14(e) of the Act for any other person who is in possession of material information relating to such tender offer which information he knows or has reason to know is nonpublic and which he knows or has reason to know has been acquired directly or indirectly from:

(1) The offering person,

(2) The issuer of the securities sought or to be sought by such tender offer, or

(3) Any officer, director, partner or employee or any other person acting on behalf of the offering person or such issuer, to purchase or sell or cause to be purchased or sold any of such securities or any securities convertible into or exchangeable for any such securities or any option or right to obtain or to dispose of any of the foregoing securities, unless within a reasonable time prior to any purchase or sale such information and its source are publicly disclosed by press release or otherwise.

(b) A person other than a natural person shall not violate paragraph (a) of this section if such person shows that:

(1) The individual(s) making the investment decision on behalf of such person to purchase or sell any security described in paragraph (a) of this section or to cause any such security to be purchased or sold by or on behalf of others did not know the material, nonpublic information; and

(2) Such person had implemented one or a combination of policies and procedures, reasonable under the circumstances, taking into consideration the nature of the person's business, to ensure that individual(s) making investment decision(s) would not violate paragraph (a) of this section, which policies and procedures may include, but are not limited to, (i)

those which restrict any purchase, sale and causing any purchase and sale of any such security or (ii) those which prevent such individual(s) from knowing such information.

(c) Notwithstanding anything in paragraph (a) of this section to contrary, the following transactions shall not be violations of paragraph (a) of this section:

(1) Purchase(s) of any security described in paragraph (a) of this section by a broker or by another agent on behalf of an offering person; or

(2) Sale(s) by any person of any security described in paragraph (a) of this section to the offering person.

(d)

(1) As a means reasonably designed to prevent fraudulent, deceptive or manipulative acts or practices within the meaning of section 14(e) of the Act, it shall be unlawful for any person described in paragraph (d)(2) of this section to communicate material, nonpublic information relating to a tender offer to any other person under circumstances in which it is reasonably foreseeable that such communication is likely to result in a violation of this section *except* that this paragraph shall not apply to a communication made in good faith,

(i) To the officers, directors, partners or employees of the offering person, to its advisors or to other persons, involved in the planning, financing, preparation or execution of such tender offer;

(ii) To the issuer whose securities are sought or to be sought by such tender offer, to its officers, directors, partners, employees or advisors or to other persons, involved in the planning, financing, preparation or execution of the activities of the issuer with respect to such tender offer; or

(iii) To any person pursuant to a requirement of any statute or rule or regulation promulgated thereunder.

(2) The persons referred to in paragraph (d)(1) of this section are:

(i) The offering person or its officers, directors, partners, employees or advisors;

(ii) The issuer of the securities sought or to be sought by such tender offer or its officers, directors, partners, employees or advisors;

(iii) Anyone acting on behalf of the persons in paragraph (d)(2)(i) of this section or the issuer or persons in paragraph (d)(2)(ii) of this section; and

(iv) Any person in possession of material information relating to a tender offer which information he knows or has reason to know is nonpublic and which he knows or has reason to know has been acquired directly or indirectly from any of the above.

[45 FR 60418, Sept. 12, 1980]

Appendix IV:
S.E.C. Regulation FD [added in 2000]

§ 243.100 General Rule Regarding Selective Disclosure

(a) Whenever an issuer, or any person acting on its behalf, discloses any material nonpublic information regarding that issuer or its securities to any person described in paragraph (b)(1) of this section, the issuer shall make public disclosure of that information as provided in § 243.101(e):

(1) Simultaneously, in the case of an intentional disclosure; and

(2) Promptly, in the case of a non-intentional disclosure.

(b)

(1) Except as provided in paragraph (b)(2) of this section, paragraph (a) of this section shall apply to a disclosure made to any person outside the issuer:

(i) Who is a broker or dealer, or a person associated with a broker or dealer, as those terms are defined in Section 3(a) of the Securities Exchange Act of 1934);

(ii) Who is an investment adviser, as that term is defined in Section 202(a)(11) of the Investment Advisers Act of 1940; an institutional investment manager, as that term is defined in Section 13(f)(6) of the Securities Exchange Act of 1934, that filed a report on Form 13F with the Commission for the most recent quarter ended prior to the date of the disclosure; or a person associated with either of the foregoing. For purposes of this paragraph, a "person associated with an investment adviser or institutional investment manager" has the meaning set forth in Section 202(a)(17) of the Investment Advisers Act of 1940, assuming for these purposes that an institutional investment manager is an investment adviser;

(iii) Who is an investment company, as defined in Section 3 of the Investment Company Act of 1940, or who would be an investment company but for Section 3(c)(1) or Section 3(c)(7) thereof, or an affiliated person of either of the foregoing. For purposes of this paragraph, "affiliated person" means only those persons described in Section 2(a)(3)(C), (D), (E), and (F) of the Investment Company Act of 1940, assuming for these purposes that a person who would be an investment company but for Section 3(c)(1) or Section 3(c)(7) of the Investment Company Act of 1940 is an investment company; or

(iv) Who is a holder of the issuer's securities, under circumstances in which it is reasonably foreseeable that the person will purchase or sell the issuer's securities on the basis of the information.

(2) Paragraph (a) of this section shall not apply to a disclosure made:

(i) To a person who owes a duty of trust or confidence to the issuer (such as an attorney, investment banker, or accountant);

(ii) To a person who expressly agrees to maintain the disclosed information in confidence;

(iii) In connection with a securities offering registered under the Securities Act, other than an offering of the type described in any of Rule 415(a)(1)(i) through (vi) under the Securities Act through (vi) of this chapter) (except an offering of the type described in Rule 415(a)(1)(i) under the Securities Act of this chapter also involving a registered offering, whether or not underwritten, for capital formation purposes for the account of the issuer (unless the issuer's offering is being registered for the purpose of evading the requirements of this section), if the disclosure is by any of the following means:

(A) A registration statement filed under the Securities Act, including a prospectus contained therein;

(B) A free writing prospectus used after filing of the registration statement for the offering or a communication falling within the exception to the definition of prospectus contained in clause (a) of section 2(a)(10) of the Securities Act;

(C) Any other Section 10(b) prospectus;

(D) A notice permitted by Rule 135 under the Securities Act;

(E) A communication permitted by Rule 134 under the Securities Act; or

(F) An oral communication made in connection with the registered securities offering after filing of the registration statement for the offering under the Securities Act.

[65 FR 51738, Aug. 24, 2000, as amended at 70 FR 44829, Aug. 3, 2005; 74 FR 63865, Dec. 4, 2009; 75 FR 61051, Oct. 4, 2010; 76 FR 71877, Nov. 21, 2011]

§ 243.101 Definitions

This section defines certain terms as used in Regulation FD (§§ 243.100–243.103).

(a) *Intentional.* A selective disclosure of material nonpublic information is "intentional" when the person making the disclosure either knows, or is reckless in not knowing, that the information he or she is communicating is both material and nonpublic.

(b) *Issuer.* An "issuer" subject to this regulation is one that has a class of securities registered under Section 12 of the Securities Exchange Act of 1934, or is required to file reports under Section 15(d) of the Securities Exchange Act of 1934, including any closed-end investment company (as defined in Section 5(a)(2) of the Investment Company of 1940, but not including any other investment company or any foreign government or foreign private issuer, as those terms are defined in Rule 405 under the Securities Act).

(c) *Person acting on behalf of an issuer.* "Person acting on behalf of an issuer" means any senior official of the issuer (or, in the case of a closed-end investment company, a senior official of the issuer's investment adviser), or any other officer, employee, or agent of an issuer who regularly communicates with any person described in § 243.100(b)(1)(i), (ii), or (iii), or with holders of the issuer's securities. An officer, director, employee, or agent of an issuer who discloses material nonpublic information in breach of a duty of trust or confidence to the issuer shall not be considered to be acting on behalf of the issuer.

(d) *Promptly.* "Promptly" means as soon as reasonably practicable (but in no event after the later of 24 hours or the commencement of the next day's trading on the New York Stock Exchange) after a senior official of the issuer (or, in the case of a closed-end investment company, a senior official of the issuer's investment adviser) learns that there has been a non-intentional disclosure by the issuer or person acting on behalf of the issuer of information that the senior official knows, or is reckless in not knowing, is both material and nonpublic.

(e) *Public disclosure.*

(1) Except as provided in paragraph (e)(2) of this section, an issuer shall make the "public disclosure" of information required by § 243.100(a) by furnishing to or filing with the Commission a Form 8-K disclosing that information.

(2) An issuer shall be exempt from the requirement to furnish or file a Form 8-K if it instead disseminates the information through another method (or combination of methods) of disclosure that is reasonably de-

signed to provide broad, non-exclusionary distribution of the information to the public.

(f) *Senior official.* "Senior official" means any director, executive officer (as defined in §240.3b-7 of this chapter), investor relations or public relations officer, or other person with similar functions.

(g) *Securities offering.* For purposes of §243.100(b)(2)(iv):

(1) *Underwritten offerings.* A securities offering that is underwritten commences when the issuer reaches an understanding with the broker-dealer that is to act as managing underwriter and continues until the later of the end of the period during which a dealer must deliver a prospectus or the sale of the securities (unless the offering is sooner terminated);

(2) *Non-underwritten offerings.* A securities offering that is not underwritten:

(i) If covered by Rule 415(a)(1)(x), commences when the issuer makes its first bona fide offer in a takedown of securities and continues until the later of the end of the period during which each dealer must deliver a prospectus or the sale of the securities in that takedown (unless the takedown is sooner terminated);

(ii) If a business combination as defined in Rule 165(f)(1) commences when the first public announcement of the transaction is made and continues until the completion of the vote or the expiration of the tender offer, as applicable (unless the transaction is sooner terminated);

(iii) If an offering other than those specified in paragraphs (a) and (b) of this section, commences when the issuer files a registration statement and continues until the later of the end of the period during which each dealer must deliver a prospectus or the sale of the securities (unless the offering is sooner terminated).

§243.102 No Effect on Antifraud Liability

No failure to make a public disclosure required solely by §243.100 shall be deemed to be a violation of Rule 10b-5 under the Securities Exchange Act.

§243.103 No Effect on Exchange Act Reporting Status

A failure to make a public disclosure required solely by §243.100 shall not affect whether:

(a) For purposes of Forms S-2, S-3, S-8 and SF-3 under the Securities Act, an issuer is deemed to have filed all the material required to be filed pursuant to

Section 13 or 15(d) of the Securities Exchange Act of 1934 or, where applicable, has made those filings in a timely manner; or

(b) There is adequate current public information about the issuer for purposes of § 230.144(c) of this chapter (Rule 144(c)).

Aug. 24, 2000, as amended Sept. 24, 2014

Appendix V:
S.E.C. Rule 10b5-1

§ 240.10b5-1 Trading "on the Basis of" Material Nonpublic Information in Insider Trading Cases

Preliminary Note to § 240.10b5-1

This provision defines when a purchase or sale constitutes trading "on the basis of" material nonpublic information in insider trading cases brought under Section 10(b) of the Act and Rule 10b-5 thereunder. The law of insider trading is otherwise defined by judicial opinions construing Rule 10b-5, and Rule 10b5-1 does not modify the scope of insider trading law in any other respect.

(a) *General.* The "manipulative and deceptive devices" prohibited by Section 10(b) of the Act and § 240.10b-5 thereunder include, among other things, the purchase or sale of a security of any issuer, on the basis of material nonpublic information about that security or issuer, in breach of a duty of trust or confidence that is owed directly, indirectly, or derivatively, to the issuer of that security or the shareholders of that issuer, or to any other person who is the source of the material nonpublic information.

(b) *Definition of "on the basis of."* Subject to the affirmative defenses in paragraph (c) of this section, a purchase or sale of a security of an issuer is "on the basis of" material nonpublic information about that security or issuer if the person making the purchase or sale was aware of the material nonpublic information when the person made the purchase or sale.

(c) *Affirmative defenses.*

(1)(i) Subject to paragraph (c)(1)(ii) of this section, a person's purchase or sale is not "on the basis of" material nonpublic information if the person making the purchase or sale demonstrates that:

(A) Before becoming aware of the information, the person had:

(1) Entered into a binding contract to purchase or sell the security,

(2) Instructed another person to purchase or sell the security for the instructing person's account, or

(3) Adopted a written plan for trading securities;

(B) The contract, instruction, or plan described in paragraph (c)(1)(i)(A) of this Section:

(1) Specified the amount of securities to be purchased or sold and the price at which and the date on which the securities were to be purchased or sold;

(2) Included a written formula or algorithm, or computer program, for determining the amount of securities to be purchased or sold and the price at which and the date on which the securities were to be purchased or sold; or

(3) Did not permit the person to exercise any subsequent influence over how, when, or whether to effect purchases or sales; provided, in addition, that any other person who, pursuant to the contract, instruction, or plan, did exercise such influence must not have been aware of the material nonpublic information when doing so; and

(C) The purchase or sale that occurred was pursuant to the contract, instruction, or plan. A purchase or sale is not "pursuant to a contract, instruction, or plan" if, among other things, the person who entered into the contract, instruction, or plan altered or deviated from the contract, instruction, or plan to purchase or sell securities (whether by changing the amount, price, or timing of the purchase or sale), or entered into or altered a corresponding or hedging transaction or position with respect to those securities.

(ii) Paragraph (c)(1)(i) of this section is applicable only when the contract, instruction, or plan to purchase or sell securities was given or entered into in good faith and not as part of a plan or scheme to evade the prohibitions of this section.

(iii) This paragraph (c)(1)(iii) defines certain terms as used in paragraph (c) of this Section.

(A) *Amount.* "Amount" means either a specified number of shares or other securities or a specified dollar value of securities.

(B) *Price.* "Price" means the market price on a particular date or a limit price, or a particular dollar price.

(C) *Date.* "Date" means, in the case of a market order, the specific day of the year on which the order is to be executed (or as soon thereafter as is practicable under ordinary principles of best execution). "Date" means, in the case of a limit order, a day of the year on which the limit order is in force.

(2) A person other than a natural person also may demonstrate that a purchase or sale of securities is not "on the basis of" material nonpublic information if the person demonstrates that:

(i) The individual making the investment decision on behalf of the person to purchase or sell the securities was not aware of the information; and

(ii) The person had implemented reasonable policies and procedures, taking into consideration the nature of the person's business, to ensure that individuals making investment decisions would not violate the laws prohibiting trading on the basis of material nonpublic information. These policies and procedures may include those that restrict any purchase, sale, and causing any purchase or sale of any security as to which the person has material nonpublic information, or those that prevent such individuals from becoming aware of such information.

[65 FR 51737, Aug. 24, 2000]

Appendix VI:
S.E.C. Rule 10b5-2

§ 240.10b5-2 Duties of Trust or Confidence in Misappropriation Insider Trading Cases

Preliminary Note to § 240.10b5-2

This section provides a non-exclusive definition of circumstances in which a person has a duty of trust or confidence for purposes of the "misappropriation" theory of insider trading under Section 10(b) of the Act and Rule 10b-5. The law of insider trading is otherwise defined by judicial opinions construing Rule

10b-5, and Rule 10b5-2 does not modify the scope of insider trading law in any other respect.

(a) *Scope of Rule.* This section shall apply to any violation of Section 10(b) of the Act and § 240.10b-5 thereunder that is based on the purchase or sale of securities on the basis of, or the communication of material nonpublic information misappropriated in breach of a duty of trust or confidence.

(b) *Enumerated "duties of trust or confidence."* For purposes of this section, a "duty of trust or confidence" exists in the following circumstances, among others:

(1) Whenever a person agrees to maintain information in confidence;

(2) Whenever the person communicating the material nonpublic information and the person to whom it is communicated have a history, pattern, or practice of sharing confidences, such that the recipient of the information knows or reasonably should know that the person communicating the material nonpublic information expects that the recipient will maintain its confidentiality; or

(3) Whenever a person receives or obtains material nonpublic information from his or her spouse, parent, child, or sibling; provided, however, that the person receiving or obtaining the information may demonstrate that no duty of trust or confidence existed with respect to the information, by establishing that he or she neither knew nor reasonably should have known that the person who was the source of the information expected that the person would keep the information confidential, because of the parties' history, pattern, or practice of sharing and maintaining confidences, and because there was no agreement or understanding to maintain the confidentiality of the information.

[65 FR 51738, Aug. 24, 2000]

Appendix VII:
SEA Section 20A [added in 1988]

Liability to Contemporaneous Traders for Insider Trading

(a) **Private Rights of Action Based on Contemporaneous Trading.** — Any person who violates any provision of this title or the rules or regulations thereunder by purchasing or selling a security while in possession of material, non-public information shall be liable in an action in any court of competent jurisdiction to any person who, contemporaneously with the purchase or sale of securities that is the subject of such violation, has purchased (where such violation is based on a sale of securities) or sold (where such violation is based on a purchase of securities) securities of the same class.

(b) **Limitations on Liability.**—

> (1) **Contemporaneous Trading Actions Limited to Profit Gained or Loss Avoided.**—The total amount of damages imposed under subsection (a) shall not exceed the profit gained or loss avoided in the transaction or transactions that are the subject of the violation.

> (2) **Offsetting Disgorgements Against Liability.**—The total amount of damages imposed against any person under subsection (a) shall be diminished by the amounts, if any, that such person may be required to disgorge, pursuant to a court order obtained at the instance of the Commission, in a proceeding brought under section 21(d) of this title relating to the same transaction or transactions.

> (3) **Controlling Person Liability.**—No person shall be liable under this section solely by reason of employing another person who is liable under this section, but the liability of a controlling person under this section shall be subject to section 20(a) of this title.

> (4) **Statute of Limitations.**—No action may be brought under this section more than 5 years after the date of the last transaction that is the subject of the violation.

(c) **Joint and Several Liability for Communicating.**—Any person who violates any provision of this title or the rules or regulations thereunder by communicating material, nonpublic information shall be jointly and severally liable under subsection (a) with, and to the same extent as, any person or persons liable under subsection (a) to whom the communication was directed.

(d) **Authority Not to Restrict Other Express or Implied Rights of Action.**—Nothing in this section shall be construed to limit or condition the right of any person to bring an action to enforce a requirement of this title or the availability of any cause of action implied from a provision of this title.

(e) **Provisions Not to Affect Public Prosecutions.**—This section shall not be construed to bar or limit in any manner any action by the Commission or the Attorney General under any other provision of this title, nor shall it bar or limit in any manner any action to recover penalties, or to seek any other order regarding penalties.

Appendix VIII:
SEA Section 21A [added in 1984]

Civil Penalties for Insider Trading

(a) Authority to Impose Civil Penalties. —

(1) Judicial Actions by Commission Authorized. — Whenever it shall appear to the Commission that any person has violated any provision of this title or the rules or regulations thereunder by purchasing or selling a security or security based swap agreement while in possession of material, nonpublic information in, or has violated any such provision by communicating such information in connection with, a transaction on or through the facilities of a national securities exchange or from or through a broker or dealer, and which is not part of a public offering by an issuer of securities other than standardized options or security futures products, the Commission — (A) may bring an action in a United States district court to seek, and the court shall have jurisdiction to impose, a civil penalty to be paid by the person who committed such violation; and (B) may, subject to subsection (b)(1), bring an action in a United States district court to seek, and the court shall have jurisdiction to impose, a civil penalty to be paid by a person who, at the time of the violation, directly or indirectly controlled the person who committed such violation.

(2) Amount of Penalty for Person Who Committed Violation. — The amount of the penalty which may be imposed on the person who committed such violation shall be determined by the court in light of the facts and circumstances, but shall not exceed three times the profit gained or loss avoided as a result of such unlawful purchase, sale, or communication.

(3) Amount of Penalty for Controlling Person. — The amount of the penalty which may be imposed on any person who, at the time of the violation, directly or indirectly controlled the person who committed such violation, shall be determined by the court in light of the facts and circumstances, but shall not exceed the greater of $1,000,000, or three times the amount of the profit gained or loss avoided as a result of such controlled person's violation. If such controlled person's violation was a violation by communication, the profit gained or loss avoided as a result of the violation shall, for purposes of this paragraph only, be deemed to

be limited to the profit gained or loss avoided by the person or persons to whom the controlled person directed such communication.

(b) Limitations on Liability.—

(1) Liability of Controlling Persons.—No controlling person shall be subject to a penalty under subsection (a)(1)(B) unless the Commission establishes that—

(A) such controlling person knew or recklessly disregarded the fact that such controlled person was likely to engage in the act or acts constituting the violation and failed to take appropriate steps to prevent such act or acts before they occurred; or

(B) such controlling person knowingly or recklessly failed to establish, maintain, or enforce any policy or procedure required under section 15(f) of this title or section 204A of the Investment Advisers Act of 1940 and such failure substantially contributed to or permitted the occurrence of the act or acts constituting the violation.

(2) Additional Restrictions on Liability.—No person shall be subject to a penalty under subsection (a) solely by reason of employing another person who is subject to a penalty under such subsection, unless such employing person is liable as a controlling person under paragraph (1) of this subsection. Section 20(a) of this title shall not apply to actions under subsection (a) of this section.

(c) Authority of Commission.—The Commission, by such rules, regulations, and orders as it considers necessary or appropriate in the public interest or for the protection of investors, may exempt, in whole or in part, either unconditionally or upon specific terms and conditions, any person or transaction or class of persons or transactions from this section.

(d) Procedures for Collection.—

(1) Payment of Penalty to Treasury.—A penalty imposed under this section shall be payable into the Treasury of the United States, except as otherwise provided in section 308 of the Sarbanes-Oxley Act of 2002 and section 21F of this title.

(2) Collection of Penalties.—If a person upon whom such a penalty is imposed shall fail to pay such penalty within the time prescribed in the court's order, the Commission may refer the matter to the Attorney General who shall recover such penalty by action in the appropriate United States district court.

(3) **Remedy Not Exclusive.**—The actions authorized by this section may be brought in addition to any other actions that the Commission or the Attorney General are entitled to bring.

(4) **Jurisdiction and Venue.**—For purposes of section 27 of this title, actions under this section shall be actions to enforce a liability or a duty created by this title.

(5) **Statute of Limitations.**—No action may be brought under this section more than 5 years after the date of the purchase or sale. This section shall not be construed to bar or limit in any manner any action by the Commission or the Attorney General under any other provision of this title, nor shall it bar or limit in any manner any action to recover penalties, or to seek any other order regarding penalties, imposed in an action commenced within 5 years of such transaction.

(e) **Definition.**—For purposes of this section, "profit gained" or "loss avoided" is the difference between the purchase or sale price of the security and the value of that security as measured by the trading price of the security a reasonable period after public dissemination of the nonpublic information.

(f) The authority of the Commission under this section with respect to security-based swap agreements (as defined) shall be subject to the restrictions and limitations of section 3A(b) of this title.

Appendix IX:
SEA Section 21A(g)/S.T.O.C.K. Act of 2012

(g) **Duty of Members and Employees of Congress.**

(1) **In General.**—Subject to the rule of construction under section 10 of the STOCK Act and solely for purposes of the insider trading prohibitions arising under this Act, including section 10(b) and Rule 10b-5 thereunder, each Member of Congress or employee of Congress owes a duty arising from a relationship of trust and confidence to the Congress, the United States Government, and the citizens of the United States with respect to material, nonpublic information derived from such person's position as a Member of Congress or employee of Congress or gained from the performance of such person's official responsibilities.

(2) **Definitions.**—In this subsection—

(A) the term "Member of Congress" means a member of the Senate or House of Representatives, a Delegate to the House of Representatives, and the Resident Commissioner from Puerto Rico; and

(B) the term "employee of Congress" means—

(i) any individual (other than a Member of Congress), whose compensation is disbursed by the Secretary of the Senate or the Chief Administrative Officer of the House of Representatives; and

(ii) any other officer or employee of the legislative branch (as defined in section 109(11) of the Ethics in Government Act of 1978 (5 U.S.C. App. 109(11))).

(3) **Rule of Construction.**—Nothing in this subsection shall be construed to impair or limit the construction of the existing antifraud provisions of the securities laws or the authority of the Commission under those provisions.

(h) **Duty of Other Federal Officials.**

(1) **In General.**—Subject to the rule of construction under section 10 of the STOCK Act and solely for purposes of the insider trading prohibitions arising under this Act, including section 10(b), and Rule 10b-5 thereunder, each executive branch employee, each judicial officer, and each judicial employee owes a duty arising from a relationship of trust and confidence to the United States Government and the citizens of the United States with respect to material, nonpublic information derived from such person's position as an executive branch employee, judicial officer, or judicial employee or gained from the performance of such person's official responsibilities.

(2) **Definitions.**—I n this subsection—

(A) the term "executive branch employee"—

(i) has the meaning given the term "employee" under section 2105 of title 5, United States Code;

(ii) includes—

(I) the President;

(II) the Vice President; and an employee of the United States Postal Service or the Postal Regulatory Commission;

(B) the term "judicial employee" has the meaning given that term in section 109(8) of the Ethics in Government Act of 1978 (5 U.S.C. App. 109(8)); and (C) the term "judicial officer" has the meaning given that term under section 109(10) of the Ethics in Government Act of 1978 (5 U.S.C. App. 109(10)).

(3) Rule of Construction. — Nothing in this subsection shall be construed to impair or limit the construction of the existing antifraud provisions of the securities laws or the authority of the Commission under those provisions.

(i) **Participation in Initial Public Offerings.** — An individual described in section 101(f) of the Ethics in Government Act of 1978 may not purchase securities that are the subject of an initial public offering (within the meaning given such term in section 12(f)(1)(G)(i)) in any manner other than is available to members of the public generally.

Table of Cases

NOTE: *Cases brought by the Department of Justice or the Securities and Exchange Commission are listed solely by the last name/entity name of the defendant.*

Index